Exam Ref AZ-304
Microsoft Azure Architect Design

Ashish Agrawal
Avinash Bhavsar
MJ Parker
Gurvinder Singh

Exam Ref AZ-304 Microsoft Azure Architect Design

Published with the authorization of Microsoft Corporation by:
Pearson Education, Inc.

ISBN-13: 978-0-13-726889-4
ISBN-10: 0-13-726889-0

Library of Congress Control Number: 2021936186

1 2021

TRADEMARKS

Microsoft and the trademarks listed at http://www.microsoft.com on the "Trademarks" webpage are trademarks of the Microsoft group of companies. All other marks are property of their respective owners.

WARNING AND DISCLAIMER

SPECIAL SALES

For information about buying this title in bulk quantities, or for special sales opportunities (which may include electronic versions; custom cover designs; and content particular to your business, training goals, marketing focus, or branding interests), please contact our corporate sales department at corpsales@pearsoned.com or (800) 382-3419.

For government sales inquiries, please contact governmentsales@pearsoned.com.

For questions about sales outside the U.S., please contact intlcs@pearson.com.

CREDITS

EDITOR-IN-CHIEF
Brett Bartow

EXECUTIVE EDITOR
Loretta Yates

SPONSORING EDITOR
Charvi Arora

DEVELOPMENT EDITOR
Rick Kughen

MANAGING EDITOR
Sandra Schroeder

SENIOR PROJECT EDITOR
Tracey Croom

COPY EDITOR
Rick Kughen

INDEXER
Cheryl Ann Lenser

PROOFREADER
Abigail Manheim

TECHNICAL EDITOR
Saabir Sopariwala

COVER DESIGNER
Twist Creative, Seattle

COMPOSITOR
codeMantra

GRAPHICS
codeMantra

Contents at a glance

Contents

Chapter 3   Design data storage   73

Acknowledgments

Ashish Agrawal   Firstly, I would like to thank my family—especially my Mom and Dad for their encouragement and blessings. I'd also like to thank my wonderful and ever-patient wife, Swapna, for putting up with my crazy schedule and letting me devote many of my weekends and evenings to this book, and my boys, Devansh and Yug, for being a continuous energy source, love, and inspiration. My Guru and inspiration, Sunil Poddar, always instilled in me the work ethic and dedication needed to get projects like this across the finish line. I'd also like to thank all my friends and elders in the family for their support and blessings.

I want to thank all people I have had an opportunity to work with at Kraft Heinz, Infosys, Patni, Cognizant, and Microsoft, as well as all my incredible client organizations for everything I learned along the way.

I am grateful to Microsoft Press and the editors at Pearson for taking on this project. Thank you, Loretta, for the opportunity to contribute to this and Charvi for excellent project management. This book has been a fantastic experience. I also want to thank my co-authors for their determination and outstanding teamwork. Finally, my special thanks go to the editors and entire Pearson team, for walking through the content with a fine-tooth comb and sharing incredible feedback.

Avinash Bhavsar   First and foremost, I would like to thank my parents for bringing me in their difficult times and making me capable of seeing this day. Thanks to them and the Almighty for the blessings. Special thanks to my wonderful wife for her support and inspiration. I want to apologize to (and thank them for their patience) my lovely kids, Atharva and Aayush, for not participating in their playtime while I devote that time to completing this project. Huge thanks to Loretta Yates and Charvi Arora for their support during this journey. Finally, I would like to thank my co-authors and the Pearson team for the opportunity to work on this project. Cheers and happy reading.

MJ Parker   I would like to thank Bryant Chrzan for having faith in me, and allowing me to work on so many wonderful Pearson projects and for introducing me to all the amazing people at Pearson that I have had the pleasure of working with, including James Manly, Loretta Yates, Laura Lewin, and Julie Phifer. I have enjoyed all my collaborations with Pearson. It has also been my honor to be counted among authors such as Ashish Agrawal, Avinash Bhavsar, and Gurvinder Singh. Another person who I am grateful for is Rick Kughen, who made all my work look great and who never gave up on me. Lastly, I would like to thank my family because they gave up the most precious commodity of all—time spent together—so that I could pursue my dream of writing.

Gurvinder Singh   I am indebted to Microsoft Press for the opportunity to co-author this book in association with Ashish Agrawal, Avinash Bhavsar, and MJ Parker. All my co-authors are well known for their professional prowess and in-depth knowledge of the Microsoft Azure Platform and need no introduction.

A 'Big Thank You' to the editors and entire Pearson team for their well-coordinated efforts and due diligence, from conceptualization to publication of this volume. I am indeed grateful to the entire Pearson Team, especially Ms. Loretta Yates and Ms. Charvi Arora, for their cooperation, support, and patience throughout this journey.

I am indeed grateful to my mother, Daljeet Kour, my wife, Jaspreet Kaur, and daughter, Amritleen Kaur, for the tremendous encouragement that helped me walk the insanely tight rope of schedules and deadlines.

Finally, I submit myself in reverence to Guru Nanak, the great spiritual Guru, whose blessings enabled an incredibly small and nondescript individual like me with wisdom and opportunity.

About the authors

ASHISH AGRAWAL is a qualified technocrat, offering two decades of multifaceted experience as a technology leader, trusted advisor, and Enterprise Cloud Architect (Infra, Apps, Data, and Security). He drives a profound influence in the cloud technology landscape with provocative thought leadership and communicates his ideas with clarity and passion. Ashish has delivered numerous successful cloud engagements for global fortune 500 companies in cloud advisory, consulting, architecture, leadership, and delivery execution roles throughout his career and is considered an Azure subject matter expert since 2010. He is a change leader with transforming teams' experience to adopt and innovate best practices leading to critical customer impacting results.

AVINASH BHAVSAR is a Microsoft certified Azure Professional with about 18 years of hands-on experience in all facets of cloud computing, such as discovery, assessment, cloud foundation build, datacenter transformation, cloud-native application development for Azure, and migration of applications and databases from on-premises to the Azure platform. He has extensive Application Development background, which includes architecture, design, development, continuous integration, and continuous delivery to Azure platform (IaaS, PaaS, and serverless).

MJ PARKER has been a programmer for 30 years and is a Microsoft Certified Trainer who has been teaching various Microsoft technologies and other platforms for 25 years. Her passion, however, is writing absolutely anything. With the help of great editors, she has published several non-technical books, as well as other technical works, including content for exams, training sessions, and courseware.

GURVINDER SINGH is a Microsoft Certified Azure Solutions Architect with about 14 years of diversified software development experience. He has a strong programming background and hands-on experience on .NET and C#. In the past few years, Gurvinder has been guiding large enterprises in the transformation of legacy applications into cloud-native architecture with a focus on migration to Microsoft Azure. He is extremely passionate about technology, especially with the Microsoft Azure platform (PaaS, IaaS, and Serverless).

Introduction

The purpose of the AZ-304 certification exam is to test your knowledge and understanding of the Microsoft Azure platform. The exam is targeted for Azure Solution Architects, including advising stakeholders responsible for translating business requirements into secure, scalable, and reliable cloud solutions. This book provides comprehensive coverage of exam domain objectives, including in-depth explanation and demonstration of real-world design scenarios. Designed for modern IT professionals, this Exam Ref focuses on the critical thinking and decision-making acumen needed for success at the Microsoft Certified Expert level.

While we've made every effort possible to make the information in this book accurate, Azure is rapidly evolving, and there's a chance that some of the screens in the Azure portal are slightly different now than they were when this book was written, which might result in some figures in this book looking different than what you see on your screen. It's also possible that other minor interface changes have taken place, such as name changes and so on.

Azure supports a wide range of programming languages, frameworks, databases, and services. Given this, IT professionals need to learn a vast range of technical topics in a short span of time. There is an overabundance of content available, which makes it difficult to find just enough study material required to prepare for the AZ 304 exam. This book will serve as prescriptive guidance for people preparing for this exam.

This book covers every major topic area found on the exam, but it does not cover every exam question. Only the Microsoft exam team has access to the exam questions, and Microsoft regularly adds new questions to the exam, making it impossible to cover specific questions. You should consider this book a supplement to your relevant real-world experience and other study materials. If you encounter a topic in this book that you do not feel completely comfortable with, use the "Need more review?" links that you'll find in the text to access more information. Take the time to research and study those topics. Great information is available on Microsoft Learn, docs.microsoft.com/azure, TechNet, and in blogs and forums.

Organization of this book

This book is organized by the "Skills measured" list published for the exam. The "Skills measured" list is available for each exam on the Microsoft Learn website: *http://aka.ms/examlist*. Each chapter in this book corresponds to a major topic area in the list, and the technical tasks in each topic area determine a chapter's organization. If an exam covers six major topic areas, for example, the book will contain six chapters.

Preparing for the exam

Microsoft certification exams are a great way to build your resume and let the world know about your level of expertise. Certification exams validate your on-the-job experience and product knowledge. Although there is no substitute for on-the-job experience, preparation through study and hands-on practice can help you prepare for the exam. This book is *not* designed to teach you new skills.

We recommend that you augment your exam preparation plan by using a combination of available study materials and courses. For example, you might use the Exam Ref and another study guide for your "at home" preparation and take a Microsoft Official Curriculum course for the classroom experience. Choose the combination that you think works best for you. Learn more about available classroom training and find free online courses and live events at *http://microsoft.com/learn*. Microsoft Official Practice Tests are available for many exams at *http://aka.ms/practicetests*.

Note that this Exam Ref is based on publicly available information about the exam and the author's experience. To safeguard the integrity of the exam, authors do not have access to the live exam.

Microsoft certifications

Microsoft certifications distinguish you by proving your command of a broad set of skills and experience with current Microsoft products and technologies. The exams and corresponding certifications are developed to validate your mastery of critical competencies as you design and develop, or implement and support, solutions with Microsoft products and technologies both on-premises and in the cloud. Certification brings a variety of benefits to the individual and to employers and organizations.

> **MORE INFO   ALL MICROSOFT CERTIFICATIONS**
>
> For information about Microsoft certifications, including a full list of available certifications, go to *http://www.microsoft.com/learn*.

Check back often to see what is new!

Quick access to online references

Throughout this book are addresses to webpages that the author has recommended you visit for more information. Some of these links can be very long and painstaking to type, so we've shortened them for you to make them easier to visit. We've also compiled them into a single list that readers of the print edition can refer to while they read.

Download the list at
MicrosoftPressStore.com/ExamRefAZ304/downloads

The URLs are organized by chapter and heading. Every time you come across a URL in the book, find the hyperlink in the list to go directly to the webpage.

Errata, updates, & book support

We've made every effort to ensure the accuracy of this book and its companion content. You can access updates to this book—in the form of a list of submitted errata and their related corrections—at

MicrosoftPressStore.com/ExamRefAZ304/errata

If you discover an error that is not already listed, please submit it to us at the same page.

For additional book support and information, please visit
MicrosoftPressStore.com/Support

Please note that product support for Microsoft software and hardware is not offered through the previous addresses. For help with Microsoft software or hardware, go to http://support.microsoft.com.

Stay in touch

Let's keep the conversation going! We're on Twitter: *http://twitter.com/MicrosoftPress*.

CHAPTER 1

Design monitoring

Monitoring is often ignored, despite being imperative for line-of-business (LOB) applications, a better user experience, and for business continuity. A common misconception is that adopting a cloud architecture removes the need for monitoring, but that is not entirely true. Depending on the cloud services you are utilizing, you must understand the shared responsibilities between you and the cloud service provider to implement a holistic monitoring strategy. If you think about the monitoring from day one, your organization can better achieve its business goals and become more responsive, productive, and competitive.

On the AZ-304 certification exam, you must demonstrate a solid understanding of the Microsoft Azure platform's monitoring capabilities. The Azure Solution Architect certification is an expert-level exam, so you are expected to have advanced-level knowledge of each of the domain objectives in this chapter.

You need to be mindful of what to monitor and why to monitor it. And you need to know what options are available. In this chapter, you learn the key design considerations you should take to develop monitoring solutions for your applications running on the Microsoft Azure platform.

Skills covered in this chapter:

- Skill 1.1: Design for cost optimization
- Skill 1.2: Design a solution for logging and monitoring

Skill 1.1: Design for cost optimization

You might think the key reason to consider is cost savings, because the cloud is cheaper than on-premises and migrating cloud could save you a significant IT spend. There is no doubt that adopting a cloud architecture empowers your business to achieve more through innovation, gain more agility and operational benefits. However, if you do not plan your transition to the cloud while considering best practices and recommendations, you might end up spending more.

In this skill, you learn the various ways you can optimize your cloud spend and how to set up cost guardrails to maximize your return on cloud investment to achieve better business outcomes.

> This skill covers how to:
> - Recommend a solution for cost management and cost reporting
> - Recommend solutions to minimize cost

Recommend a solution for cost management and cost reporting

Cost management is a set of processes that you develop as part of your organization's governance model. It takes extensive upfront planning of cloud resources and aligning them effectively with your business requirements. Keeping your cloud spend under control and maximizing your cloud investment requires you to consider the critical aspects described in the following sections.

Planning

Identifying clear business and technical requirements and understanding your organization's business goals for cloud adoption help you design a cost-effective solution by selecting the appropriate Azure services and choosing the right Azure regions that are aligned with your organization's goals and budget constraints. First, you should evaluate the available billing models for Azure services and choose the right fit:

- **Free**   In this billing model, you get 12 months of access to several popular free services. Additionally, you receive a $200 credit against your cloud spends for 30 days.

- **Student Account**   Microsoft helps students learn the technology by providing them with a $100 Azure credit to spend over twelve months when creating a new free student account.

- **Pay-As-You-Go**   This is a consumption-based pricing model that allows you to pay for what you use. You can cancel it anytime.

- **Enterprise Agreement**   With this option, enterprise customers work directly with Microsoft. With EA, you get a special discount on Azure services through an upfront commitment on Azure spend. You also get dedicated premier support from the Azure Rapid Response (ARR) team.

- **Cloud Solution Provider (CSP)**   Cloud Solution providers are companies that have partnered with Microsoft under the CSP licensing program. They customize the cloud services and bundle them to provide customized cloud solutions to customers. With this purchasing option, you work directly with a CSP partner instead of Microsoft to build and deploy a cloud solution for you. You get the necessary support from CSP cloud experts, not directly from Microsoft.

> *NEED MORE INFO?*   **MICROSOFT AZURE OFFER DETAILS**
>
> From time to time, Microsoft updates its offers. To get the most up-to-date information on the available active offers, see *https://azure.microsoft.com/en-us/support/legal/offer-details/*.

Estimating cloud spend

Estimating your overall cloud spend and keeping business stakeholders informed helps create a budget for your organization's cloud journey. You can use the following Azure tools to get an estimate of your cloud infrastructure requirements:

- **Azure Pricing Calculator**   The Azure pricing calculator is a tool that you must use to assess the cost of your cloud workload and tailor your design or adopt different ways to implement a solution to minimize spending.

- **Azure Total Cost of Ownership (TCO) Calculator**   The TCO calculator is a much more sophisticated tool that helps organizations estimate cost savings by migrating to Azure Cloud. The TCO calculator is an online tool provided by Microsoft that supplies existing on-premises datacenter workload details, such as databases, virtual machines, storage capacity, and so on. The TCO calculator then gives you a comparative report of on-premises versus Azure estimated spending.

- **Azure Migrate**   Azure Migrate is an assessment service that helps you to assess an on-premises datacenter. Using an Azure Migrate assessment, you get a better understanding of cloud resources that you need as part of an Azure replacement solution for your on-premises workload.

Organization structure

Cost management is an iterative process that defines the right team structure responsible for efficient cloud spending. Specifically, when your organization's goal is to reduce the on-premises datacenter cost, it becomes crucial for you to set up a cost-conscious organization for your cloud journey. You start by inviting people with the right level of accountability and visibility of your cloud spend and cost-related data. The critical process-related attributes that you should consider when defining a cost-conscious organization are as follows:

- **Visibility**   Visibility requires constant reporting of cost-related data; for example, the finance team is responsible for approving a budget for cloud spend and applications, and management teams are accountable for spending. Visibility can be achieved using the right tools and services, such as Azure Cost Management and Billing. Visibility includes granting proper access controls, such as Role-Based Access Control (RBAC), using clear tagging for the cloud resources, using a well-structured resource organization, and using the right reporting scope.

- **Accountability**   Like visibility, accountability is also a critical aspect that helps you understand your cloud spend. Good organization structure facilitates ways to optimize your cloud spend and hold people accountable for the efficient use of cloud resources to ensure that the cloud spend remains in your organization's cloud adoption budget.

- **Optimization**   Optimization is an ongoing process that requires involvement from all key stakeholders in the cost management lifecycle. As part of this ongoing process, you look for an opportunity to reduce your cloud spend by optimizing cloud resources through the use of best practices and recommendations. Sometimes, you might need to make a trade-off between cost control and performance by keeping your key stakeholders informed.

Organizing Azure resources

You must organize your cloud resources considering the recommended guidelines and best practices so that you have full visibility of the different environments within your organization and the costs associated with them. Remember, cost management within your organization's cloud portfolio is all about cloud governance and the cloud operation process.

Microsoft Cloud Adoption Framework (CAF)'s enterprise-scale design principles provide you a good starting point to take in reference to the Azure landing zones deployment approach. Cost management is an essential aspect of the CAF recommendation for the landing zone.

Figure 1-1 depicts the simplest Azure environment hierarchy model for management groups, subscriptions, and resource groups. This model allows each team to set and track an Azure spend budget at a particular scope. This hierarchy model also allows you to set up a policy with a specific scope for managing the Azure resources you create; this also allows you to control cloud spend.

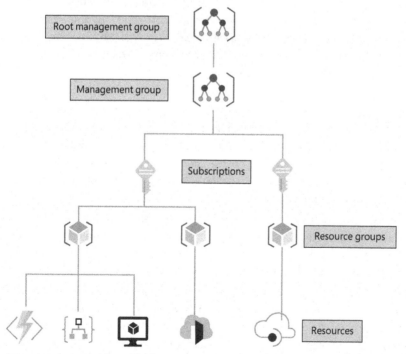

FIGURE 1-1 A sample hierarchy of Azure resources for governance using management groups and a subscription.

You can create up to six levels of management groups in your hierarchy. The top-level management group is tied to the Azure Active Directory tenant and is also called the root management. Once the root management group is created, all existing management groups and subscriptions in the directory become children of the root management group.

You should also create a separate management group and a subscription to segregate Azure environments across your organization structure. For example, you can create a separate management group and a subscription for production and non-production environments for better control over managing access control and policies defined for different environments.

You create Azure resources into resource groups under the environment-specific subscriptions that define the boundaries for your organization's projects and business units. You then use Azure policies in your governance model, such as limiting the size or tier of resources provisioned to control undesirable spending. For example, you might not want to have someone create virtual machines with expensive tiers in a dev/test environment. If needed, costly resources should be vetted and go via an approval process that you may want to set up as part of your overall Azure governance model.

The well-structured hierarchy of your Azure resources also enables you to abide by the principle of least privilege. It allows you to ensure that the right people get access to only the required privileges to perform their job duties. For example, non-production subscriptions may grant contributor access to developers, while in the production subscription, developers should only have read access. Ultimately, a well-structured environment and granular policies make your cloud governance model robust and prevent your organization from seeing unexpected large bills.

> **IMPORTANT** **ACCESS POLICIES INHERITANCE**
>
> Azure policies or access control applied to one level in the hierarchy are inherited by the levels below. For example, if you define RBAC and Azure policies at the management group level, all subscriptions beneath it would inherit the same.

Resource tagging

Tagging is a key-value pair and one of the easiest ways to classify resources in your Azure subscription. It is highly recommended that you tag all your cloud resources. You can tag on pretty much everything in the Azure resource hierarchy model described earlier in this chapter. Fundamentally, resource tagging is a primary way to understand data in any cost reporting system. For example, within your organization, you have several Azure subscriptions. For the chargeback and cost management reporting, you would use tags such as business unit, department, billing code, environment type, location, etc.

Cost reporting and monitoring

In the Azure portal, the **Cost Management + Billing** feature is your go-to tool to perform your billing-related activities and have full insights into Azure consumption and spend. It helps manage Azure spend at no additional cost. You can perform many cost management activities, such as reporting, alerting, and spending by setting up budgets using recommendations to reduce cost by optimizing cloud resources.

In the Azure portal, navigate to the **Cost Management + Billing** screen by searching for it in the global search box on the top. On the **Cost Management + Billing** screen, in the left menu, click **Cost Management**. The **Cost Analysis** menu appears, as shown in Figure 1-2.

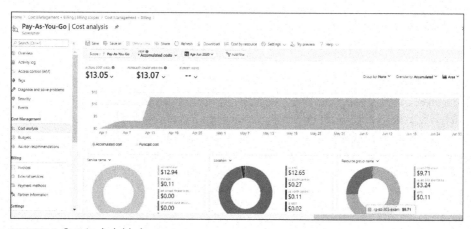

FIGURE 1-2 Cost Analysis blade

In addition to the default view, which provides an elegant summary of your Azure consumption and spends for the previous month, you can also perform the following activities:

- **Cost analysis**   Establish a periodic process to check on your Azure spending. The **Cost Analysis** menu under **Cost Management** (see Figure 1-2) gives you a detailed view of the total accumulated cost for the current month under the scope you are in. You drill down further based on inbuilt grouping and filtering options, such as resources, tags, subscription, billing period, and so on.

- **Configure budget alerts**   You can set up a budget to manage costs and control spending. You can also create alerts that automatically notify the stakeholders of spending threshold breaches.

- **Export data**   The **Export** option on the settings menu allows you to schedule an auto-export of your cost and usage data to a storage account based one of the following schedules:

  - **Daily**   Export of month-to-date costs

  - **Weekly**   Export of costs for the last seven days

  - **Monthly Export Of Last Month's Cost**   Export of previous month's cost

  - **One Time Export**   Export of historical cost data up to a maximum of 90 days in the past

- **Use Azure Advisor recommendations**   The easiest way to get started with cost optimization is to use the built-in Azure Advisor service to get recommendations on the Azure spend. Azure Advisor keeps track of your deployed services and analyzes them for cost optimization, such as pointing out under-utilized virtual machines, unprovisioned Express Route circuits, idle virtual network gateways, unused public IPs, and much more.

Recommend solutions to minimize cost

As we briefly discussed previously, cost optimization is an ongoing activity, and planning is the critical starting point for your cloud journey. You start by identifying the right Azure services and best practices to make the right design decisions that could maximize return on your cloud investment.

In this skill, you learn the critical aspects of minimizing your cloud spend.

Azure services and design choices

The Azure migration journey for any organization starts with evaluating the available Azure services to find the best cloud counterpart for the existing on-premises workload. During the initial planning phase, it is crucial to select the right size of cloud services and the right tier to meet your application scalability and performance requirements while adhering to the organization's budget for the cloud spend. The cloud is all about elasticity and the consumption-based billing model, which means you're better off scaling out and scaling in your cloud resources, as opposed to the traditional way of scaling up your on-premises infrastructure.

Depending on the organization's digital transformation journey—which means adding more business capabilities to evolve faster and be always ahead in the game with other competitors. You want to explore ways to utilize cloud and its off-the-shelf features efficiently. If you choose to do a lift-and-shift or rehost your existing application on the cloud, you might not see much benefit in cost, scalability, and performance. Therefore, having a good understanding of various Azure resource types and solution options is imperative for designing scalable and cost-efficient solutions in the cloud.

Generally, on-premises workloads are often over-provisioned because of a lack of monitoring infrastructure, legacy application design, and little or no visibility into infrastructure resource usage patterns. That means you are likely to scale up on-premises resources by adding more capacity, such as more CPU cores, more memory, etc. However, in the cloud, because of its ability to scale dynamically, the cloud provides much better options for cost-efficient scaling by adding more instances during peak hours and removing them during off business hours to pay for what you use. This scaling type is also known as *horizontal scaling*, which is more cost-efficient and resilient than an on-premises vertical scale.

The second key aspect for minimizing your cloud spend is to choose managed services (Platform as a Service [PaaS], Software as a Service [SaaS], or serverless) over Infrastructure as a service (IaaS). The managed services (SaaS and PaaS) help you significantly reduce the operations, security, and data center maintenance cost. Additionally, switching to managed services opens doors to try out new advanced architecture patterns that could further optimize your cloud spending.

Azure regions

The cost of the Azure services may vary depending upon the location they are provisioned into. Therefore, you should use the Azure calculator to get the cost insights for the selected resources in different regions, making a better choice.

Bandwidth

This is another crucial aspect you need to consider while designing cost-efficient solutions in Azure. The data flow in (ingress) and out (egress) of Azure is *bandwidth*. The inbound (ingress) data flow is always free, but the outbound (egress) data flow has a cost associated with it.

Azure zones

Azure zones, sometimes called *billing zones*, are the geographical grouping of Azure regions for billing purposes. The data transfer charges are based on the zones. Therefore, it makes sense to consider zones when designing your Azure solution to get an idea of the associated cost. Billing zones are different from Availability Zones. There are five billing zones available at the time of writing of this book. See the Microsoft documentation for the latest information.

Minimize Blob Storage cost

Azure Blob Storage is one of the most cost-effective and popular storage options in Azure, required in almost all applications. Azure Blob Storage is a utility service, and you pay only for the data you store. As the data grows, so does the cost. Azure blob storage provides **Hot**, **Cool**, and **Archive** access tiers to store data, with the storage costs being highest in the Hot tier and lowest in the Archive tier.

The **Hot tier** is used for storing data that is frequently accessed and has a high storage and a low access cost, whereas the **Cool tier** is used for infrequently accessed data, but it has a low storage cost and a high access cost.

The **Archive tier** is the cheapest data storage option, and it is meant to be used for rarely accessed data. The Archive access tier has the lowest storage cost but has the highest access cost.

Another avenue for cost optimization is wisely selecting geo-redundant storage. Azure Storage provides three options to strengthen data resiliency and visibility:

- **Local redundant storage (LRS)**   LRS is the least-expensive option that keeps three copies of your data replicated synchronously within the same region.
- **Zone-redundant storage (ZRS)**   More expensive than LRS, ZRS keeps an additional three copies of your data replicated synchronously across the availability zones within the primary region.
- **Geo-redundant storage (GRS) or read-access geo-redundant storage (RA-GRS)** This option copies the data asynchronously to a single physical location in the secondary region. Like LRS, GRS keeps three copies in the primary region.
- **Geo-zone-redundant storage (GZRS) or read-access geo-zone-redundant storage (RA-GZRS)**   GZRS copies your data synchronously across three Azure availability zones in the primary region using ZRS and then copies your data asynchronously to a single physical location in the secondary region.

The latter two options—GRS and GZRS—do not give default read access to the replicated data in the secondary region unless a failover is initiated to the secondary region. However, the read access on the secondary region can be enabled by configuring a storage account to use read-access geo-redundant storage (RA-GRS) or read-access geo-zone-redundant storage (RA-GZRS). The cost of data storage increases as you move from LRS to ZRS or GRS, so you need to be mindful of choosing the best replication option while considering tradeoffs between lower cost and high availability. For example, suppose your application is hosted in a multi-datacenter serving user traffic by the application instance closest to the user's geo-location. In this case, you already have a data presence across two different regions that would prevent you from regional disaster. This means if you are using Azure storage, local redundant storage (LRS) is good enough, and you do not need to have additional expensive replication options enabled.

Minimize infrastructure cost

The Azure DevTest labs feature provides a self-service cloud environment to minimize investment. You can also control cost by setting up auto-shutdown policies, setting the number of virtual machines per user, determining allowed VM sizes, and so on. Some of these policies are discussed below:

- **Spot instances** Spot VMs allow you to take advantage of unused Azure capacity at a steep discount. You request spot VMs at a maximum price that you set, or you can request them based on the capacity you need to run a given workload. The Spot VMs do not have SLAs and are automatically evicted when the price or capacity threshold is exceeded. Spot VMs are recommended for workloads that can handle interruptions, like dev/test environments.

- **Rightsizing the underutilized virtual machines** Virtual machines in Azure are often over-provisioned and seen as highly cost-intensive resources. Many SKUs of virtual machines are available, such as general-purpose, compute-optimized, and memory-optimized, and each is designed to meet specific workload requirements. It is crucial that you carefully look at all available options, map those options to your scalability and performance requirements, and make sure you do not over-provision them. Azure Advisor recommendations should be your starting point to look at oversized and underutilized VMs to optimize them and save on cost. The B-series tier, also known as *burstable low-cost VMs*, is an excellent cost-efficient offering for the steady-state workload that usually needs less CPU utilization and needs an intermittent burst situation with significantly higher CPU demand.

- **Deallocate virtual machines when not in use** Virtual machines that are meant for occasional use only, such as VMs used for the development environment, should be deallocated when not in use. You can also implement hibernate and wakeup schedules to deallocate them during off-business hours or over the weekend to minimize the compute cost. However, you continue to incur storage charges. This is similar to the Azure DevTest environment, where you do not need VMs running at all times and when environment policies allow you to auto shutdown when not in use.

> **IMPORTANT** **DISKS ATTACHED TO VM ARE NOT AUTOMATICALLY DELETED**
>
> By default, when you delete a virtual machine (VM) in Azure, any disks attached to the VM are not automatically deleted. After a VM is deleted, you continue to pay for unattached disks unless you manually delete them as needed.

- **Azure Reservations and Azure Hybrid benefits** Azure Reservations is a promising option for organizations to save significant costs with an upfront purchase commitment for a one- or three-year period. If you have a steady-state workload that runs 24 hours a day, it makes sense to go with the Azure Reservations option to save up to 72 percent of the cost compared to a pay-as-you-go option. Azure Reservations is available for Azure virtual machines (reserved instances) and Azure reserved capacity for database services, such as Azure SQL, Cosmos DB, Azure Synapse Analytics, and Azure Storage. In addition to Azure Reservations, Azure Hybrid benefits allow you to use your on-premises Windows server or SQL server license to save license costs on Azure. For example, if you already have an on-premises SQL server license, you could use it with a vCore-based model and save up to 55 percent of the Azure SQL Database cost. With a Windows server license, you save on the OS cost and pay only for the base compute cost. Combining both the Azure Reservations and Azure Hybrid benefits could save you up to 80 percent of Azure spend.

- **Keep an eye on Azure updates**   Azure is continuously evolving. New services and features are regularly released. You can check the Azure updates page or subscribe to the Azure updates blog to get the latest updates on Azure products and services. For example, Microsoft rolled out a new autoscaling feature for Cosmos DB in May 2020 that helped many organizations optimize database request units (RU)/second usage and cost usage by scaling down when not in use.

Skill 1.2: Design a solution for logging and monitoring

Designing a solution for keeping your operations team in mind plays a vital role in business continuity and happy application users. As an architect, ask yourself a couple of questions:

- How do you make your operations team's job easier when it comes to troubleshooting issues proactively when things go wrong in production?
- How can your operations team have visibility into what's going on under the hood when users start reporting problems?

The answer to all such questions is the robust logging and monitoring strategy of your solutions that helps you have visibility into anomalies that can affect application availability, performance, or other SLAs. This is where Azure Monitor comes into play.

Azure Monitor is a unified, end-to-end monitoring solution for applications and resources in the cloud and on-premises environments.

In this chapter, you learn how Azure Monitor provides a single pane of glass to collect and analyze logs across a broad spectrum of Azure resources and applications running in the cloud. Having your monitoring data all in one place helps you seamlessly detect and diagnose issues, drill down into telemetry data, and act on issues proactively. You can also stream data into external tools such as your organization's custom security information and event management (SIEM) products.

This skill covers how to:

- Determine levels and storage locations for logs
- Send platform logs to different destinations
- Plan for integration with monitoring tools including Azure Monitor and Azure Sentinel
- Recommend appropriate monitoring tool(s) for a solution
- Security monitoring
- Choose a mechanism for event routing and escalation
- Recommend a logging solution for compliance requirements

Determine levels and storage locations for logs

The critical element of any monitoring system is enabling visibility across the different environments by collecting the right amount of data, analyzing it, and converting it into actionable work. Azure Monitor makes this whole process simple by providing a comprehensive suite of monitoring tools. Azure Monitor facilitates data collection from a broad spectrum of cloud and on-premises resources under its common data platform, where you have a variety of tools available to analyze, visualize, and report on it.

The data collected in Azure Monitor falls into these two categories:

- **Metrics**   Metrics are numerical values that describe some aspect of a system at a particular time and are collected at a regular interval, which allows you to have near real-time alerting.

- **Logs**   Logs are raw telemetry that contains a different type of data captured from various sources providing detailed diagnostic and auditing information collected sporadically, typically in the form of an event.

In this skill, you learn about the different tiers and categories of log and metrics data you send into Azure Monitor to monitor specific requirements.

Logs in Azure are categorized into the following types that provide a wide array of insights into performance, health, and operations performed on the Azure resources.

- **Activity logs**   Activity logs provide insight into subscription-level events such as administrative actions on Azure resources, Azure events such as alerts, auto-scale operation, and service health events. Activity logs are generated and collected in Azure Monitor automatically without any additional configurations. Typically, Activity Log is used to determine what, who, and when for any write operations (PUT, POST, DELETE) taken on the resources in your subscription. For example, an activity log would log when someone modifies the SKUs of an existing virtual machine or when someone creates a new resource under the resource group. You can view the activity logs by logging in to the Azure portal under Monitor Resource or using PowerShell or Azure CLI.

- **Resource logs**   Azure resource logs, previously known as *diagnostic logs*, come from deployed resources such as Azure SQL Database, Cosmos DB, VMs, and network interfaces. Resource logs provide detailed insights into operations performed within the resource, such as IIS logs, crash dump data, and error logs. Unlike activity logs, resource logs are not collected automatically. You need to create a diagnostic setting for each supported resource to send resource logs to either a Log Analytics workspace or Azure storage. You can also stream the same log data to Event Hubs to further send data to third-party analytics solutions. The content of the resource log data varies based on the resource type.

- **Azure Active Directory logs**   Azure AD logs provide a full insight into sign-in activity and the audit trail of changes made in Azure Active Directory.

Send platform logs to different destinations

The Azure platform allows you to send platform logs and metrics, including automatically captured activity logs, to the following destinations for longer retention and other reporting requirements. The diagnostic settings allow you to select the list of categories of platform logs or metrics that you want to collect from a resource and send it to one or more destinations listed below.

- **Log Analytics Workspace** You can send log and metric data to a Log Analytics Workspace, which allows that data to be retained for up to 730 days.
- **Azure Storage Account** Archiving logs and metrics to an Azure Storage Account is useful for audit, static analysis, or backup. Compared to a Log Analytics Workspace, Azure Storage is a less expensive option to store data indefinitely.
- **Event Hubs** Using Event Hubs, you can stream log and metrics data to external systems, such as third-party SIEMs and other log analytics solutions.

> **NEED MORE INFO?**   **CONFIGURE DIAGNOSTIC SETTINGS IN AZURE MONITOR**
>
> Because the resource log data varies by resources, each Azure Resource requires you to configure its diagnostic setting within Azure Monitor. The diagnostic settings also allow you to send platform metrics and log data to a different destination for longer retention. See the Microsoft document at *https://docs.microsoft.com/en-us/azure/azure-monitor/platform/ diagnostic-settings.*

EXAM TIP

The default retention for Application Insights data is 90 days. If you need to retain it beyond 90 days, you can send it to the Log Analytics Workspace. You can configure the data retention of a Log Analytics Workspace from 30–730 days. See *https://docs.microsoft.com/en-us/ azure/azure-monitor/platform/manage-cost-storage#default-retention.*

EXAM TIP

The Log Analytics Workspace has different data sources to collect log data from Windows and Linux virtual machines. You would need to manually configure them as per your need. To learn more about configuring data sources, see the Microsoft documentation at *https:// docs.microsoft.com/en-us/azure/azure-monitor/platform/agent-data-sources#configuring- data-sources.*

Plan for integration with monitoring tools including Azure Monitor and Azure Sentinel

In today's digital transformation era, organizations are in a race to reshape their IT operations and line-of-business (LOB) applications to become more innovative and agile. Digital transformation initiatives have led to an exponential growth in data volume over the past few decades, which has resulted in an ever-evolving threat landscape wherein organizations face growing complexity when it comes to securing their application data and datacenter resources.

Many organizations already use third-party security information and event management (SIEM) solutions to mitigate the risks posed by these modern-day threats. It also becomes crucial for you as an Azure solutions architect to help organizations understand the Azure platform's available capabilities to make their threat detection and response smarter and faster with overall reduced IT spending.

In this skill, you learn how organizations can keep their security hygiene intact for cloud applications either by leveraging their existing SIEM solutions or adapting to new cloud-native SIEM solutions such as Azure Sentinel. Azure Sentinel provides built-in machine learning and AI capabilities to detect, investigate, and respond to threats at cloud scale.

Stream Azure log and metrics data to external systems

As you learned earlier in this chapter, with Azure Monitor, you can capture logs and metrics data that help you monitor the performance and availability of your applications and services on the cloud and in on-premises environments. The Azure monitor data comes from a variety of sources, as shown in Figure 1-3.

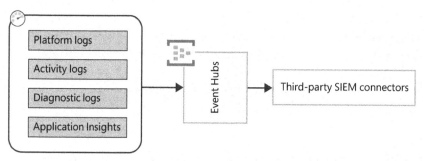

FIGURE 1-3 Export Azure platform and metrics logs to external SIEM systems

Azure Monitor collects logs and metrics data across every layer of the infrastructure and application stack. The data collection starts with the Azure platform when you spin up Azure resources, including activity logs at the subscription level, sign-in activity logs from Azure AD, logs related to Azure services' health, and much more.

You can also capture even more detailed level logs for your Azure resources with a little more configuration. The resource-level diagnostics settings and insights option available in the Azure Monitor blade give you further visibility into the health and performance of Azure resources.

To help organizations collect the log data inside Azure and feed it to their custom monitoring and SIEM solutions, route the monitoring data from Azure Monitor to Event Hubs. Event Hubs output can be easily integrated with SIEM tools such as Splunk, IBM QRadar, and ArcSight. Splunk already has a built-in connector for Azure Event Hubs to consume data that gets routed from Azure Monitor logs into Azure Event Hubs.

> ***NEED MORE REVIEW?*** **STREAM AZURE MONITORING DATA TO AN EVENT HUB**
>
> **To learn more about streaming data for different sources to Azure Event Hub, see** *https://docs.microsoft.com/en-us/azure/azure-monitor/platform/stream-monitoring-data-event-hubs.*

Integration with Azure Sentinel

Microsoft Azure Sentinel is a cloud-native, massively scalable security information event management (SIEM) and security orchestration automated response (SOAR) solution. Azure Sentinel allows you to ingest data from a wide variety of sources, including servers, users, devices, on-premises, and other clouds, and it can deliver intelligent security analytics, threat detection, investigation, and proactive threat hunting and response across the enterprise. The built-in AI and machine-learning capabilities empower Azure Sentinel to proactively perform threat hunting and provide the organization's security operations (SOC) team with a single pane of glass to see security anomalies that are important to them. Azure Sentinel filters the massive log data to just a handful of cases; more than 90 percent of alert fatigue and false positives are reduced. Figure 1-4 shows the four key aspects of Azure Sentinel security operations.

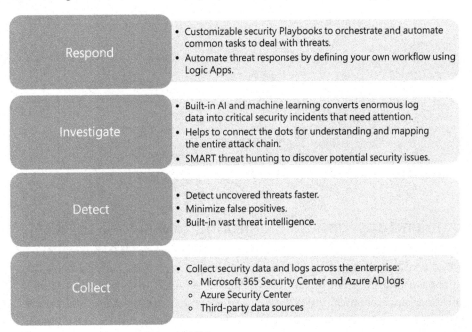

Respond
- Customizable security Playbooks to orchestrate and automate common tasks to deal with threats.
- Automate threat responses by defining your own workflow using Logic Apps.

Investigate
- Built-in AI and machine learning converts enormous log data into critical security incidents that need attention.
- Helps to connect the dots for understanding and mapping the entire attack chain.
- SMART threat hunting to discover potential security issues.

Detect
- Detect uncovered threats faster.
- Minimize false positives.
- Built-in vast threat intelligence.

Collect
- Collect security data and logs across the enterprise:
  - Microsoft 365 Security Center and Azure AD logs
  - Azure Security Center
  - Third-party data sources

FIGURE 1-4 Azure Sentinel built-in capabilities

Azure Sentinel is built on highly scalable and high-performance Azure Monitor Logs that allow you to use a rich Kusto Query Language (KQL) query experience to filter and aggregate data and get insights blazingly fast. Azure Sentinel comes with built-in connectors (see Figure 1-5) that provide real-time integration with many industry solutions, including Microsoft services such as Office 365, Azure Active Directory, and Azure Security Center.

Where Azure Sentinel does not have a connector, you can also ingest data into Azure Sentinel using Common Event Format (CEF) and Syslog REST-API. You can also push data to Azure Monitor's workbooks to create interactive reports and customize the dashboard. The built-in workbook templates, such as Azure AD sign-in logs and Azure activity logs, provide a quick reference guide for getting reports to have visibility into anomalies and critical data sources. Azure Sentinel helps you spend more time responding to real issues instead of trying to determine what to do.

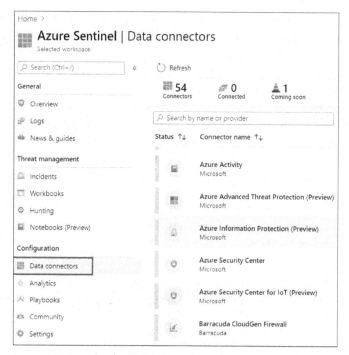

FIGURE 1-5 Azure Sentinel Data Connector pane

Recommend appropriate monitoring tool(s) for a solution

As we learned earlier in this chapter, continuous monitoring is paramount for business continuity. Traditionally, with on-premises datacenters, the monitoring is mostly focused on applications and infrastructure to determine whether the system is up and running. But with the cloud-based applications and infrastructure—where we have a wide variety of choices to use services that best fit our needs—you must use the right tools designed for monitoring a specific use case for a given service offering.

As an Azure Solutions Architect, you are responsible for vetting an application's design to ensure the monitoring aspects are not overlooked. There are many monitoring solutions, tools, and services within Azure, each with its use cases for a given Azure service model (PaaS, IaaS, and serverless).

In this skill, you learn some of the monitoring options available to you, what they monitor, and how to configure them. The following are the key aspects you consider when you are choosing the available monitoring tools and services as part of your monitoring strategy:

- **Application Monitoring** Application monitoring helps you keep track of application performance metrics, usage patterns, and exceptions. It also helps you monitor the application's availability, and it notifies the operations team using Azure Monitor alerts when there are anomalies.

- **Application Insights** Application Insights go beyond monitoring to give you detailed insights into problems and help you find the root cause(s) of the underlying issues. Following are some of the critical capabilities of Application Insights:

  - It provides you a sophisticated default dashboard with essential metrics, such as availability and performance metrics.

  - Code instrumentation helps you visualize both client and server performance statistics.

  - Smart detection keeps you informed when anomalies happen.

  - Application Map provides full visibility into other remote calls, such as database or external API calls.

  - Use either codeless monitoring by merely enabling an agent that requires no code change or by using code-based monitoring by using available SDKs for the programming language of your choice to send custom user telemetry from the application code.

- **Infrastructure Monitoring** Azure Monitor automatically collects the platform-level metrics for Azure services such as virtual machines, containers, databases, and storage accounts when they are created. But depending upon the type of service, you might need to perform additional configuration to collect the desired logs to monitor the service's health and performance. For example, the host-level monitoring data is automatically collected when you create a virtual machine. However, to monitor the guest-level operating system metrics, you would need to install an agent on the virtual machines that sends data to Azure Monitor logs. There are different agents available, such as Azure diagnostics extension, Log Analytics agent, Dependency agent, and Telegraf agent. These agents are used for specific monitoring requirements and collect the different monitoring data on Windows and Linux virtual machines. Azure Monitor unifies the infrastructure monitoring experience for many services in a feature called **Insights**, which helps you customize the monitoring experience for supported services. You can enable Azure Monitor for VMs either by navigating to the **Insights** menu option under the resource (in this case, a virtual machine) or navigating to the **Insights** options from the Azure Monitor. Azure Monitor Insights sends data to the Log Analytics workspace, also known as Azure Monitor logs. You are not charged for enabling this feature, but you incur charges for ingesting data into the workspace and its storage duration. Data retention can be configured from 30 to 720 days, except for the free pricing tier.

> **NOTE   AZURE MONITOR INSIGHTS**
>
> In this section, we covered only the virtual machine. The Insights feature is continuously evolving for other services, such as containers and databases. To learn more, see *https://docs.microsoft.com/en-us/azure/azure-monitor/insights/insights-overview.*

- **Network monitoring**   Network monitoring is a challenging and daunting task for getting insights into underlying network traffic logs, primarily to troubleshoot problems when things go wrong. Network Watcher is the Azure Monitor component that manages the infrastructure and network components such as VMs, virtual networks, application gateways, and load balancers. Network Watcher provides you with the tools for monitoring, troubleshooting, and diagnosing network problems. (These tools are discussed in the following sections.)

Monitoring tools

Following are Network Watcher's monitoring tools:

- **Topology**   The network watcher's topology capability helps you view the simplified version of your network components and resources.
- **Network Performance Monitor (NPM)**   NPM is a cloud-based network monitoring tool that helps you monitor the network connectivity between on-premises and the cloud or across cloud-deployment components.
- **Connection Monitor**   Connection Monitor provides a unified end-to-end connection monitoring experience that supports hybrid and Azure cloud deployments. You can diagnose and view connectivity-related metrics for your resources running in Azure and on-premises with this feature.

Network diagnostics tools

Following are Network Watcher's network diagnostic tools:

- **IP Flow Verify**   This helps you detect overall packet flow between two IP endpoints.
- **Next Hop**   As the name suggests, Next Hop tells you the next destination IP address. Next Hop gets the next hop type and the packet IP address from a specific VM and NIC. It helps you determine whether traffic is being directed to the intended destination.
- **Network Watcher**   Network Watcher allows you to troubleshoot the most common VPN Gateway and Connections issues.

- **Connection Troubleshoot** The connection troubleshoot feature allows you to detect connectivity issues such as traffic packet loss, misconfigured networking routes, DNS resolution failures between source and destination virtual machines.
- **Variable Packet Capture** This is a virtual machine extension in which Network Watcher starts to initiate a packet capture session, enabling tracking traffic to and from a virtual machine.

EXAM TIP

Network Watcher's IP Flow Verify tool helps you to detect whether packets are allowed or denied between the source and destination VMs. To learn more about configuring data sources, see the Microsoft documentation at *https://docs.microsoft.com/en-us/azure/network-watcher/network-watcher-ip-flow-verify-overview.*

Logging tools

Following are Network Watcher's logging tools:

- **NSG flow logs** Network security group (NSG) flow logs provide you with detailed insights into the ingress and egress of IP traffic passing through NSGs that are connected to either VMs or VNETs.
- **Traffic Analytics** Traffic analytics analyzes Network Watcher network security group (NSG) flow logs to provide insights into traffic flow in your Azure cloud.

EXAM TIP

The Application Map feature of Application Insights provides an in-depth visibility of distributed application components, so you can spot anomalies and failure hotspots. To learn more, see the Microsoft documentation at *https://docs.microsoft.com/en-us/azure/azure-monitor/app/app-map?tabs=net.*

Security monitoring

Securing applications, infrastructure, and data in the cloud is a shared responsibility between customers and cloud vendors. As far as Azure platform-level security goes, Microsoft is committed to keeping Azure Datacenter secure from attackers. It also provides several capabilities as part of a service offering to help design and implement reliable solutions in Azure to detect and respond to threats even before they appear. Azure Security Center is one of the prominent service offerings that empower you to strengthen your cloud environment's security posture and protect your infrastructure and Azure services against security threats. The security center comes in two tiers: the free tier, and the standard tier.

- **Free tier** The free tier is enabled by default on your Azure subscription and provides actionable security recommendations on supported Azure resources.

- **Standard tier**   The standard tier comes with additional monitoring and vulnerability assessment capabilities and can also be leveraged for your hybrid workloads. Security Center standard tier supports Azure resources, including VMs, VM scale sets, App Service, SQL servers, and Azure Storage Accounts.

Choose a mechanism for event routing and escalation

To this point, you have learned that Azure Monitor is the all-in-one place for all your monitoring data that is coming in at a massive scale from Azure resources, including both on-premises environments and other cloud environments. Now, the question is, how do you decide what to do with this data and take appropriate actions proactively, such as notifying your operations team when there are anomalies or when problems have occurred on the deployed resources or applications?

Azure Monitor alerts provide you unified, end-to-end alerting experience across the different environments. In Azure Monitor, you can define alerts rules to trigger an action for event routing, and you can define escalations based on conditions for monitoring data so that you always remain informed about the state of your deployed resources.

Alert rules in Azure Monitor can be defined on metrics, platform logs, or custom logs that you collect from different sources. Alert rules are mainly made up of the following three categories:

- **Scope**   The first thing you select in the scope is a target resource for the alert rule. A target resource can be a virtual machine, an Azure SQL Database, Application Insights, or a Log Analytics workspace.

- **Condition**   After you have selected a resource to monitor, the next step is to define alert criteria or the condition on the selected resource. The alert condition comprises a combination of an alert signal and logic defined on a selected resource. For example, you want to trigger an alert when a virtual machine's CPU goes beyond 90 percent for a specified time.

- **Action group**   Action groups define the actions that need to be taken when an alert is fired for a given alert rule. You can set one or more actions to be performed when an alert is fired. Following are the types of actions you can set up in the action group:

  - Run an Azure function.
  - Trigger an Azure automation runbook.
  - Send email/SMS/voice or push notification.
  - Trigger a Logic App.
  - Invoke a webhook.
  - Integrate with your ITSM ticketing system, such as ServiceNow.

Recommend a logging solution for compliance requirements

Multinational organizations face numerous regulatory and compliance requirements to comply with the relevant local government laws worldwide. Many organizations, when adopting cloud, are particular about the need to meet their compliance obligations. The obligations might be internal to the organization, or they could be external industry-standard regulations enforced by local government laws. One of the most common compliance requirements that organizations must address in the cloud is a robust logging, auditing, and monitoring strategy.

In this skill, you learn different types of log data that you capture for various Azure services and how to retain it to meet the compliance and regulatory requirements specific to the organization's business model.

Azure provides a wide variety of options to capture logs across different types of services. At a high level, the logs in Azure are categorized as follows:

- **Control/Management logs** These provide information about the activity performed on Azure Resource Manager (ARM) resources such as CREATE, UPDATE, and DELETE operations. An example of this log would be creating a new virtual machine.

- **Data plane logs** These provide information about events raised by Azure resource usage. Examples of such logs are application performance logs generated by Application Insights, diagnostics logs configured in Azure Monitor, Azure Active directory sign-in logs, etc.

- **Processed events** These provide information about analyzed events or alerts that have been processed on your behalf. Examples of this type include Azure SQL Database advanced threat protection (ATP) alerts, where ATP analyzes the databases on the SQL Server and generates alerts for anomalies and vulnerability.

Based on your organization's compliance requirements for logging and auditing, you must understand different Azure layers and capabilities to extract logs for Azure services. Understanding each one of them helps organizations make informed decisions for compliance requirements. For instance, let's say you want to have visibility on who created a virtual machine in Azure or who updated an existing virtual machine. You can look at Azure activity logs for the operations performed on the Azure resources. Similarly, to get information about the history of sign-in activity and an audit trail of changes made in the Azure Active Directory for a particular tenant, you can look at Azure Active Directory logs.

Figure 1-6 shows the different categories of data sources and logs available in Azure that can be captured in various scopes to address compliance.

To meet your organization's compliance requirements for data retention, you use the Log Analytics workspace to retain the log data for up to 730 days. You can seamlessly integrate and ingest the data from within Azure Monitor to the Log Analytics workspace. If you want to retain the log data beyond two years, use Azure Storage Accounts.

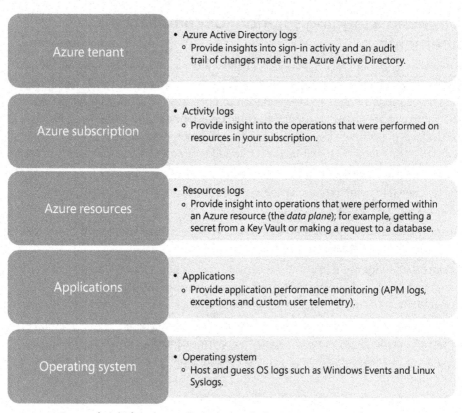

FIGURE 1-6 Sources for platform logs and metrics logs in Azure

Chapter summary

- Cost management is a set of processes and tools that you apply to your organization's governance model. It takes extensive upfront planning of cloud resources to align them effectively with your business requirements.

- Azure Cost Management + Billing is a free tool in Azure that helps you track, analyze, manage, and optimize Azure services and resource costs.

- Use appropriate Azure purchasing options (free, pay-as-you-go, enterprise agreements, Cloud Solution Provider (CSP), Azure Regions, Azure Reservations, and hybrid benefits) to help keep your Azure spend down.

- The platform logs in Azure (activity logs, resource, and Azure AD logs) provide you with detailed diagnostics and auditing information for Azure resources.

- You can choose to send the platform logs to one or more destinations such as a Log Analytics workspace, Azure storage, or external log analytics or monitoring system using Event Hub.

- Azure Sentinel is a cloud SIEM and SOAR solution that delivers intelligent security analytics and threat intelligence across the enterprise.

- Azure Sentinel is built on highly scalable and high-performance Azure Monitor logs that allow you to use a rich KQL query experience to filter and aggregate data and get insights blazingly fast.

- Azure Monitor provides a unified platform for monitoring solutions in Azure that span across applications, the infrastructure, and the network.

- Azure Monitor alerts use action groups to notify the user when an alert is triggered. Action groups allow integrating notifications to your enterprise ticketing systems, such as ServiceNow.

- Within Azure, you can track logs across different Azure environment service layers for logging and auditing requirements. You can also meet the data retention compliance requirements by sending data to storage services such as a Log Analytics workspace or Azure Storage.

Thought experiment

In this thought experiment, you need to demonstrate the skills and knowledge of the objectives covered in this chapter. You can find an answer to the thought experiment in the "Thought experiment answers" section at the end of this chapter.

You are an Azure Solutions Architect for a fictitious company named Contoso. The company wants to migrate its on-premises infrastructure to Azure, but it is skeptical about the cost and cloud infrastructure management. The company also wants to know if there would be any changes in monitoring existing on-premises applications and infrastructure after migrating to Azure.

You have had several meetings with Contoso leadership for the Azure Migration project, and you have recorded the following requirements:

1. The Contoso leadership wants to know the high-level cost estimates for the Azure Migration project for budgeting purposes.

2. The team of stakeholders also wants to understand what capability is there in Azure to be leveraged to minimize the cost of infrastructure that they only need on an on-demand basis.

3. The company wants to empower its security operations teams to act promptly and respond to threats more proactively.

4. For business-critical applications, the company wants to automate alerting and monitoring capability so that its operations team remains on top of problems when they occur.

Thought experiment answers

This section contains the solutions to the thought experiment in the previous section:

1. Regarding getting the high-level cost estimate for on-premises infrastructure with the compatible replacement of Azure services, you would use the Azure calculator and the Azure total cost of ownership (TCO) calculator.

2. To minimize the cost of infrastructure you use occasionally, you would use Azure Dev/Test labs that facilitate quick provisioning of Dev and Test environment and automate the shutdown when not in use. Implement auto-scaling to meet the spiking behavior and then revert to the capacity required for consistent usage.

3. Azure provides a SIEM solution called Azure Sentinel that operates at a cloud scale to hunt for built-in AI and machine learning threats. You would use Azure Sentinel to empower your SOC team to respond to threats much faster by reducing alert fatigue to a larger extent.

4. To empower your operations team to act proactively when an anomaly is detected within the application, you would use Azure Monitor alerts and action groups. Azure Monitor can monitor both application and infrastructure and provide a sophisticated dashboard and an elegant view of the application and infrastructure health. Additionally, you can integrate Azure Monitor alerts with existing ITSM tools such as ServiceNow or send notifications to operations teams via SMS or email.

CHAPTER 2

Design identity and security

The challenge of migrating to a cloud-centered architecture forces us to think of new ways to protect data, resources, and services. Companies have become comfortable protecting legacy, on-premises environments against threats from the outside world, but now it is expected that those same resources must be equally protected, even though they are moving to the cloud. In this chapter, we will cover the core concepts of how to protect all resources, so that all data and services can safely be accessed from anywhere, by all users.

Skills covered in this chapter:

- Skill 2.1: Design authentication
- Skill 2.2: Design authorization
- Skill 2.3: Design security for applications

Skill 2.1: Design authentication

Designing a cloud-based solution for authentication is not an easy task. It must include assurance that users and applications are properly verified before they can access data, services, and resources in the cloud, and on-premises. While offering the most stellar verification, user requests for data and services must remain seamless and high-performing, even when there are many simultaneous requests, working over both on-premises and in the cloud. Azure provides all that you need for the purposes of Authentication.

This skill covers how to:

- Single sign-on solutions (SSO)
- Authentication
- Multifactor authentication
- Network access authentication
- Create a virtual network and a network security group
- Azure AD Connect and Azure AD Connect Health
- Self-service
- Azure Active Directory B2B

Single sign-on solutions (SSO)

Traditionally, IT staff individually created and updated user accounts in each application, which meant that users had to remember a password for each such application. Single sign-on means being able to access all the applications and resources that a user needs to do business by signing in only once using a single user account. Once signed in, the user can access all needed applications without being required to authenticate (type a password) a second time.

Single sign-on, which is depicted in Figure 2-1, offers several benefits:

- Enabling single sign-on across applications and Office 365 provides a superior log in experience for existing users, which reduces or eliminates multiple log in prompts.

- Coupling Azure AD SSO with conditional access policies can offer significantly improved security experiences.

- Auditing access requests and approvals for the application, as well as understanding overall application usage, becomes easier with Azure Active Directory. Azure AD supports native audit logs for every application access request performed.

- Replacing current access management and provisioning process and migration to Azure Active Directory to manage self-service access to the application (as well as other SaaS applications in the future) will allow for significant cost reductions related to running, managing, and maintaining the current infrastructure.

- Eliminating application specific passwords eliminates costs related to password reset for that application and lost productivity while retrieving passwords.

- Single sign-on across Azure, Microsoft 365, and many SaaS applications is available in the Azure AD free tier.

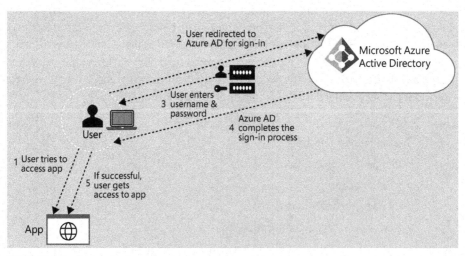

FIGURE 2-1 Single sign-on flow

Figure 2.1 illustrates all the components and steps involved when a user tries to sign in to an application secured by Azure AD and if password hash sync used. This is a cloud-based authentication flow. As depicted in the figure, when a user tries to sign in to an application secured by Azure AD (and if the user is authenticating directly with Azure AD), the following steps occur:

1. The user tries to access an application such as the Outlook web app or Box.

2. If the user is not already signed in, the user is redirected to the Azure AD User Sign-In page.

3. The user enters their username and password into the Azure AD sign-in page and then clicks the **Sign In** button.

4. Azure AD evaluates the response and responds to the user as appropriate. For example, Azure AD either signs the user in immediately or makes an Azure multifactor authentication request.

5. If the user sign-in is successful, the user can access the application.

Figure 2-2 shows the point-and-click Azure portal options for setting up single sign-on. In this case, using Enterprise Applications, the Google Docs app is being set up for single sign-on.

Also, if external users are allowed in your organization, it is not a requirement that they implement Azure Active Directory in their own environments. Log in screens can be customized to include company logos and text that will extend a comfort level to all users because the log in screen is intuitive, and users will know that the only requirements are a username and password.

FIGURE 2-2 Single sign-on options in Azure Active Directory Enterprise Applications

Azure AD provides the following topologies for SSO solutions. You should choose the one that most closely matches your specific scenario:

1. Azure AD Single Sign-On with Password Hash Sync or cloud-based user authentication.
2. Azure AD Single Sign-On with AD FS or other federation as the IDP (identity provider). This solution is a combination of hybrid identity sync that uses Azure AD Connect and maintains a trust with an on-premises federation service as the identity provider for Azure Active Directory. Azure Active Directory acts as the IDP for the application, while acting as the SP (service principal) for the on-premises federation service.
3. Azure AD Single Sign-on with Pass-through Authentication, which allows your users to sign in to both on-premises and cloud-based applications using the same passwords.

In addition to authentication being managed with the Azure portal, it can be managed with command-line tools, PowerShell, Microsoft Graph API, and .Net Languages, such as C# and VB.Net, using libraries, such as ADAL.

Authentication

Once a user has populated a log-in screen, authentication is the next step in the process. Authentication can take place as a result of a variety of scenarios and various types of applications, such as web apps, mobile apps, desktop apps, and web APIs.

The Microsoft Authentication Library (MSAL) can be used to acquire security tokens, so that web APIs can be protected and acquire security tokens from APIs or web apps.

Although most authentication methods include users who are signed in with previously mentioned app types, some apps known as *daemon* apps can acquire tokens without a user. Apps and services can be automated so that the flow is triggered in a flow of tasks and activities. These apps use the OAuth 2.0 standard. Examples of a daemon app include web applications that are used to perform batch or background processing.

As companies are migrating to the cloud, there is a focus on empowering users to be productive anywhere and at any time. Conditional access, which is an AAD service, is a great way to apply the proper access controls without a heavy-handed obstruction process. Conditional access policies can be put into place that will check signals (users, groups, locations, devices, applications, and real-time risks). Signals will verify every access attempt and determine if access should be allowed, blocked, or will require more information to make that determination.

Conditional access policies address concerns that are common to most companies. Some examples of the most common policies include:

- Requiring multifactor authentication for users with administrative roles
- Requiring multifactor authentication for Azure management tasks
- Blocking sign-ins for users attempting to use legacy authentication protocols
- Requiring trusted locations for Azure AD multifactor authentication registration
- Blocking or granting access from specific locations

- Blocking risky sign-in behaviors
- Requiring organization-managed devices for specific applications

In the past, both users and IT professionals struggled with repetitive authentication procedures to get users and/or applications authenticated. With the innovation of Microsoft's Identity Platform, users and applications can prove who they are with various protocols through Azure Active Directory's "store" of user and application data. Delegating Azure Active Directory as the single point of authentication alleviates a high administration burden for IT professionals by using the Microsoft Identity Platform.

Microsoft Identity Platform provides Identity as a Service (IaaS), which supports industry-standard protocols, including:

- OAuth (for authorization)
- OpenID Connect (open standard for authentication access)
- SAML (Security Assertion Markup Language) for exchanging authentication and authorization between identity and service providers.

Azure Active Directory uses Conditional Access policies to make decisions about which users and devices can access Azure resources. Conditional Access uses policies that work with signals, decisions, and enforcement. To better understand these components, see Table 2-1.

TABLE 2-1 Conditional Access components

Common Signals	Common Decisions	Common Enforcements
User or group membership	Block access	Requiring multifactor authentication for administrators
IP location Information	Grant access	Requiring multifactor authentication for Azure management tasks

Common Signals	Common Decisions	Common Enforcements
Devices		Blocking sign-ins for legacy authentication (using legacy authentication protocols)
Applications		Requiring trusted locations for Azure multi-factor authentication registration
Risk detection (real-time and calculated)		Blocking or granting access from specific locations
Microsoft Cloud App Security (MCAS)		Requiring organization-managed devices for specific applications

NEED MORE REVIEW? **CONDITIONAL ACCESS**

To review further details about Conditional Access, see *https://docs.microsoft.com/en-us/ azure/active-directory/conditional-access/overview.*

Multifactor authentication

Azure multifactor authentication (see Figure 2-3) can be enabled so that users are required to provide additional verification methods to sign in. Examples of additional access methods are a call to a phone, a text message to a phone, or to send a mobile app verification code. Multifactor authentication can be managed through the Azure portal, command-line tools, scripts, or code.

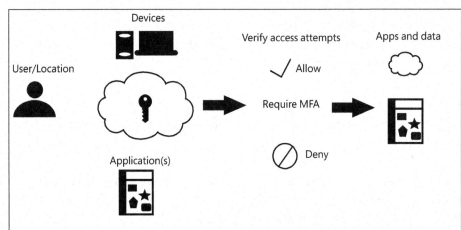

1. User attempts to access a resource from a specific location with a device or an application.
2. Depending on the business rules, the user might be required to provide additional information through MFA (text, phone call, and the like).
3. The user is allowed access once the user, device, or location has been verified by MFA.
4. If MFA does not verify the user, device, or location, conditional policies can outline what should be done next.

FIGURE 2-3 Conditional access using MFA

Users must register their own selected methods for MFA. The most efficient approach is to use Azure Directory Identity Protection. This service will prompt users to register for MFA on their next log in.

An alternative approach is to enforce MFA registration through Conditional Access Policies for an "All Users" group in your company. This method is not as efficient, as it requires some manual setup and periodic review.

Assigning multifactor authentication (MFA) to an existing user

Follow these steps to assign multifactor authentication to an existing user:

1. From the Azure portal, go to Azure Active Directory.
2. Click **All Users**.
3. Click the ellipsis (**...**) at the top right.
4. Choose **Multi-Factor Authentication**, as shown in Figure 2-4.

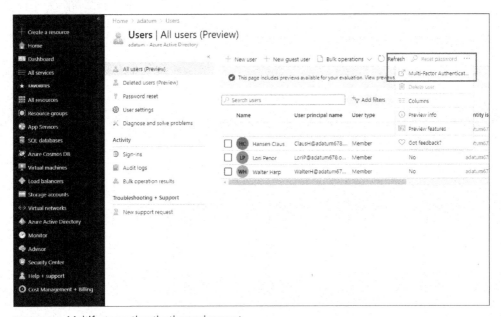

FIGURE 2-4 Multifactor authentication assignment

5. Choose a user by clicking the user's name and then choose **Enable** > **Service Settings**, as shown in Figure 2-5.

FIGURE 2-5 Choosing a user for whom to enable MFA

6. From the **Service Settings** blade, observe the MFA Options available to validate users, as shown in Figure 2-6.

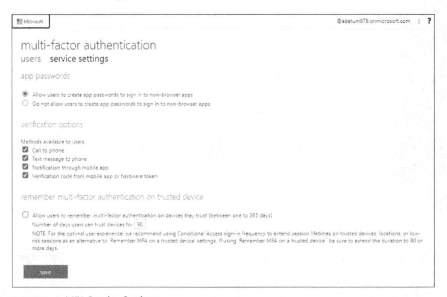

FIGURE 2-6 MFA Service Settings

Network access authentication

When the need arises in Azure to control or limit connectivity to and from networks (Example: devices or subnets), Azure supports isolation techniques for the purpose of allowing only intended connections to the network.

Similar to Azure Policy, Azure uses Network Security Groups to assist with filtering network traffic to and from Azure resources, as well as services in an Azure virtual network. Like Conditional Access policies, Network Security Groups (NSGs) contain security rules to allow or deny inbound and/or outbound traffic to and from Azure resource in the virtual network.

NSGs are assigned to either network interfaces or subnets. Any rules that have been created will apply to all network interfaces in a subnet. Using a subnet as an NSG target can reduce management and administration. Network Security Groups support:

- **TCP (Transmission Control Protocol/Internet Protocol)** TCP establishes and maintains the network conversation.
- **UDP (User Datagram Protocol)** UDP is a communication protocol used across the Internet for especially time-sensitive transmissions, such as video playback or DNS lookups.
- **ICMP (Internet Control Message Protocol)** ICMP protocol is most commonly used by network devices to send error and operational messages. It is also used for troubleshooting network connectivity issues.

> **NOTE NETWORK SECURITY GROUP–SUPPORTED PROTOCOLS**
>
> Each subnet and network interface can have one network security group applied to it.

> **NEED MORE REVIEW? PROCESSING INBOUND AND OUTBOUND RULES**
>
> To understand how Azure processes inbound and outbound rules for network security groups (NSGs), see *https://docs.microsoft.com/en-us/azure/virtual-network/network-security-group-how-it-works*.

Security rules

Network Security Groups (NSGs) contain one or more security rules that are defined to allow or deny traffic to and from the network. All NSG rules start by identifying properties, including priority, which is used to evaluate NSG rules.

Azure also creates several default rules that cannot be deleted as listed in Table 2-2. While you cannot remove these default rules, you can override them by creating higher priority rules.

TABLE 2-2 Inbound and outbound default traffic rules when NSGs are created in Azure

Inbound traffic default rules		
Priority	**Rule name**	**Description**
65000	AllowVnetInbound	Allow inbound traffic from all VMs in VNET VNet.
65001	AllowAzureLoadBalancerInbound	Allow inbound traffic from Azure Load Balancer.
65500	DenyAllInBound	Deny all inbound traffic.
Outbound traffic default rules		
Priority	**Rule name**	**Description**
65000	AllowVnetOutbound	Allow outbound traffic from all VMs to all VMs in a VNET.
65001	AllowInternetOutBound	Allow outbound traffic from all VMs to the Internet.
65500	DenyAllOutBound	Deny all outbound traffic.

Service tags

Service tags allow access restriction by resources or services. Service tags represent a group of IP addresses and simplify rule configuration. When using tags, you do not need to know the IP address or port details. Microsoft creates and manages service tags. Listed below are the most-used service tags:

- VirtualNetwork
- AzureLoadBalancer
- Internet
- AzureTrafficManager
- Storage
- SQL
- AppService

Create a virtual network and a network security group

Although both VNets and NSGs can be created and managed with the Azure portal, a common way to create and manage NSGs is with Azure CLI, using the Azure Cloud Shell.

Listing 2-1 shows the command-line snippets that can be used to create a VNet and an NSG:

LISTING 2-1 Create a virtual network and an NSG

```
//Sample of Azure CLI command line code
//Create Resource Group
$rg = "lucernerg"
```

```
az group create --name $rg --location
 'East US'
```

//Create Virtual Network/Servers

```
az network vnet create --resource-group $rg --name Lucerne-servers --address-prefix
10.0.0.0/16 --subnet-name LucerneApps --subnet-prefix 10.0.0.0/24
```

//Create Lucerne Servers NSG Group

```
az network nsg create --resource-group $rg --name Lucerne-SERVERS-NSG
```

The following steps show the quick creation method for creating a virtual network. If you have custom IP addresses and subnet addresses, you can use the detailed creation method, which is explained separately after this set of steps.

1. In the Azure portal's left menu, click **Virtual Networks**.

2. Click **+Create**.

3. For a quick create, choose **Add Resource Group** > **Name** > **Region**, and click **Review And Create**. (Azure will create default properties for the remaining entries.)

4. Click **Review + Create**. Azure will run a final validation. If everything has been filled out correctly, the portal will display **Validation Passed** and a green check mark, and the **Create** button will appear.

5. Click the **Create** button to create the new Azure virtual server.

> **NOTE** **QUICK CREATION METHOD**
>
> The quick creation method will create an Azure Virtual Server with default names, IP addresses, subnets, security options, and tags.

> **NOTE** **DETAILED CREATION METHOD**
>
> If you want to use custom or business standard names, you should use the detailed creation method (see below).

Detailed creation method:

1. In the Azure portal's left menu, click Virtual Networks.

2. Click **+Create**.

3. Across the top, you will see tabs for each set of items. Click each tab and fill the information as shown here:

   ■ **Basics**   Subscription Name, Resource Group (new or existing), Name, and Region.

   ■ **IP Addresses**   IPv4 or IPv6 Address Space (choose either), Subnet Names (if using), and optional Default IP Address.

   ■ **Security**   You are offered both **Disable** or **Enable** options for Bastion Host, DDoS Protection Standard, and Firewall.

- **Tags** Tags act like custom labels and are designed to help users find tagged items at any time by using the search bar located at the top of the Azure portal.

- **Review + Create** Submits the above details for validation.

4. Once **Review + Create** has been selected, Azure will run a final validation. If everything has been filled out correctly, the portal will display **Validation Passed** and a green check mark, and the **Create** button will appear.

5. Click the **Create** button to create the new Azure Virtual Server.

As is always true in Azure, there are alternative ways to accomplish the same goal:

1. The **+Create A Resource** option in the left hub menu will take you to the Azure Market-place. Typing **Network Security Group** in the Azure Marketplace search bar will show a choice of NSGs. Use the **Create** button to launch a wizard that will allow you to create an NSG.

2. The **All Services** option in the left hub menu will take you to the most commonly used, or featured items. In the filter box, enter **Network Security Group**. The choices will be filtered, and **Network Security Group** will appear first in the list. When using the **All Services** option, you will see the **+Add** option, which begins the process of creating an NSG.

NOTE **BOTH CHOICES LEAD TO THE NSG WIZARD**

Both the **+Create** option (Azure Marketplace), and the **All Services** option will eventually end up in the same NSG wizard. As is true in all Azure services, the wizards offer quick creation and detailed creation methods. The difference between the two is always the same. The quick creation method will name and choose all default options for you, which is great for develop-ment and testing. For production, the best practice is to use the detailed creation method so that you can name and choose options which are specifically designed for your company.

Follow these steps to create an NSG:

1. From the Azure portal choose **All Services** or open the **Azure Marketplace** and type **Network Security Group**.

2. Click **+Add**.

3. Fill in the **Resource Group Name**, **Instance Name**, and **Region**.

4. Click **Review + Create**.

5. Once the green validation check appears, your choices have been validated and are ready for submission.

6. Click **Create**.

Follow these steps to associate an NSG to a subnet:

1. From the Azure portal, click **Virtual Networks**.

2. Click the network to which you want to associate the NSG.

3. Click the **Subnets** option from the **Settings** section.

4. Click on the desired subnet. The screen will show all subnets available, including the default subnets.

5. The pop-up menu will contain an option to choose an NSG. This drop-down menu contains all NSGs that have been created in this subscription. Choose the desired NSG that will be associated with the subnet chosen above.

6. Click **Save**.

Azure AD Connect and Azure AD Connect Health

Active Directory Domain Services and Azure Active Directory are identity services that can be effective when identities are consistent in both on-premises and cloud environments in a hybrid cloud scenario.

Azure AD Connect addresses this need by creating and managing the synchronization of identities across on-premises and cloud environments. Installation is quick, and a wizard allows verification of both cloud and on-premises administrative accounts. Once AD Connect verifies the administrator, it walks the administrator through a series of screens that will perform initial setup of AD Connect. Subsequent walk-throughs allow the administrator to adjust the settings. Azure AD Connect provides following features:

- **Password hash synchronization** Password hash synchronization acts like an extension to the directory synchronization feature that is implemented by Azure AD Connect Sync. Password hashes allow you to sign in to an Azure service using the same password that you use to sign in to your on-premises Active Directory instance. This option reduces the number of passwords that users will need to maintain and improve productivity. Behind the scenes, these passwords are synced when Azure AD Connect syncs on-premises and cloud directories. Therefore, the passwords will remain the same, but you cannot enforce user-level Active Directory security policies during sign-in.

- **Pass-through authentication (PTA)** This feature is an alternative to password hash synchronization even though it will seem the same to end users. Pass-through authentication also allows users to sign in to both on-premises and cloud-based applications using the same passwords. Like password hash synchronization, users only have to remember one password, which will improve productivity. The main difference with pass-through authentication is that organizations want to enforce on-premises Active Directory security and policies, which cannot be accomplished with password hash synchronization.

- **Synchronization** The process of synchronization is completed using AD Connect too, which is installed in minutes and has a tiny footprint (which makes it very efficient). Administrators are required to sign in with two sets of credentials:
  - On-premises administrative credentials
  - Cloud-based administrative credentials

Once the administrator is signed in, a walk-through wizard gives the administrator choices such as pass-through authentication versus federated authentication. It also allows the administrator to choose which OUs (organization units) they wish to sync. Although Azure Active Directory does not implement OUs, the wizard knows how to pull items from OUs and sync them to Azure Active Directory. The Administrator can also choose to sync up the entire Active Directory implementation (all OUs). However, if a company is very large and has an extremely large number of objects/entries in Active Directory, it might behoove the Administrator to sync OUs in chunks. Doing so will reduce the amount of time it takes for objects to sync, and will allow testing in chunks, rather than finding errors after syncing the entire enterprise at once. AD Connect also offers schedulers that will help to automate the sync process at desired points in time, as well as filtered/grouping options to make your syncs more efficient.

- **AD Connect Health** AD Connect Health is a tool that can be installed with the AD Connect software suite and is used to monitor and collect insights into on-premises identity infrastructure. In other words, it will ensure reliability of syncing objects from on premises to the cloud. This monitoring feature has no extra charge, but it requires a minimum of a P1 license. AD Connect Health will make administrators aware of any issues and/or errors that will take place during sync, therefore allowing administrators to proactively troubleshoot issues before they become a bigger problem.

Azure AD Connect allows organizations to:

- Enable users to use a single identity to access both cloud and on-premises applications and services (Microsoft 365 being one of the most common applications).
- Use one tool to deploy and manage the synchronization of identities.
- Use the most sought-after identity management capabilities.

Identity management is the backbone of a company's user community. To be certain that your identity management is always up to date and without error, Azure provides Azure AD Connect Health, which is a portal to view usage analytics, alerts, performance, and other pertinent on-premises, identity infrastructure–related information.

AD Connect Health allows organizations to

- Use enhanced security to view trends regarding lockouts and failed sign-in attempts.
- Use one tool to receive alerts on all critical identity management performance and connectivity issues.
- Use one tool to monitor per-server metrics such as top application usage, network locations, and connectivity.

Figure 2-7 depicts the placement of AD Connect and AD Connect Health.

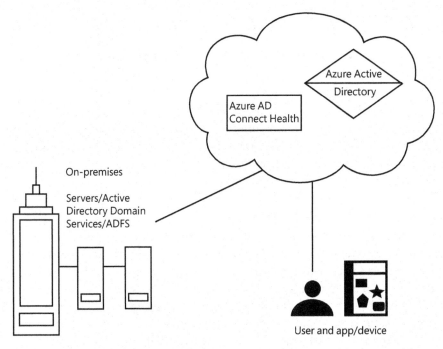

FIGURE 2-7 Placement of Azure Active Directory, Azure AD Connect, and Connect Health

User Self Service solutions

Azure provides some ways that users can help themselves, thereby reducing calls to company administrators or help desk employees. Administrators can also perform access reviews to ensure security standards. Self-service options include:

- Self-Service Reset for Azure multifactor authentication verification options
- Azure Active Directory self-service password reset
- Self-service group and application access
- Self-service sign-up user flow
- Azure AD access review

Self-Service Reset for Azure multifactor authentication verification options

Self-service password reset (SSPR) allows users to self-serve multifactor authentication options without the intervention of an IT professional. This service also allows users to reset verification options such as:

- **Call To Phone**   Users can reset their phone numbers.
- **Text Message To Phone**   Users can reset their mobile phone numbers.

- **Notification Through Mobile App**   Users can reset some mobile app notification settings.
- **Verification On Code From Mobile App Or Hardware Token**   Users can reset some app notifications.

Azure Active Directory self-service password reset

SSPR or self-service password reset empowers users to self-serve with password resets in Azure Active Directory. This includes password locking and resets. Azure provides detailed reporting that tracks user password locking and resets, including alert notifications to users on password reset and to all admins when other admins reset their passwords.

Self-service group and application access

Azure Active Directory provides non-administrators the ability to manage access to resources such as groups, application roles, Microsoft 365 groups, security groups, and access package catalogs. These users are not required to hold an administrative role. For example, in Microsoft 365, a user may create a SharePoint site that would automatically give him or her the Owner role. While this is not a Global Administrator role—or even a specialized Administrator role—it would allow the owner to perform any changes, additions, or deletions of that SharePoint site. In addition, this owner could delegate rights for this site to users of their choosing. The same applies to other Microsoft 365 services, such as Teams and OneDrive using for Business.

Azure AD access review

Azure administrators can maintain security standards by using Azure AD access reviews. This service allows administrators to efficiently review and manage group memberships, access enterprise applications, and make role assignments, and it allows administrators to be certain the users do not retain access for extended periods of time (if they no longer need it).

> **NEED MORE REVIEW?   AZURE AD ACCESS REVIEWS**
>
> To review further details about Azure AD access reviews, see *https://docs.microsoft.com/en-us/azure/active-directory/governance/access-reviews-overview*.

EXAM TIP

To protect your users, you can configure risk-based policies in Azure Active Directory that automatically respond to risky behaviors. Azure AD Identity Protection policies can automatically block a sign-in attempt or require additional action, such as require a password change or prompt for Azure AD Multi-Factor Authentication. These policies work with existing Azure AD Conditional Access policies as an extra layer of protection for your organization.

Azure Active Directory B2B

With Azure Active Directory B2B, administrators can now provide access to your company's Azure resources to external users and partners using a simple invitation/redemption process.

External users do not need to remember or learn anything new when it comes to logging in to company Azure resources. Azure AD B2B provides the following features:

- Allows partners to use their existing identities and credentials.
- Allows partners to take advantage of Azure AD, without requiring them to use it in their own environments.
- Allows administrators to manage resources for the partners, without having to manage any external accounts or passwords, or lifecycles (syncing accounts).
- Allows administrators to protect company resources with Conditional Access policies.

To invite a guest/partner user, click **Azure Active Directory** in the Azure portal and click **Users > New Guest User** (see Figure 2-8).

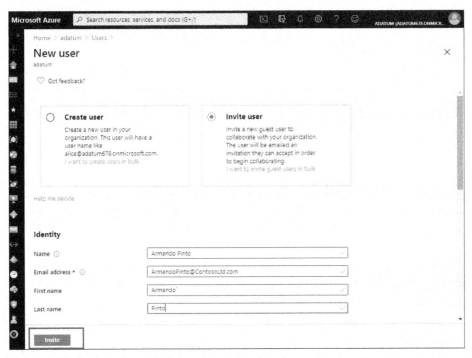

FIGURE 2-8 Inviting guest users to Azure resources

In Figure 2-8, Armando Pinto was added as a guest user. Once the **Invite** button is clicked, Armando will receive an email containing an invitation link. When Armando accepts the invitation, he will be listed as **Guest** in Azure Active Directory and will have access to Azure resources that the administrator or self-serve user gives him. Keep in mind that Conditional Access policies (including the requirement for MFA) can be used further as per your security needs.

Skill 2.2: Design authorization

Authorization is the process of granting permissions for authenticated parties. It encompasses what data the user can access and what the user can do with the data. Microsoft Identity Platform implements the OAuth 2.0 protocol to handle authorization, as discussed in the "Design authentication" section earlier in this chapter. In this section, we will cover key concepts for delegating authorization for Azure services in the most seamless way.

This skill covers how to:
- Choose an authorization approach
- Hierarchical structure
- Design governance

Choose an authorization approach

The Microsoft identity platform implements authorization for application developers by providing open-source libraries for different platforms. In the Microsoft identity platform, the Azure Active Directory (Azure AD) acts as a single pane of glass for authentication (AuthN) and authorization (AuthZ) using industry-standard protocols Open ID Connect (OIDC) and OAuth 2.0.

The Microsoft identity platform issues the following types of security tokens used by the OAuth2 and OpenID Connect protocols

- **Access token** An access token is a security token that is issued by an authorization server (Azure AD) as part of an OAuth 2.0 flow.
- **Refresh token** Refresh tokens are timebound access tokens; authorization servers sometimes issue a refresh token while the access token is issued to allow the client app to use it while requesting a new access token.
- **ID token** ID tokens are sent to the client application as part of an OpenID Connect flow.

Depending upon the type of client application, such as Web apps, Web APIs, Mobile Apps, Desktop Apps, and the application architecture, it can use more than one of the authentication flows supported by the Microsoft identity platform. These flows can issue one or more security tokens and authorization codes for the client application to work. The Microsoft identity platform supports the following implementation of OAuth2 and Open ID Connect flows for different app scenarios

- **Authorization Code flow:** The OAuth 2.0 authorization code grant flow is recommended and can be used in native mobile or desktop apps, single-page apps, and web apps to gain access to protected resources, such as web APIs. In this flow, the client app securely acquires the access tokens that can be used to access protected resources and refresh tokens to get additional access tokens and ID tokens for the signed-in user.

- **Implicit Flow:** The implicit grant is a simplified version of authorization code flow that is optimized for single-page applications. Instead of issuing the client an authorization code in the implicit flow, the client is issued an access token directly. The silent SSO features of the implicit flow do not work across different browsers because of the removal of third-party cookies, causing applications to break when they attempt to get a new access token. Therefore, the authorization Code flow is recommended because it now supports single-page applications as well.

Hierarchical structure

As you can infer from the section **organizing Azure resources** on page 4 of Chapter 01, nearly everything in Azure security can be viewed in a hierarchical manner. Depending on your business rules and compliance, you can choose from a variety of levels in Azure to efficiently manage access, polices, and compliances. Following are the levels available in Azure:

- **Tenant**   This represents an organization when signing up for Azure. Organizations may purchase more than one Azure account and can have several tenants. Also, private government tenants can be purchased, such as Azure Germany, Azure US, and so on.

- **Management Group(s)**   This is considered to be the top-level management in Azure and allows the management of one or more subscriptions. There is a single top-level "root" management group in Azure for each directory. All other management groups and subscriptions fold up into this root management group. The root management group allows the application of global polices and role assignments at the directory level.

- **Subscription(s)**   Subscriptions are logical containers that are used to provision resources for an organization. Companies can have one or more subscriptions that are categorized in various ways. Cost can be managed for large companies much more easily when separate subscriptions are created based on department, region, budget group, and so on.

- **Resource Group(s)**   Resource groups are logical containers for related Azure resources. You can create resource groups if it makes sense for your specific grouping needs. Resources in a resource group can be deployed and deleted as a group. Also, RBAC can be applied at the resource group level to control access to the resources within the resource group.

- **Resource Group Locking**   Resource groups are required for all Azure resources, and when a resource is created, it must belong to a resource group. From a security perspective, resource groups can be locked, which can help protect them from user deletion.

- **Read-Only** Read-only lock means authorized users can read a resource, but they can't delete or update the resource. Applying this lock is similar to restricting all authorized users to the permissions granted by the Reader role. The great news is that Azure shows a very visible pop-up warning to any user who is trying to violate the read-only lock. If users attempt to edit a read-only resource group, they will receive a warning.

- **Delete locking** Setting this option prevents the resource group from being deleted, as shown in Figure 2-9.

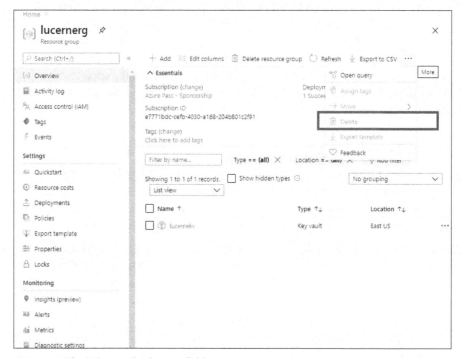

FIGURE 2-9 The Delete option is unavailable

- **Resource(s)** These are the individual IaaS and PaaS services, such as VMs, databases, functions, and so on, that have been created in a resource group.

Azure's hierarchical structure is flexible in the sense that different organizations may structure and categorize management groups, subscriptions, resource groups, and resources, in any way they see fit. The planning of said architecture is often based upon business rules, or compliance. The planning should be carefully orchestrated by teams of people, including stakeholders. Once the architecture is in place, manipulating it can be a daunting task.

Table 2-3 shows an example of the hierarchical structure for the fictitious company, Lucerne Publishing:

TABLE 2-3 Azure hierarchical structure

Management Groups				
IT	Human Resources	Finance	Sales	Marketing
Subscriptions				
Dev Test Production	Apps Databases	Apps Databases Power BI Dashboards	Apps Databases Websites	Apps Databases
Resource groups				
Dev–East US Test–West US Production–East and West US	East Region only	East Region only	East and West Regions	North, South, East, and West Regions

RBAC (role-based access control)

Azure role-based access control (RBAC) assists administrators by allowing them to manage who can access resources and what they can do with those resources. By designating groups or individual roles, Azure will circumvent confusion and misplaced access. RBAC is built on top of Azure Resource Manager and provides granular access management of Azure resources. In addition, administrators have a central place to create and manage role-based access control from within Azure Active Directory.

SECURITY PRINCIPAL

A security principal is an object that is representative of users, groups, services, or managed identities that are requesting access to Azure Resources.

ROLE DEFINITIONS/ROLE ASSIGNMENTS

A role definition is set of permissions that are simply called *roles*. These permissions indicate what a user associated with a particular role has access to and what they can do. There are built-in roles (such as Owner, Contributor, Reader, and so on), but administrators can create custom roles in Azure RBAC as well. There are many ways to create custom role definitions, including PowerShell, Azure CLI, REST API, and the Azure portal. Custom roles in Azure have an orange resource icon, which makes them stand out from built-in roles. Listing 2-2 shows how to make a custom role in Azure with JSON:

LISTING 2-2 JSON custom role

```
//JSON Custom Role Definition
{

  "Name": "Resource Group Custom Editor",
```

```json
    "Id": "00000000-00000000-00000-0000000000000",

    "IsCustom": true,

    "Description": "Can monitor resource groups, read resources, start resources, edit and
    add resources. In addition the Custom Editor can create alert rules, and read/write or
    delete diagnostic settings.",

    "Actions": [

      "Microsoft.Storage/*/read",

      "Microsoft.Network/*/read",

      "Microsoft.Compute/*/read",

      "Microsoft.Compute/virtualMachines/start/action",

      "Microsoft.Compute/virtualMachines/restart/action",

      "Microsoft.Authorization/*/read",

      "Microsoft.ResourceHealth/availabilityStatuses/read",

      "Microsoft.Resources/subscriptions/resourceGroups/write",

      "Microsoft.Insights/alertRules/*",

      "Microsoft.Insights/diagnosticSettings/*",

      "Microsoft.Support/*"

    ],

    "NotActions": [],

    "DataActions": [],

    "NotDataActions": [],

    "AssignableScopes": [

      "/subscriptions/{subscriptionId1}",

      "/subscriptions/{subscriptionId2}",

      "/providers/Microsoft.Management/managementGroups/{groupId1}"

    ]

  }
```

Access control (IAM)

Each Azure Resource has an option called Access Control (IAM), as shown in Figure 2-10. This Identity Access Management option includes the ability for those with permissions to do the following things:

- View their level of access to the resource
- Check access for users, groups, service principals, or managed identities
- Add role assignments
- View role assignments
- View deny assignments

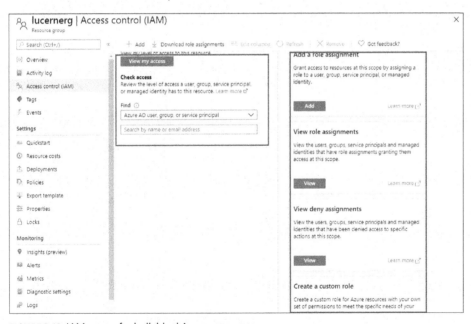

FIGURE 2-10 IAM access for individual Azure resources

Privileged Identity Management (PIM)

PIM is a service that is part of Azure Active Directory. This service allows administrators to manage, control, and monitor access to important resources in Azure AD, Azure, and other Microsoft Online Services such as Microsoft 365 or Microsoft Intune.

Some key terms to be familiar with regarding PIM are shown in Table 2-4:

TABLE 2-4 Key PIM terms

Term	Role assignment category	Description
Assigned	State	User with an active role assignment.
Activated	State	User with an eligible role assignment and who has activated the role. User can use the role for a pre-configured period of time.
JIT (Just in Time)		Users receive temporary permissions, for the purpose of performing privileged tasks. Access is granted only when users need it or "on the fly".
Least Privilege Access		User is given the least privilege to do his or her job. With least privilege, we assume that it is better for a user to have to call IT or the help desk to access a resource, rather than to receive too much permission for a resource. Least Privilege is a best-practice technique.
Expire Eligible	Duration	Users can activate a role with specified beginning and end dates.
Expire Active	Duration	This is a role assignment where a user can use the role without performing any actions within specified start and end dates.
Eligible	Type	If a user has been made eligible for a role, it means that the user can activate the role when he or she needs to perform privileged tasks.

EXAM TIP

Azure AD Privileged Identity Management (PIM) helps you minimize account privileges by helping you:

- Identify and manage users who have been assigned to administrative roles.
- Identify and manage unused or excessive privilege roles that you should remove.
- Establish rules to make the user require multifactor authentication for activating a privileged role.
- Establish rules to make sure privileged roles are granted only long enough to accomplish the privileged task.

Azure AD Identity Protection

Azure Identity Protection was designed to assist with protecting organization identities. Policies can be created to block behavior entirely, or initiate remediation triggers, such as forcing password change, and requiring multifactor authentication (MFA). Policies can be created with identity protection that are considered "risk-based," meaning these policies can respond to behavior that your organization deems as risky.

User risk is calculated based upon detections through Conditional Access policies, which were discussed in Skill 2-1. User risk policies evaluate the risk level to a specific user or a group: low, medium, or high risk.

INVESTIGATE RISK

From the Azure Active Directory Security Center (accessed by clicking **Security** in the Azure Active Directory left menu), you can receive automatic reports on risk detection. These reports are very helpful and can be downloaded and shared for further analysis.

There are three reports that Azure provides to assist with investigating identity risks in an organization's environment.

All three reports can be downloaded for sharing and/or further analysis:

Risky Users (can download the most recent 2,500 entries): This report is meaningful to an Azure Administrator because it allows them to view:

- Which users are at risk, have had risk(s) remediated, or have had risks dismissed
- Details about risk detection (date, type of risk, location, application signed into, and more)
- History of all risky sign-ins (to establish possible patterns of risk)

Using a risky user report, Administrators can take appropriate actions by choosing to:

- Reset user passwords
- Confirm user compromise
- Dismiss user risk
- Block users from signing in
- Investigate further

Risky Sign-ins (can download the most recent 2,500 entries): This report contains data that can be filtered for up to the past 30 days. Administrators use this report to find:

- Which sign-ins are classified as at-risk, confirmed compromised, confirmed safe, dismissed, or remediated
- Real-time and aggregate risk levels associated with sign-in attempts
- Detection types triggered
- Conditional Access policies applied
- MFA details
- Device information

- Application information
- Location information

Using a risky sign-in report, Administrators can take appropriate action by choosing to:

- Confirm a sign-in compromise
- Confirm that a sign-in is safe

Risk Detections (can download the most recent 5,000 entries): This report contains data that can be filtered for up to the past 90 days. Administrators use this report to find:

- Information about each risk detection including type
- Other risks triggered at the same time
- Sign-in attempt location
- Links out to more detail from Microsoft Cloud App Security (MCAS)

Using a risk detection report, administrators can take appropriate action by choosing to return to the user's risk or sign-in reports to take action based on any/all information gathered by those reports.

> **NOTE   OTHER USES**
>
> Risk detection reports can also help identify false positives, or they can identify which users have already been remediated by using a "risk state," which will report safe or not safe.

> **NEED MORE REVIEW?   RISK REPORTS**
>
> For detailed information on risk reports, see *https://docs.microsoft.com/en-us/azure/active-directory/identity-protection/howto-identity-protection-investigate-risk*.

> **NEED MORE REVIEW?   MICROSOFT CLOUD APP SECURITY**
>
> To review further details about Microsoft Cloud App Security, see *https://docs.microsoft.com/en-us/cloud-app-security/what-is-cloud-app-security*.

> **EXAM TIP**
>
> Microsoft Identity Protection is available in the **Security** area of Azure Active Directory and requires an Azure AD Premium P2 license. If this license is not in place, the **Identity Protection** link will redirect you to *docs.microsoft.com*, where identity protection is discussed in detail.

Azure Identity Score

Azure Active Directory provides an Identity Score that helps you effectively measure your identity security posture, plan improvements, and review successes (after improvements). The Identity Score is calculated every 48 hours and compares your security settings with recommended best practices. It is based upon your Azure AD configuration and is a number between 1 and 223 overall; it provides detailed information about all risks. Microsoft uses the range of 1–223 to help administrators measure security, according to the best-practice recommendations. When scores are lower than 223, the Identity Secure Score dashboard will contain detailed information and recommendations on how to improve the score to 223. The dashboard includes the following information:

- Your Identity Secure Score
- A comparison graph showing how your Identity secure score compares to other tenants in the same industry and of similar size
- A trend graph showing how your Identity Secure Score has changed over time
- A list of possible improvements

The outcome is designed to help improve security posture and therefore, the overall score.

EXAM TIP

To view the Identity Secure Score, you must hold one of the roles below:

- **Global Admin role**
- **Security Admin role**
- **Security Readers role**

In Figure 2-11, Azure depicts a Secure Score of 203, based upon 12 items that were used to gain this score. Secure Scores have a range of 1–223, with 223 being the ideal score.

FIGURE 2-11 Identity Secure Score

In Figure 2-12, you can see the result of clicking the Secure Score shown in Figure 2-11. Once you click a Secure Score, you will be transferred to the recommendation screen where you see Improvement Actions that should be taken to achieve a higher score. This screen also depicts the impact of each action on the final score.

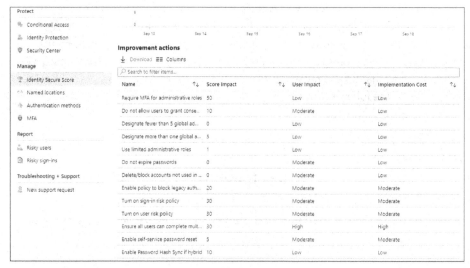

FIGURE 2-12 Identity Secure Score–Improvement Actions

Design governance

After putting all the work in regarding policies, investigations, mitigating risk, and the like, you must be aware of any compliance standards that your organization must follow. For example, you need to know if your organization going to be monitored, audited, or reported.

Make sure you are aware of the specific compliance that dictates adherence to security controls, such as:

- Industry compliance
- Government compliance
- Regulatory compliance

Make sure you are you aware of the specific standards and controls, including:

- **ISO27001**   Ensures that a comprehensive system for collecting data and managing threats is in place.
- **NIST**   This stands for the National Institute of Standards and Technology, which develops standards for technology and metrics to drive competition and innovation.

- **PCI-DSS**   This stands for the Payment Card Industry Data Security Standard, which adheres to policies and procedures to prevent misuse of personal information by credit card holders.

The role of organizations to manage security standards uses a lifecycle process. The lifecyle includes three steps that should be done when creating and managing security standards. These processes should be repeated with each iteration:

- **Define**   Set organization standards for technologies, practices, configurations, culture, assets, initiatives, and internal and external factors.

- **Improve**   Continually push standards toward their ideal state, while continually reducing risk.

- **Sustain**   Make sure security standards do not degrade.

Tagging strategy

Tags are useful for many things, including:

- You can quickly locate tagged items with the Azure search feature.

- You can list tagged resources by categories to investigate access.

- You can work with cost centers, using tags as a means to identify which budget areas pay for what. Also, cost centers help monitor cost.

RESOURCE TAGGING

Tagging is a key-value pair, and it is one of the easiest ways to classify resources in your Azure subscription. We highly recommend that you tag all your cloud resources. You can tag pretty much everything in the Azure resource hierarchy model described earlier in this chapter.

Fundamentally, resource tagging is a primary way to understand data in any cost reporting system. For example, within your organization, you might have several Azure subscriptions. For charge-back and cost management reporting, you would use tags such as business unit, department, billing code, environment type, location, and so on.

You can also view costs for specific tags in Azure's **Cost Management + Billing** center.

Follow these steps to view costs for a specific tag:

1. From the Azure portal, click **Azure Cost + Billing Center** from the left-side menu.

2. Click **Cost Management** and then click **Cost Analysis**.

3. You will see a list of filters that can be applied, and you can choose any filter to view the detailed cost information for that tag, by choosing **Add Filter (Tag)**. Figure 2-13 shows the **Tag** filter.

FIGURE 2-13 Tag filter

Azure policy

While we are speaking of governance and compliance, this is a good place to talk about Azure policy, how it can help you to work toward standards, and how to be sure your organization is complying.

Azure policies can be created and assigned for the purpose of enforcing rules for your Azure resources that will assist you with remaining compliant, as well as staying in line with any standards and service-level agreements (SLAs) that a company has agreed to with their clients (internal or external). Azure policies can specifically evaluate Azure resources for non-compliance. For example, your company compliance might forbid the creation of an Azure Storage Account in a more expensive region. (Some regions are more costly than others.) After this policy is put into place, a user who tries to create a Storage Account in the forbidden region will be blocked from doing so.

CREATING A POLICY

Azure policies can be created in the Azure portal with PowerShell code, command-line tools, and REST API.

NEED MORE REVIEW? **REST API**

To see an example of creating a policy assignment to identify non-compliant resources with a REST API, see *https://docs.microsoft.com/en-us/azure/governance/policy/ assign-policy-rest-api.*

The process to create and enforce a policy is as follows:

1. Create a policy definition.
2. Assign a definition to a scope of resources.
3. View the policy evaluation results.

The most common policy definitions are associated with:

- Allowed storage account pricing (SKU)
- Allowed resource types
- Allowed locations
- Allowed VM size (SKUs)
- NOT allowed resource types

Policies are represented with JSON format. JSON files can be imported into Azure, or they can be created in the Azure portal.

Azure Blueprint

Azure Blueprint takes Azure policy further in that it is made up of artifacts, including Azure policy assignments. Azure Blueprint is like a container for policy assignments, resource groups, ARM templates, and role assignments. It allows us to establish and maintain patterns to protect ongoing compliance.

Azure Blueprints are repeatable sets of patterns and requirements that make it possible for IT Teams to confidently stand up (bring online or put into service) new environments that are already compliant. In addition, Azure Blueprints contains common templates for nearly every type of compliance that an organization will need. Blank templates are also provided for architects who want to customize an Azure Blueprint. Figure 2-14 shows Azure Blueprint templates.

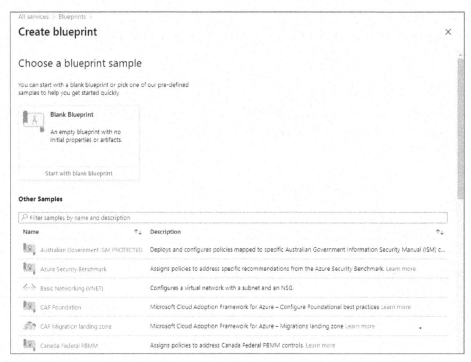

All services > Blueprints >

Create blueprint ✕

Choose a blueprint sample

You can start with a blank blueprint or pick one of our pre-defined
samples to help you get started quickly

Blank Blueprint

An empty blueprint with no
initial properties or artifacts.

Start with blank blueprint

Other Samples

🔍 Filter samples by name and description

Name	↑↓	Description	↑↓
Australian Government ISM PROTECTED		Deploys and configures policies mapped to specific Australian Government Information Security Manual (ISM) c...	
Azure Security Benchmark		Assigns policies to address specific recommendations from the Azure Security Benchmark. Learn more	
Basic Networking (VNET)		Configures a virtual network with a subnet and an NSG.	
CAF Foundation		Microsoft Cloud Adoption Framework for Azure – Configure Foundational best practices Learn more	
CAF Migration landing zone		Microsoft Cloud Adoption Framework for Azure – Migrations landing zone Learn more	
Canada Federal PBMM		Assigns policies to address Canada Federal PBMM controls. Learn more	

FIGURE 2-14 Azure Blueprint templates

From the Azure portal, follow these steps to create an Azure Blueprint:

1. Click **All Services**.

2. Type **Blueprints** in the search box.

3. Three options appear:

   - **Getting Started**   This is a document page that provides an overview of the ways to create, apply, and track Azure Blueprints.

   - **Blueprint Definitions**   This is the blade used to create Azure Blueprints.

   - **Assigned Blueprints**   This is the blade used to view and track Azure Blueprints assignments.

SAVING AZURE BLUEPRINTS

Azure Blueprints can be saved to a management group or subscription. The Azure Blueprint creator must have Contributor access to create a Blueprint. However, if the Contributor has access rights to the management group, he or she also has access to any children subscriptions of the management group.

PUBLISHING AZURE BLUEPRINTS

Azure Blueprints are created in Draft mode. At the time of assignment, the Blueprint must be published. Publishing requires the version information and change notes. Azure Blueprints maintains a history that can be accessed if necessary. This is called *versioning*. When an initial

Blueprint is created, it is considered to be in Draft mode. With each additional change, each published version still exists and so do unpublished changes. Once an unpublished version is published, the updated blueprint will also have a new version.

AZURE BLUEPRINTS PERMISSIONS

To use Azure Blueprints, permission must be granted through role-based access control (RBAC), which was discussed in Skill 2.1. The RBAC permissions that are needed for Azure Blueprints are as follows:

Creating Azure Blueprints:

- `Microsoft.Blueprint/blueprints/write`   Creates a Blueprint definition.
- `Microsoft.Blueprint/blueprints/artifacts/write`   Creates artifacts on a Blueprint definition.
- `Microsoft.Blueprint/blueprints/versions/write`   Publishes a Blueprint.

Deleting Azure Blueprints:

- `Microsoft.Blueprint/blueprints/delete`   Allows a user to delete a Blueprint.
- `Microsoft.Blueprint/blueprints/artifacts/delete`   Allows a user to delete a Blueprint artifacts.
- `Microsoft.Blueprint/blueprints/versions/delete`   Allows a user to delete any and all versions of Blueprints (to alleviate confusion of past history)

Assigning or Unassigning Azure Blueprints:

- `Microsoft.Blueprint/blueprintAssignments/write`   Assigns a Blueprint.
- `Microsoft.Blueprint/blueprintAssignments/delete`   Unassigns a Blueprint.

RBAC has a list of built-in roles that administrators can use for tasks on specific resources. For Azure Blueprint, the built-in roles are shown in Table 2-5.

TABLE 2-5 Azure Blueprint roles

Azure RBAC Role	Detail
Owner	Includes all Azure Blueprint permissions, in addition to any other permissions.
Contributor	Contributors are allowed to create and delete Blueprint definitions, but cannot assign Blueprint permissions to another user.
Blueprint Contributor	Can manage Blueprints but cannot assign them.
Blueprint Operator	Can assign existing published Blueprints but can't create new Blueprint definitions. Blueprint assignment only works if the assignment is done with a user-assigned managed identity.
Custom Role	If any of the above roles do not fully satisfy the needs of your organization, you can create a custom role, by opening Azure Active Directory and clicking **Roles And Administrators** from the left menu in Azure. These roles can be completely new, or you can use one of the existing roles to begin and then customize it with the necessary assignments.

Skill 2.3: Design security for applications

Azure Key Vault is a secure, centralized Azure service that is used for storing secrets, keys, and certificates. As with other services, it has built-in security controls for network, monitoring and logging, identity, data protection, and access control. In the past, when developers needed to store keys, secrets, or certificates, they would need to do so for each application. If the keys, secrets, or certificates changed over time, developers would be saddled with having to edit each application, to reflect the changes. Azure Key Vault eliminates all the extra burden by storing this information outside the application—with encryption.

> **This skill covers how to:**
> - Key Vault solutions
> - Azure AD–managed identities
> - Use a custom logo for applications

Key Vault solutions

Typically, keys, secrets, and certificates are used to keep applications as secure and compliant as possible. In this section, we will discuss each of the components, along with the Key Vault container that holds them.

Key Vault terminology

To better understand Key Vaults and what goes inside them, let's look at some terminology that we will use going forward to describe and use key vaults.

VAULTS

Azure Key Vault is an Azure service that is used for securely storing and accessing secrets. A secret is anything that you need to tightly control access to. Vaults group secrets together, and therefore are a logical container of secrets. Vaults are encrypted, and when components (key, secret, or certificate) are created within the key vault, they are represented by a URI. Therefore, when an application needs a Key Vault component, the application can use the URI to refer to the component, instead of specifically identifying all the information to access the component in each application. If any changes take place to the component in the Key Vault, it is not necessary to make changes to each application. Instead, the new changes will flow directly to any application through the URI.

> **NEED MORE REVIEW?** **AZURE KEY VAULT BASIC CONCEPTS**
>
> To review further details about Azure Key Vault Basic Concepts, including a diagram of Key Vault, see *https://docs.microsoft.com/en-us/azure/key-vault/general/basic-concepts*.

Figure 2-15 depicts the **Keys**, **Secrets**, and **Certificate** settings available in the Azure Key Vault service. These three settings can use existing keys, secrets, and certificates by importing them, or they can be created from scratch.

FIGURE 2-15 Azure Key Vault

Secrets

Secrets are anything you want to store in a vault that has to do with accessing Azure resources or any other services. Imagine that you are signing in to your banking website and are asked to validate your credentials with additional information, such as the name of your first pet or your parent's middle name(s). This is information that only you should know. Secrets are stored and protected by Azure. In this case, protection means that all secrets will be encrypted and/or masked so they are never available in clear text. Therefore, this information is protected, and it would be difficult for hackers to get to the actual answers that a user has entered. They could be keys, certificates, or actual secrets, such as passwords. They are divided into categories of secrets, certificates, and keys. Secrets can also store and protect database connection strings, or strings of username information.

All secrets are encrypted in storage. Developers or users of the secrets can use them without any explicit encryption or decryption. Azure Secrets are automatically encrypted when they are added, and automatically decrypted when they are read. All encryption keys are unique.

Access Control is provided at the level of the Key Vault. Permissions for secrets management are:

- Get   Read a secret.
- List   List the secrets or versions of secrets.
- Set   Create a secret.
- Delete   Delete a secret (can be recovered by Restore).
- Recover   Recover a deleted secret.
- Backup   Back up a secret.
- Restore   Restore a backed-up secret.
- Purge   Permanently delete a deleted secret (cannot be recovered by Restore).

EXAM TIP

- Conditional Access in Azure Active Directory controls access to cloud apps based on specific conditions that you specify. To allow access, you create Conditional Access policies that allow or block access based on whether or not the requirements in the policy are met.
- Use Managed Service Identity in conjunction with Azure Key Vault to simplify and secure secrets management for your cloud applications. Ensure that Azure Key Vault soft-delete is enabled.

Keys

Azure Key Vault has support for various key types, including HSM (High Security Modules) for high-value keys. Multiple algorithms are also supported. Keys can be created from Azure Key Vault, or already existing keys can be imported.

From a developer standpoint, keys in the Azure Key Vault are a feature that makes all applications more secure, and they are easier to manage because they are centralized. In the past, developers would include key values in web.config files and/or machine.config files. The management of these keys took excessive effort because keys change, and developers would have to change each web app with every change.

CRYPTOGRAPHIC PROTECTION

Key Vault only supports RSA and elliptic curve keys.

> **NEED MORE REVIEW?** **CRYPTOGRAPHIC PROTECTION**
>
> To review more details about Azure Key Vault basic concepts, including a diagram of Key Vault, see *https://docs.microsoft.com/en-us/azure/key-vault/keys/about-keys*.

NEED MORE REVIEW? **CREATED DATE AND UPDATED DATE ATTRIBUTES**

See *https://docs.microsoft.com/en-us/azure/key-vault/secrets/about-secrets* for detailed information about Created Date and Updated Date for Azure Key Vault attributes.

Access Control is provided at the level of the Key Vault. Permissions for key management are:

- `Get`   Read the public part of a key, along with its attributes.
- `List`   List the keys or versions of keys.
- `Update`   Update key attributes.
- `Create`   Create new keys.
- `Import`   Import an existing key.
- `Delete`   Delete a key.
- `Recover`   Recover a deleted key.
- `Backup`   Backup a key.
- `Restore`   Restore a backed-up key.
- `Purge`   Permanently delete a deleted key (cannot be recovered by `Restore`).

Following are the permissions for cryptography operations:

- `Decrypt`   Use the key to unprotect a sequence of bytes.
- `Encrypt`   Use the key to protect an arbitrary sequence of bytes.
- `UnwrapKey`   Use the key to unprotect wrapped symmetric keys.
- `WrapKey`   Use the key to protect a symmetric key.
- `Verify`   Use the key to verify digests.
- `Sign`   Use the key to sign digests.

Certificates

Certificates can be created in Azure Key Vault, or they can be imported if they already exist. Key Vault supports x509 certificates and includes both self-signed and Certificate Authority–generated certificates.

Key Vault certificate owners can implement secure storage and management of certificates without interaction with private key material. Owners can also manage the lifecycle of certificates, from within Key Vault in the Azure portal. Lastly, owners can provide information and notifications about lifecycle events, including certification information (such as expiration and/or renewal of certificates).

Certificate access control

Like secrets and keys, certificate permissions can be managed for all operations. The permissions for certificate management operations are shown in the following list. Note that there are more permissions than secrets and keys because of the certificate metadata.

- **Get** Get the current certificate version or any version of a certificate.
- **List** List the current certificates or versions.
- **Update** Update a certificate.
- **Create** Create a certificate.
- **Import** Import certificate material into a Key Vault certificate.
- **Delete** Delete a certificate, its policy, and versions (not permanent).
- **Recover** Recover a deleted certificate.
- **Backup** Back up a certificate.
- **Restore** Restore a certificate if it has been backed up.
- **Manage Contacts** Manage certificate contacts.
- **Manage Issuers** Manage certificate authorities/issuers.
- **Get Issuers** Read a certificate's authorities/issuers.
- **List Issuers** List a certificate's authorities/issuers.
- **Set Issuers** Create or update a certificate's authorities/issuers.
- **Delete Issuers** Delete a certificate's authorities/issuers.
- **Purge** Permanently delete a deleted certificate.

Azure Key Vault regions

You cannot move any Azure Key Vault (and its secrets) from one Azure Region to another. There might be circumstances that require you to move an Azure Key Vault across regions (such as a compliancy or business need). There are two workaround options:

- **Azure Key Vault Backup and Restore** Secrets, keys, and certificates can be backed up with backup commands (or the Azure portal). When they are backed up, the components are encrypted and downloaded as a blob. The blob can then be restored into the new Key Vault. There are limitations to backing up and restoring Azure Key Vault Secrets, Keys, and Certificates, including:
  - Keys cannot be backed up in one geography and then restored into another.
  - Backups include all versions of each secret. This version information can be set to include less version history. If the history includes more than 500 versions, the backup information can fail because the maximum size limit has been exceeded.
- **Azure Key Vault Download and Upload** Some secret types can be downloaded manually (such as a PFX file). Downloads and uploads eliminate any geographical restrictions for some secret types, such as certificates. PFX files can be uploaded to any Key Vault, in any region.

> *NOTE* **AZURE KEY VAULT COMMANDS**
>
> For a complete list of Azure Key Vault commands, see *https://docs.microsoft.com/en-us/azure/key-vault/secrets/quick-create-powershell.*

Individual keys, secrets, and certificates permissions should be used only for specific scenarios such as:

- Multi-layer applications that need to separate access control between layers
- Sharing individual secret between multiple applications

Azure AD–managed identities

There are two types of managed identities in Azure:

- **System-assigned managed identities**   Azure enables identities for service instances, and automatically provisions credentials. If the service instance is deleted, the credentials/identity is automatically cleaned up in Azure Active Directory.

- **User-assigned managed identities**   These identities are created as a standalone Azure resource. When a user creates a user-assigned managed identity in Azure through the create process, an identity is created by Azure in the Azure AD tenant that is trusted by the subscription being used. Once created, identities can be assigned to one or more Azure service instances.

Table 2-6 compares system-assigned managed identities to user-assigned managed identities:

TABLE 2-6 System-assigned versus user-assigned managed identities

Property	System-assigned managed identity	User-assigned managed identity
Create	Created when an Azure Resource is created, such as an Azure virtual machine or Azure App Service.	Created as a standalone Azure resource.
Most Common Use Cases	Workloads that are contained within a single Azure resource. Workloads for which you need independent identities, such as an application that runs on a single virtual machine.	Workloads that run on multiple resources but can share a single identity. These workloads need pre-authorization for provisioning. Workload for which permissions should stay consistent, even if there are frequent recycles. Might be used for a workload where multiple virtual machines need to access the same resource.
Sharing across Azure resources	Not Shareable. Can only be associated with a single Azure resource.	Shareable. Can be associated with more than one Azure resource.
Lifecycle	Shared lifecycle with the Azure resource that the managed identity is created with (if the parent resource is deleted, the managed identity is also deleted).	Independent life cycle. Must be explicitly deleted.

Support for managed identities in Azure

The following services support managed identities in Azure:

- Azure APIs
- Azure App Service
- Azure Arc Enabled Kubernetes
- Azure Blueprints
- Azure Cognitive Search and Services
- Azure Container Instances and Registry Tasks
- Azure Data Explorer
- Azure Data Factory V2
- Azure Event Grid
- Azure Functions
- Azure IoT Hub
- Azure Import/Export
- Azure Kubernetes Service (AKS)
- Azure Logic Apps
- Azure Policy
- Azure Service Fabric
- Azure SignalR Services
- Azure Spring Cloud
- Azure Virtual Machines and Virtual Machine Scale Sets
- Azure VM Image Builder

Support for Azure Active Directory authentication

The following services support Azure Active Directory authentication:

- Azure Resource Manager
- Azure Key Vault
- Azure Data Lake
- Azure SQL
- Azure Event Hubs
- Azure Service Bus
- Azure Storage Blobs and Queues
- Azure Analysis Services

> **NOTE** **AZURE AD AUTHENTICATION SUPPORT**
>
> Support for Azure AD authentication is different based on the region in which the service is provisioned.

Azure App Service

Azure App Services support both system-assigned and user-assigned managed identities. These identities can be managed through:

- Azure portal
- Azure CLI
- Azure PowerShell
- Azure Resource Manager Template

Azure App Service can use Managed Identity Types (both system- and user-assigned), in all generally available regions.

> **NEED MORE REVIEW?** **MANAGED IDENTITIES**
>
> For a detailed table outlining the differences between the two types of managed identities, see *https://docs.microsoft.com/en-us/azure/active-directory/managed-identities-azure-resources/overview.*

Integrating applications into Azure Active Directory

Applications can be new, existing, on-premises, or enterprise applications and can still be integrated with Azure Active Directory.

Azure AD must be configured to integrate with an application. In other words, it needs to know what apps are using it for identities. Making Azure AD aware of these apps and how it should handle them is known as application management.

> **NEED MORE REVIEW?** **IDENTITY AND ACCESS MANAGEMENT**
>
> For details on application management as it applies to identity and access management, see *https://docs.microsoft.com/en-us/azure/active-directory/manage-apps/what-is-application-management.*

Enterprise applications

Enterprise applications (see Figure 2-16) will enhance your users' experience, allowing them to use applications without having to start from scratch. Azure Active Directory allows you to add the following:

- Applications that your organization is developing that are custom or proprietary.
- On-premises applications (such as those that present reports), data from on-premises databases, or even applications such as SharePoint apps.
- Non-gallery applications which can be purchased from external or third-party companies.
- Gallery applications that are included in Azure Active Directory; these can be added from the Azure portal.

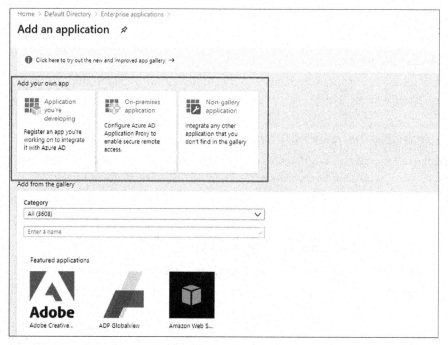

FIGURE 2-16 Adding applications to Azure Active Directory

In this example, we will add a Twitter gallery application, so that a user can sign in to your application with Twitter.

1. Choose **Azure Active Directory** > **Enterprise Applications**.

2. Click **+New Application**.

3. Click the **Enter A Name** option and enter **Twitter** into the text box.

4. Select the Twitter icon.

5. The name will default to **Twitter**, but it can be changed.

6. Click **Add**.

7. Your application is now ready for valid Twitter users to attach to when signing in to your Azure Application.

Note that these steps also can be completed with Azure PowerShell, Azure CLI, or REST API.

> **IMPORTANT**   **ENTERPRISE TWITTER APPLICATION**
>
> You can now assign users and groups, set up single sign-on, provision user accounts, set up conditional access policies, and set up self-service requests for using the new Enterprise Twitter application.

EXAM TIP

You can provide access to internal applications, which are located inside your private network, securely from anywhere using Microsoft Azure AD Application Proxy.

Configuring properties for an application in Azure Active Directory

When you add an application to Azure Active Directory, your tenant is now aware that it is the identity provider for your application. Once the application has been added, you can configure properties for the application. To manage these properties, you will need to:

- Possess an Azure Account that has an active Subscription
- Be in one of the following roles:
  - Global Administrator
  - Cloud Application Administrator
  - Application Administrator
  - Owner of the service principal

Figure 2-17 shows the application **Properties** configuration blade in Azure Active Directory.

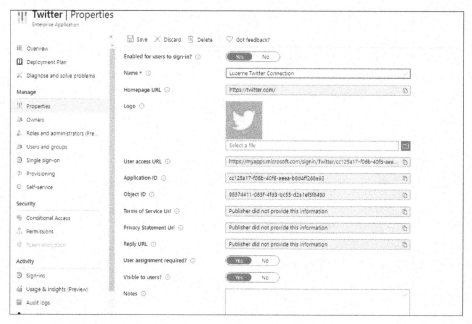

FIGURE 2-17 Application configuration in Azure Active Directory

Conditional Access for application properties

When using Conditional Access policies for your added application, your users will have a streamlined experience using any device (BYOD—Bring Your Own Device). This will also provide the control and protection for any business rules, standards, or compliance that you need to keep your application data secure. In addition, restrictions can be applied to external users, networks, or devices to meet the policy objectives.

Conditional access for applications is useful in several scenarios:

- You can secure your applications, and you can require multifactor authentication for internal or external users and administrators.

- You can be aware of risky sign-ins through the risky sign-in report offered from the Microsoft Security Center, located directly in the left menu of the Azure portal.

- You can secure your data by requiring devices to be marked as compliant. Also, you can allow Hybrid Azure Active directory–joined devices to have access to your company resources.

NOTE **PREMIUM ACCESS OR CONDITIONAL ACCESS POLICIES REQUIRED**

You must have a premium subscription to use Conditional Access policies for applications.

Use a custom logo for applications

When inviting external users (or internal users from other areas of your organization) to your application, you can customize the log-in screen to include custom logos, so that the external users will have no doubt that they are signing onto your application with their organization's credentials.

Follow these steps to use a custom logo:

1. Create the logo first and save it in `.png` format. The pixel size should be 215x215 pixels.
2. Click **Azure Active Directory** from the Azure portal.
3. Click **Enterprise Applications**.
4. Choose the desired application.
5. Click **Properties** (from the **Managed** section).
6. Click the **Upload** button to upload the new logo (see Figure 2-18).
7. Click **Save**.

> **NOTE** **CHECK THE IMAGE SIZE**
>
> If you receive an error, make sure that your logo is sized to 215x215.

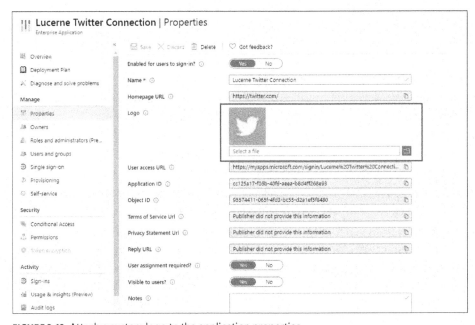

FIGURE 2-18 Attach a custom logo to the application properties

Chapter summary

- Azure provides many solutions for authentication design, authorization design, and designing security. When planning an architecture for your organization, you should develop a checklist and include any items related to:
    - Business rules
    - Business standards
    - Compliances
    - Best practices for your organization
- As a best practice, it is a good idea to involve not only the IT professionals in your company to plan security, but also any business professionals, and stakeholders who can assist in helping you to keep compliant.
- Azure Active Directory is the backbone for identity management in the cloud. The levels that can benefit from role-based access control (RBAC) are:
    - Tenant-level isolation
    - Management groups
    - Subscriptions
    - Resource groups
    - Resources
- Azure Active Directory provides Identity Management resources for internal, on-premises, and external solutions. Every user, web API, and application can take part in being secure to help protect sensitive company data and resources.
- Authentication options in Azure include single sign-on, Conditional Access, multifactor authentication, network access, self-service, B2B integration, and more.
- Authorization options in Azure include design for hierarchical structures and being able to authorize at every level, including management groups, subscriptions, resource groups, and resources.
- Resource tagging in Azure allows you to categorize resources and view consolidated billing by applying the same tag to multiple resources and resource groups.
- Azure Policy helps you to enforce organization-wide resource governance for existing or future resource deployments, set guardrails, and make sure future configurations are compliant with organizational or external standards and regulations. Blueprints allow you to create environment designs that deploy Azure resources from Resource Manager templates, configure Azure RBAC, and enforce and audit configuration by assigning Azure Policy.
- AD Connect and AD Connect Health will work together to keep your Azure Active Directory solution synchronized between on-premises and the cloud. AD Connect Health will specifically allow you to monitor the health of your environment, regarding the syncing

of data from point A to point B, such as syncing contacts from an on-premises Active Directory to Microsoft 365 or syncing contacts from Google into Exchange.

- The Azure Key Vault service increases the security posture of your Azure-hosted workload by securely storing and accessing secrets, keys, and certificates.

- This protection is offered using a URI. If any information in the above components changes, developers will not have to rewrite configurations for the applications. They will automatically be updated.

- Managed Identity eliminates the need of storing and managing credentials.

- Azure also contains options to integrate security for internal apps, external apps, and even includes apps from the Azure Enterprise gallery.

Thought experiment

In this thought experiment, demonstrate your skills and knowledge of the topics covered in this chapter. You can find answers to thought experiment questions in the following sections labeled "Thought experiment answers."

You are an Azure solutions architect working for a large enterprise looking to migrate their on-premises line of business (LoB) applications into Azure. The company wants to allow users to log in to cloud-based applications and on-premises applications with the same password for a seamless single-sign-on experience.

The company's security team expressed some concerns over storing passwords outside the organization's Active directory. Additionally, the company's administrators want to use more than one authentication method to log in to cloud-based applications.

Considering the above requirements, answer the following questions:

1. How would you address the security team's concern about account passwords?

2. How would you address the administrators' concerns about implementing more than one method of authentication?

Thought experiment answers

This section contains the solution to the thought experiment for this chapter. Please keep in mind that there might be other ways to achieve the desired results. Each answer explains why the answer is correct.

1. There are two ways we can address the security team's concern. The security team can review and opt-in for one of these solutions:

   a. **Password hash synchronization with Azure AD:** In Azure AD, we can use password hash synchronization instead of storing the plain text, on-premises user account password. This is one of the sign-in methods used to accomplish hybrid identity. Azure AD Connect synchronizes a hash of a user's password from an on-premises Active Directory instance to a cloud-based Azure AD instance.

   b.   **Pass-through authentication:** Pass-through authentication is an alternative in which you keep the password on-premises. When users signs in to cloud-based Apps, this feature validates users' passwords directly against your on-premises Active Directory.

2.   Azure AD provides out-of-the-box support for multifactor authentication (MFA). However, it is recommended that you should use conditional or just-in-time access policies for administrators. The conditional access capability comes with the Azure Active Directory (Azure AD) Privileged Identity Management (PIM) product. To use PIM, you must have a premium P2 licenses for your administrators in your Azure Active Directory tenant.

CHAPTER 3

Design data storage

In today's information era, data is growing rapidly and exponentially. This vast amount of data also opens a door for organizations to use it effectively to make business decisions. Like a wide variety of IoT devices, and social networking sites, database applications generate a massive amount of data. Handling such massive data with a traditional relational database approach sometimes becomes challenging and inefficient. The heterogeneity and complexity of the data—also known as *big data*—emitted by numerous connected devices also make managing traditional database storage solutions challenging.

Because the AZ-304 exam is an expert-level exam, you need to thoroughly understand Microsoft's data storage services, use your architectural thinking, and design the precise data storage solution. In this chapter, you will learn the critical concepts of designing storage and data integration on the Microsoft Azure Cloud platform.

Skills covered in this chapter:

- Skill 3.1: Design a solution for databases
- Skill 3.2: Design data integration
- Skill 3.3: Select an appropriate storage account

Skill 3.1: Design a solution for databases

A database is the foundation of any application. An accurate database design provides consistent data, high performance, scalability, less management, and ultimately, user satisfaction. A modern database needs to address new challenges, such as massive data, diverse data sources, multi-region deployment, and so on. The Azure Cloud platform helps overcome these challenges by providing sets of Azure database services.

In this skill, we look at the various database deployments available today in Azure.

> **This skill covers how to:**
> - Select an appropriate data platform based on requirements
> - Recommend database service tier sizing
> - Database scalability solutions
> - Encrypting data at rest, data in transmission, and data in use

Select an appropriate data platform based on requirements

First, you need to understand these vital requirements for selecting a data platform:

- **Data types**   What kind of data are you going to store? Is the data relational or non-relational?

- **Manageability**   Are you ready to completely manage your database, or would you like to offload manageability to the Microsoft Azure platform?

- **Encryption**   What different encryption methods are required for securing your data?

- **Data volume**   How much data do you need to store?

- **Ease of migration**   How quickly can you migrate databases from on-premises to Azure?

- **Feature set**   Does the platform support reporting such as SQL server reporting services (SSRS) and analytics like SQL Server Analytics Services (SSAS)? Does it support ETL (extract, transform, load), such as SQL Server Integration Services (SSIS)?

- **Database backup service**   Do you need to make an explicit backup of the database?

- **Cost**   How cost-effective is your database solution?

- **Security**   Is the database in a cloud-exposed public endpoint, or is it completely deployed in a private network?

- **Scalability**   Is the database scalable to support your growing demands? Does it also support horizontal scaling?

- **High availability**   Is your database highly available? How much availability will you get?

- **Read Intensive or transactional data**   Does the database need to support read-intensive or transactional data?

Now let's consider the options available on the Azure Cloud platform. Table 3-1 compares the capabilities of each of the Azure services discussed in the following sections.

TABLE 3-1 Azure services

	Azure Table Storage	Azure Cosmos DB	Azure SQL Database	Azure SQL Database Managed Instance	SQL Server on VM
Database size	500 TB per table.	Maximum storage across all items per (logical) partition: 20 GB.	Up to 4 TB in DTU and VCode model and 100 TB in hyperscale.	Max 8 TB.	SQL Server limit: 524,272. Database files on VM disk: maximum size of the disk supported by the VM. Database Files on Azure Storage: Azure storage size limit.
Scalability	Yes.	Horizontal.	Vertical.	Vertical.	Vertical.

	Azure Table Storage	Azure Cosmos DB	Azure SQL Database	Azure SQL Database Managed Instance	SQL Server on VM
Availability	99.99 percent for RA-GRS and 99.9 percent for other tiers.	99.999 percent for multi-region account, and 99.99 percent for single region account.	99.99 percent.	99.99 percent.	99.99 percent.
Data type	Key-value.	Key-value pair, column-family, document, graph.	Relational database that supports non-relational data, such as graphs, JSON, spatial, and XML.	Relational database that supports non-relational data, such as graphs, JSON, spatial, and XML.	Relational database that supports non-relational data, such as graphs, JSON, spatial, and XML.
Features (SSRS, SSIS, SSAS)	No.	No.	No.	No.	Yes.
Encryption	256-bit AES encryption using a Microsoft-managed key, as well as the customers' managed keys.	256-bit AES encryption using a Microsoft-managed key, as well as the customers' managed keys.	Transparent data encryption (TDE). Always encrypted for data in motion data at rest, and data in use.	Transparent data encryption (TDE). Always encrypted for data in motion, data at rest, and data in use.	Transparent data encryption (TDE). Always encrypted for data in motion, data at rest, and data in use.
Disaster recovery solution	Geo-replication at the storage account level.	Yes.	Active-geo replication. Auto-failover group.	Auto-failover group.	AlwaysOn Availability Groups, database mirroring, and log shipping.

Azure Table Storage

Azure Table Storage is a NoSQL data store where you can store key-value pairs with a schema-less design. Data stored in Azure Table Storage is in the form of entities, and entities are like rows. An entity can have maximum of 252 properties; additionally, entities have system properties that specify a partition key, row key, and a timestamp. Each entity can be of a maximum 1 MB in size. In Azure Table Storage, you can store terabytes of semi-structured data. Data stored in Azure Table Storage is highly available, as Azure internally maintains three replicas in the primary region, and if the storage account is geo-redundant, then the data is replicated in the secondary region. Azure Table Storage is highly scalable; there is no manual need to shard a dataset. A table can span up to the maximum size of the storage account. (Sharding is covered later in this chapter.) By default, all data stored in Azure Table Storage (data at rest) is encrypted. Following are some scenarios in which you would use Azure Table Storage:

- Store and query a huge set of non-relational, schemaless data

- Non-relational data that does not require any complex joins or foreign keys
- Faster retrieval of data using the key (partition key)
- As a cost-effective data storage solution

Azure Cosmos DB

Azure Cosmos DB is also a NoSQL, multi-model, fully managed, globally distributed, and high-throughput database. Cosmos DB supports key-value pair, column-family based, document-based, and graph-based databases. It provides 99.999 percent availability for multi-region accounts and 99.99 percent availability for a single-region account. Azure Cosmos DB guarantees less than 10-millisecond latencies for both reads (indexed) and writes at the 99th percentile. Azure Cosmos DB supports multiple APIs, such as MongoDB API, Graph API, Cassandra API, Gremlin API, SQL API, and Cosmos DB Table API. It also provides SDKs for multiple programming languages, including Python, .NET, Java, Node.js, JavaScript, and the like. Following are some scenarios in which you would use Azure Cosmos DB:

- Non-relational data that can be in key-value, document-based, graph-based, or column-family–based forms
- A business-critical application that requires very-high, near-real response time in milliseconds and high throughput
- An application that requires a massive and global scale with high availability and disaster recovery
- A social media application or IoT and telematics application that requires enormous data ingestion or unpredictable loads

Azure SQL Database

Azure SQL Database is a fully managed, scalable, and highly available relational database service on Azure Platform as a Service (PaaS). It is a multi-model database that allows you to store relational data, graphs, JSON documents, key-value pairs, and XML data. The maximum database size supported by the Azure SQL Database is 4 TB. Microsoft has introduced a new Hyperscale tier, which is a highly scalable storage and compute tier. This tier supports 100 TB of data. By default, all new databases that are deployed in Azure SQL Database are encrypted at rest using transparent data encryption (TDE). (TDE must be manually enabled for Azure SQL Databases created before May 2017.) The database, its backup file, and transaction logs are encrypted and decrypted in real-time by the Azure platform without requiring any application changes. Microsoft also offers the Always Encrypted feature to protect data at rest, data in transit, and data in use. This feature uses column granularity to encrypt data inside client applications and does not reveal encryption keys to the database engine. Thus, it provides separation between those who own the data and those who manage it, and it keeps data confidential from administrators and cloud operators.

Following are some scenarios when you would use Azure SQL Database:

- For storing relational data when the database schema is known before actual implementation of the application

- When you need high availability and quick disaster recovery of the database
- When you want to offload management tasks to the Microsoft Azure platform
- Artificial Intelligence (AI)–based tuning of databases
- A database that requires Always Encrypted functionality to protect sensitive data

Azure SQL Managed Instance

Azure SQL Managed Instance is fully managed and scalable, and it is nearly 100 percent compatible with the latest SQL Server (Enterprise Edition) database service. Azure SQL Managed Instance only supports the vCore-based purchasing model. You can manually scale from 4 vCore to 80 vCore. Azure SQL Managed Instance is completely isolated and is deployed to VMs in a dedicated subnet. Azure SQL Managed Instance provides 99.99 percent uptime, and it ensures that committed data is never lost because of failures. Similar to the Azure SQL Database, it also supports TDE encryption and the Always Encrypted feature. SQL Managed Instance databases created before February 2019 are not encrypted by default, so you would need to manually enable encryption. Azure SQL Managed Instance eases the migration from an on-premises Azure SQL Server. Azure SQL Server Database backups from on-premises SQL Server can be restored on the Managed Instance without needing any tools. Azure SQL Managed Instance supports the auto-failover group for data replication. It also provides the following standard features of SQL Server Database engines:

- SQL Server Agent
- Database Mail
- Native database backup and restore
- Linked Servers
- Cross-database transactions
- SQL CLR modules
- Row-Level Security
- SQL Audit
- Service Broker
- In-memory optimization
- DBCC statement
- SQL Server Analysis Services (SSAS)
- SQL Server Integration Services (SSIS)
- SQL Server Reporting Services (SSRS)

Following are some scenarios in which you would use Azure SQL Managed Instance:

- When you want to easily migrate a database from on-premises to Azure
- When you want to migrate an on-premises database to Azure with minimal downtime
- When an application uses lots of cross-database queries

- When an application requires a scheduled job to be executed inside the database using an SQL agent

- When you want to store relational data and you know the database schema before the actual implementation of the application

- When you need high availability and quick disaster recovery of the database

- When you want to offload management tasks to the Microsoft Azure platform

- When you have a database that requires Always Encrypted functionality to protect sensitive data

SQL Server on Azure Virtual Machine (VM)

SQL Server on Azure Virtual Machine is Microsoft's SQL Server database engine for Azure VMs. You can vertically scale SQL Server on a VM to the maximum VM size supported by the Azure platform. The maximum size of the database depends on the maximum disk size supported by the Azure VM. When you host a database on infrastructure (Azure VM), you become responsible for managing and implementing the high-availability and disaster recovery of the database solution, while Microsoft owns the high availability of Azure VMs. Following are some scenarios in which you would use SQL Server on a VM:

- When an application requires full compatibility with the SQL Server (Enterprise Edition) database engine

- When an application needs top features of SQL Server, such as SQL Server Reporting Services (SSRS); analytics, such as SQL Server Analytics Services (SSAS); and ETL, such as SQL Server Integration Services (SSIS)

- When you want to migrate an on-premises database to Azure with minimal changes

- When complete isolation is required at the infrastructure level

Recommend database service tier sizing

The selection of service tiers for the Azure platform's database depends on the database type and whether it is a single database, elastic pool, or Managed Instance. Also, in a single instance or an elastic pool, the selection of service tiers depends on the purchasing model—Virtual Core (vCore) or Database Transaction Unit (DTU)–based. Let's start with database types:

Single database

Following are the database service tiers based on the purchasing model:

- **DTU-based purchasing model:**
  - Basic
  - Standard
  - Premium
- **vCore-based purchasing model:**
  - General purpose

- Business critical
- Hyperscale

Elastic pool

Following are the database service tiers based on the purchasing model:

- **DTU-based purchasing model:**
  - Basic
  - Standard
  - Premium
- **vCore-based purchasing model:**
  - General Purpose
  - Business Critical

Let's look at the DTU-based purchasing model. DTU stands for Database Transaction Unit, and it blends CPU, memory, and I/O usage. The more DTUs, the more powerful the database. This option is suitable for customers who would like to use a simple preconfigured resource bundle.

While migrating a database from on-premises to Azure, you can get the current CPU, disk read/write, log bytes, and flushed/sec information from the current on-premises server and calculate the required DTU value on the target Azure SQL Database.

Table 3-2 lists the characteristics of DTU-based service tiers:

TABLE 3-2 DTU-based service tiers

	Basic	Standard	Premium
Maximum storage size	2 GB	1 TB	4 TB
CPU	Low	Low, Medium, High	Medium, High
Maximum DTUs	5	3,000	4,000
IO throughput	1–5 IOPS per DTU	1–5 IOPS per DTU	25 IOPS per DTU
Uptime SLA	99.99 percent	99.99 percent	99.99 percent
IO latency	Read: 5 ms Write: 10 ms	Read: 5 ms Write: 10 ms	Read/write: 2 ms
Maximum backup retention	7 days	35 days	35 days
Columnstore indexing	N/A	S3 and above	Supported
In-memory OLTP	N/A	N/A	Supported

Table continued on next page...

	Basic	Standard	Premium
Active geo-replication	Yes	Yes	Yes
Read scale-out	No	No	Yes

In the vCore purchasing model, you have the flexibility to independently pick compute, memory, and storage based on your workload needs. So, with this flexibility, you can easily map the on-premises database's vCore, memory, and storage and choose the matching Azure database tier. The vCore-based purchasing model offers Azure Hybrid Benefits (AHB), which allows you to use existing licenses for a discounted rate on Azure SQL Database and Azure SQL Managed Instance. Azure Hybrid allows you to save 30 percent or more on your SQL Database and SQL Managed Instance by using your existing SQL Server licenses with Software Assurance.

> **NEED MORE INFO?** **AZURE HYBRID BENEFITS CALCULATOR**
>
> For more details, see the AHB calculator at *https://azure.microsoft.com/en-us/pricing/hybrid-benefit/.*

Table 3-3 lists the characteristics of vCore-based service tiers:

TABLE 3-3 vCore-based service tiers

	Database	General Purpose	Business Critical	Hyperscale
Database Size	SQL database	5GB–4 TB	5GB–4 TB	Up-to 100 TB
	SQL managed instance	32 GB–8 TB	32 GB–4 TB	N/A
Compute Size	SQL database	1 to 80 vCores	1 to 80 vCores	1 to 80 vCores
	SQL managed instance	4, 8, 16, 24, 32, 40, 64, an 80 vCores	4, 8, 16, 24, 32, 40, 64, and 80 vCores	N/A
Availability	All	99.99 percent	99.99 percent; 99.995 percent with zone redundant single database	99.95 percent with one secondary replica; 99.99 percent with more replicas
Storage Type	All	Premium remote storage (per instance)	Super-fast local SSD storage (per instance)	De-coupled storage with local SSD cache (per instance)
Backup	All	RA-GRS, 7–35 days (7 days by default)	RA-GRS, 7–35 days (7 days by default)	RA-GRS, 7 days, constant time, point-in-time recovery (PITR)
In-memory OLTP	All	N/A	Available	N/A
Read Scale-out	All	No	Yes	No

Database scalability solutions

One of the objectives of moving an application to the cloud is to support a growing load. An application should be able to increase resources (compute, storage, and so on) to sustain the on-demand load and should be able to decrease resources when demand goes down. This flexibility is called elastic scaling. With elastic scaling, you can use optimal resources and pay only for what you use.

Following are two methods of scaling:

- **Vertical scaling** In this method, the capacity of the same resource is changed to meet the requirement. For example, you can increase (scale up) VM size from Standard_D2_v2 to Standard_D3_v2 and similarly decrease (scale down) VM size from Standard_D3_v2 to Standard_D2_v2. When you change the size of the same VM , a restart is required, which means the application deployed on the VM is unavailable until the VM restarts and comes back online. Therefore, this method is generally not automated. This method is also called *scale-up and scale-down*.

- **Horizontal scaling** In this method, capacity is increased or decreased by adding and removing instances of resources. For example, you can add one more VM to the load balancer set to meet the increasing load on the application. Similarly, you can remove the existing VM from the load balancer set when there is less load on the application. During this scaling, the application does not become unavailable or experience downtime. Therefore, this is the preferred method for auto-scaling. All Azure services that support auto-scaling are based on this method only.

Auto-scaling is a feature of Azure services that automatically adds or removes resources based on the actual load on the services. Auto-scaling eliminates the overhead of the operation team to monitor utilization and adjust resources.

The following sections examine the options available to scale databases:

Azure SQL Database Serverless

Serverless is a vertical scaling option that has been introduced as a new compute tier called **Serverless**. This tier automatically scales up or scales down the database's compute based on the actual load. You can specify the minimum and maximum vCore range that the database can use. Memory and IO limits are proportional to the specified vCore range. The cost of the Serverless tier is the sum of compute and storage cost. The compute cost is calculated based on the number of vCore used per second. This Serverless tier is available under the General-Purpose tier in the vCore purchasing model.

Another exciting feature of the Serverless tier is auto-pause. When the database is inactive, the Serverless compute tier pauses the database automatically, and it resumes the database when activity returns. There is no compute cost when the database is in the paused state, but you pay for storage cost.

Auto-pause delay is the time duration for which the database must be in an inactive state before it is automatically paused. The minimum auto-pause delay is one hour. Figure 3-1 depicts the minimum and maximum vCore configuration, actual CPU utilization, auto-pause delay period, and auto-pause.

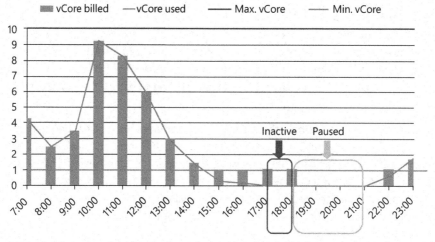

FIGURE 3-1 Serverless database configuration and its vCore utilization

In this example, between 7:00 to 14:00 hours, the number of vCores used is more than 1. During this period, vCores used and vCores billed is the same. From 15:00 to 18:00, the vCore used is below 1, but even though it is below 1 vCore, it will be billed as 1 vCore because that is the minimum vCore configuration. From 17:00 to 18:00 hours, vCore utilization is 0 because of database inactivity. The Azure SQL Database Serverless tier monitors this for one hour, which is called auto-pause delay. After one hour, the database is paused at 19:00 hours. At 21:00 hours, SQL Database resumes responding to activity.

Following are scenarios in which you would use an SQL Serverless Database:

- A new single database (either migrated from on-premises or freshly deployed on Azure) in which vCore and memory requirements are unknown.

- A single database with an unpredictable usage pattern with an inactive period and below-average vCore utilization.

Sharding

Sharding is an architecture pattern in which a large set of data is distributed into multiple and identically structured databases deployed into separate compute nodes called a *shard*. Data is distributed into shards based on the list of values or ranges of values called *sharding keys*. This metadata information (mapping) about data distribution is stored in a separate database called a *shard map manager.*

List-based mapping is called *list mapping*, whereas range-based mapping is called *range mapping*. The shard map manager database is used by the application to identify the correct database (shard) using the sharding key to perform database operations. This sharding method is most suitable for Software as a Service (SaaS) applications. SaaS application developers created sharding patterns to support a large volume of data and a large user base. Customers of the SaaS application are referred to as tenants. If all the data pertaining to one customer is stored in a single database, then it is called a *single-tenant model.* For this model, Shard Map

Manager stores the global mapping information using a list of tenant IDs. This mapping is called *list mapping*. Figure 3-2 depicts the single-tenant model.

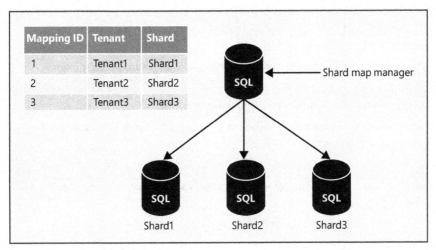

Mapping ID	Tenant	Shard
1	Tenant1	Shard1
2	Tenant2	Shard2
3	Tenant3	Shard3

FIGURE 3-2 Single tenant model

When the application needs a small amount of data for one tenant, then data from multiple tenants is stored in one database using a *multi-tenant model*. This model uses range mapping in which the Shard Map Manager keeps the mapping between ranges of tenant ID and the shard. Figure 3-3 shows the multi-tenant model.

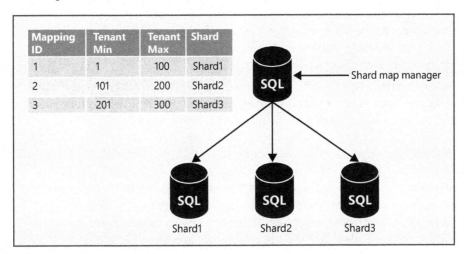

Mapping ID	Tenant Min	Tenant Max	Shard
1	1	100	Shard1
2	101	200	Shard2
3	201	300	Shard3

FIGURE 3-3 Multi-tenant model

The Elastic Database tools are a set of libraries and tools that create and manage shards:

- **Elastic database client library** This is a .NET and Java library that is used to create and maintain sharded databases.
- **Elastic database split-merge tool** This tool is useful for moving data between sharded databases.

- **Elastic database jobs**   This tool helps to easily manage large number of databases by performing administrative operation such as schema changes, credential management, data collection, reference data update by using jobs.

- **Elastic database query**   This tool allows you to run a transact-SQL query that spans multiple databases.

- **Elastic transactions**   This tool allows you to run transactions that span multiple databases.

Following are some scenarios in which you would use sharding:

- Customers' data needs to be stored in different geographies for geopolitical, performance, or compliance reasons.

- The volume of data is enormous and cannot fit into one single database.

- The transaction throughput requirement is very high and cannot be accommodated using a single database.

- Customers' data needs to be isolated from other customer's data.

Sharding provides high availability, more bandwidth, more throughput, and faster query response and processing. It also helps to mitigate the outage impact in the following scenarios:

- When databases are stored in different geographies, and one of the locations is having some outage.

- All databases are stored in one single region, and one of the databases is having some issue/outage.

In the above scenarios, only one customer (tenant) will be affected if you have chosen the single-tenant model, and only a few customers will be affected if you have chosen a multi-tenant model. Thus, the application's overall impact will be less than the non-sharding application in which the whole application will crash.

While sharding offers many benefits, it also adds complexity to create and manage shards and move data between shards. You must carefully design your sharding architecture and choose the right sharding keys, which are discussed in the following sections.

READ SCALE-OUT

There might be some scenarios in which the latest data is not immediately available in the read-only replica because of some latency issues. You need to consider this small latency when selecting read-only replicas for your application. You can use sys.dm_database_replica_states dynamic management views (DMVs) to monitor the replication status and synchronization statistics. When the client/application tries to connect the database, the gateway internally checks connection strings for the ApplicationIntent parameter. If the value of the parameter is ReadOnly, then it routes the request to a read-only replica. If the value of the parameter is ReadWrite, then it routes that request to a read-write replica. ReadWrite is the default value of the ApplicationIntent parameter.

Following are some scenarios when you would use read scale-out:

- An analytics workload, which only reads data for analysis purposes.
- A reporting application, which only reads data and generates various reports
- An integration system, which only reads data

ELASTIC POOL

An elastic pool is a collection of databases that are deployed on a single server that shares resources allocated to the pool. The capacity of the pool is fixed and does not change automatically. So, within a fixed capacity of the pool, databases scale automatically within a minimum and maximum capacity defined by the **Per Database** setting on the **Configure** blade in the elastic pool settings in the Azure portal. The Elastic Pool can use either DTU-based or vCore-based models. In the DTU-based model, databases can scale between a minimum and maximum DTU that is specified by the **Per Database** setting. Similarly, in the vCore-based model, a database can scale between a minimum and maximum vCore that is specified by the **Per Database** setting.

The size of the elastic pool can be changed with minimal downtime. A database can be added or removed from an elastic pool. The cost of the elastic pool depends on the size of the pool and not on the individual databases allocated in the pool. So, more databases in the pool means more cost savings.

Following are some scenarios in which to use an elastic pool:

- It is more suitable for an application or with a group of applications with a large number of databases having low utilization and few infrequent spikes.
- It can be used for an SaaS application that requires multiple databases with low to medium utilization.

Table 3-4 provides a quick comparison of scaling methods.

TABLE 3-4 Scaling methods

	Azure SQL Database Serverless	Sharding	Read Scale-Out	Elastic Pool
Scaling method	Vertical	Horizontal	Horizontal	Vertical
Auto-scaling	Yes	No	No	Auto-scaling within the minimum and maximum defined settings
Ease of Implementation	Yes	No	Yes	Yes
Manageability	Fully managed	Customer managed	Fully managed	Fully managed
Auto-pause to save compute cost	Yes	No	No	No
Read-only versus read-write replica	Read-write	Read-write	Read-only	Read-write

Encrypting data at rest, data in transmission, and data in use

Encryption is the process of scrambling or encoding data so that only authorized users can decrypt and read the data. Encryption is required when data is stored, data is in motion, or when data is in use. Effective encryption is the key to secure an organization's confidential data at rest, transit, and use. Encryption adds an additional layer of data protection. Even if unauthorized users gain access to encrypted data storage, they can't read data from encrypted storage. In this skill, you learn how you can protect the data storage on Azure platforms using encryption for data at rest, in transit, and in use.

Symmetric and asymmetric key encryption

There are two main types of encryption—symmetric and asymmetric encryption. In symmetric encryption, the same key is used to encrypt and decrypt data. Asymmetric encryption uses two keys—a public key and a private key. The public key is used to encrypt data, which is shared with everyone, whereas the private key is used to decrypt data, and it is kept securely and shared with only intended users.

Encrypting data at rest

Encryption at rest is the data protection method for data stored in persistent storage on physical media. Microsoft uses symmetric key encryption for data at rest. Encryption at rest is mandatory for an organization to be compliant with HIPAA, PCI, and FedRAMP standards. Microsoft uses key hierarchy models for implementing data at rest. It has two types of keys:

- **Data encryption key (DEK)**   This key is used to encrypt and decrypt actual data.
- **Key encryption key (KEK)**   This key is used to encrypt the data encryption key.

These keys need to be secured, and it is recommended that you store them in Azure Key Vault. You can use Azure Active Directory to manage and control access to keys stored in the Azure Key Vault. Encryption can be done at the client-side or server-side, based on your needs. The encryption models shown in the following sections provide more details about the implementation of encryption:

- Client-side encryption model
- Server-side encryption model

Client-side encryption model

In this model, encryption is done at the client-side before storing data in the Azure services. You need to handle the encryption, decryption, and key management (such as key rotation) in the client application.

Server-side encryption model

In this model, encryption and decryption is performed by the Azure service, and you or Microsoft can manage the encryption keys. The server-side encryption model is classified into the following three types:

- **Using service-managed keys**   The Azure service performs encryption, decryption, and key management.

- **Using customer-managed keys in Azure Key Vault**   You need to manage keys using Azure Key Vault. The Azure service performs encryption and decryption using the Key Vault.

- **Using customer-managed keys on customer-controlled hardware**   The Azure service performs encryption and decryption, and you need to manage keys using your hardware.

Microsoft's Azure platform supports encryption at rest for Platform as a Service (PaaS), Infrastructure as a Service (IaaS), and Software as a Service (SaaS).

Encrypting data in transmission

Encrypting data in transmission is the data protection method for the data that is actively moving from one component to another. It could be moving across the Internet or through a private network.

Microsoft offers the following features for encrypting data in transmission:

- **Transport Layer Security (TLS)**   TLS is a cryptographic protocol that provides data integrity, privacy, and authentication during communication between two components over the network. Microsoft protects data using TLS when data is traveling between cloud services and client systems.

- **Azure App Services**   In the Azure App services, you can enforce an encrypted connection by setting the HTTPS value to ON. Once enabled, any HTTP connection to your Azure App Service is redirected to an HTTPS URL.

- **Azure SQL Database and SQL Managed Instance**   Both the Azure SQL Database and SQL Managed Instance feature always enforce an SSL/TLS connection, irrespective of the encrypt or TrustServerCertificate setting in the connection string.

- **Azure Storage**   Azure Storage supports both HTTP and HTTPS protocols. You can enforce HTTPS by enabling the secure transfer required property. Once you have enabled it, any call to Azure Storage using the HTTP protocol is rejected. Similarly, any SMB connection without encryption to the Azure file share will also be rejected. By default, this property is enabled when you provision a new storage account.

- **Azure Virtual Machine**   The remote desktop protocol (RDP) connection to Azure VMs uses TLS to protect data in transit. Also, data in transit is encrypted when you connect to a Linux VM using the Secure Shell (SSH) protocol.

- **VPN Connection** A site-to-site VPN connection uses IPsec, while a point-to-site VPN connection uses the secure socket tunneling protocol (SSTP) to encrypt the communication.
- **Data-link Layer Encryption** Microsoft is using the IEEE 802.1AE MAC Security Standard for data in transit between datacenters. This encryption method is also known as MACsec. This encryption is enabled for all the traffic within a region or between regions.

Encrypting data in use

Data in use means data that is actively being used by the user or system for processing. This data is stored in non-persistent storage such as RAM.

Always Encrypted is a client-side encryption technique that protects sensitive data, such as social security numbers (SSN), credit card numbers, and personally identifiable information (PII) stored in SQL Server databases and SQL Azure databases. A database driver inside the client application encrypts data before storing it in the database, and it decrypts encrypted data retrieved from the database. Because encryption is happening at the client-side, the keys used to encrypt data are never revealed to the database. Thus, by using this feature, even a database administrator or cloud database operator who manages the database server and who has full control of the database cannot see original decrypted data.

The Always Encrypted feature uses the following keys:

- **Column encryption keys** These keys are used to encrypt data before storing it in the database.
- **Column master keys** Column encryption keys are encrypted by using column master keys.

The column encryption keys are stored into the database in encrypted form, and column master keys are stored outside the database like a local key management system or Azure Key Vault.

This feature encrypts data at rest, in transit, and in use. Hence, this feature is called Always Encrypted. However, transparent data encryption (TDE) is the recommended option for encrypting data at REST.

Skill 3.2: Design data integration

In the current information age, large amounts of data are generated by many applications, and the amount of data being generated is growing exponentially. An organization needs to collect data from multiple sources such as business partners, suppliers, vendors, manufacturers, customers, social media, and so on. This exploding volume of data, disparate data sources, and cloud adoption are crucial factors when it comes to organizations that must redesign or adopt a new integration solution to meet business needs. In this skill, we look at various options available in the Microsoft Azure cloud platform for data integration.

Data flow to meet business requirements

Data flow is movement of data from one component/system to another. During the lifecycle of the data, it flows through four phases: collection, processing, archiving, and destruction. While data moves from one phase to another, you need the right set of tools and services to meet the business requirements.

Figure 3-4 shows the lifecycle of the data, how data is flowing into the different systems during its lifecycle, and how to choose the right set of tool/services to manage the data to meet the business requirements/goals.

The following sections discuss each of the four data lifecycle phases.

Collection

In this phase, data is collected from various disparate systems. This data comes in one of three formats—unstructured, semi-structured, and structured. The data can be collected from multiple sources, such as

- Signal reception (transmitted by a sensor or IoT data)
- Logs collected from various systems
- Data collected from social media
- Data entered by the user into business or custom applications
- Spatial and GPS data
- Business data received from vendors, suppliers, or business partners

Following are the critical business requirements for data collection:

- A data platform should be able to collect data from various disparate systems.
- It should support real-time ingestion of data.
- It should allow collecting all types of data—unstructured, semi-structured, and structured.
- It should support a large volume of data.

Microsoft offers the following services to meet these business requirements:

- **Azure Data Factory (ADF)**   Azure Data Factory is a fully managed, highly scalable, and serverless data integration service on the Azure Cloud platform. ADF provides flexibility to collect data from various disparate systems. It runs on scheduled time or based on the event. We explore the Azure Data Factory in detail in the next section.

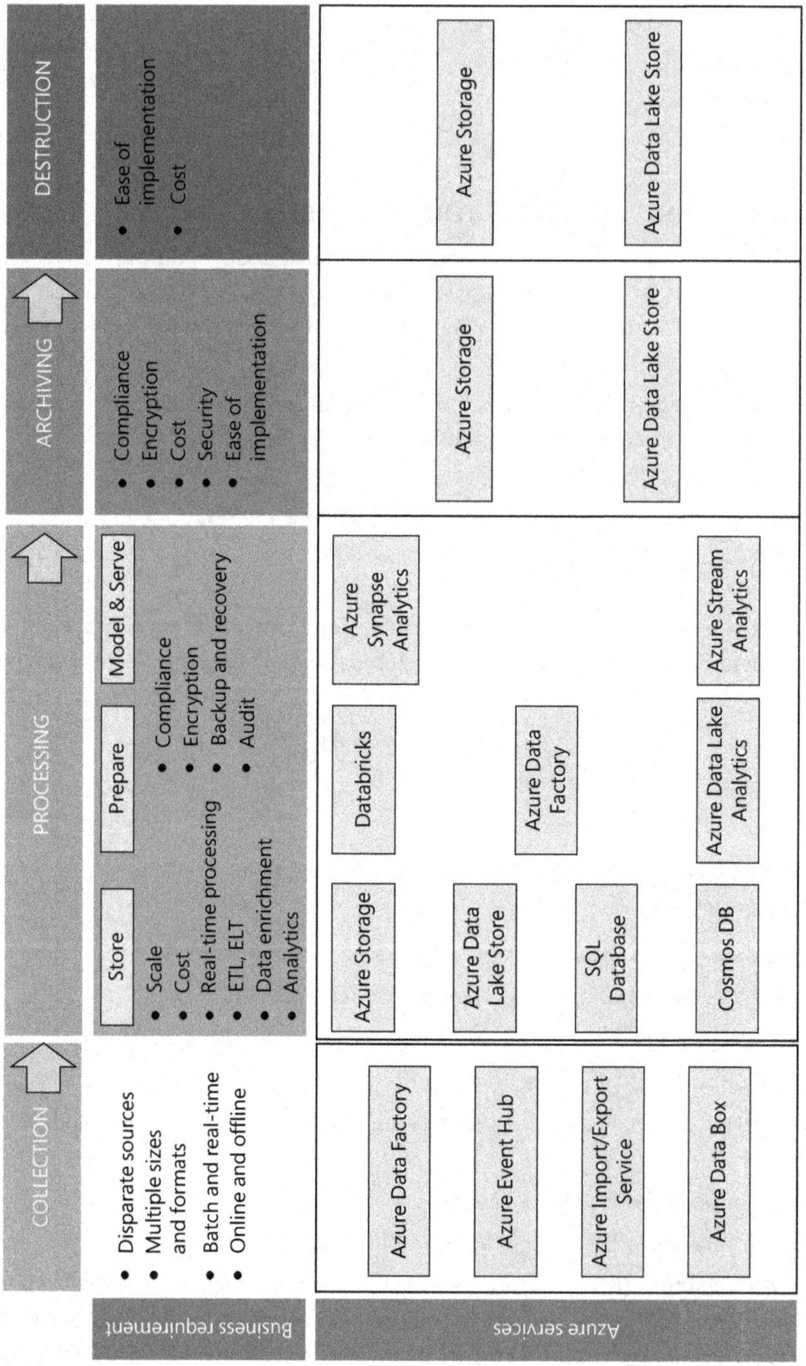

FIGURE 3-4 Data lifecycle and Azure services

- **Azure Event Hub**   Azure Event Hub is a big data–streaming platform and real-time event-ingestion service that is a highly scalable, fully managed service on the Azure Cloud platform. Azure Event Hub can stream millions of events per second with low latency.
- **Azure Import/Export Service**   You can use Azure Import/Export Service to transfer a large amount of data into Azure Blob and file storage. You need to copy data to hard drives and encrypt it with BitLocker. Then you need to create a job in the Azure portal and ship the disk drives to the Microsoft Azure datacenter. This option is mostly suitable for one-time data copied in offline mode or for when you have a low-bandwidth network.
- **Azure Data Box**   Azure Data Box is a family of products designed to transfer a massive amount of data. This family includes Azure Data Box, Azure Data Box Disk, Azure Data Box Heavy, Azure Data Box Edge, and Azure Data Box Gateway. Of these, Azure Data Box, Azure Data Box Disk, and Azure Data Box Heavy are designed to transfer data offline by shipping disks/appliances to Microsoft datacenters. These products are suitable for one-time migration, initial bulk transfer, or periodic upload. Table 3-5 provides a glance at the features of these products.

TABLE 3-5 Azure Data Box products

	Azure Data Box	Azure Data Box Disk	Azure Data Box Heavy
Total devices per order	1	5	1
Total capacity	100 TB	40 TB	1 PB
Usable capacity	80 TB	35 TB	800 TB
Supported Azure Storage services	Block Blob, Page Blob, Azure Files, or Managed Disk	Block Blob, Page Blob, Azure Files, or Managed Disk	Block Blob, Page Blob, Azure Files or, Managed Disk
Interface	1x1/10 Gbps RJ45 and 2x10 Gbps SFP+	USB/SATA II and III	4x1/10 Gbps RJ45 and 4x40 Gbps QSFP+
Encryption	AES 256-bit	AES 128-bit	AES 256-bit

Azure Data Box Gateway and Azure Data Box Edge are online data transfer methods.

- **Azure Data Box Edge**   Azure Data Box Edge is a hardware appliance provided by Microsoft to be placed at the on-premises end. It acts as a storage gateway linking the on-premises world to Azure Storage. It caches data locally, and then it writes to Azure Storage.
- **Azure Data Box Gateway**   Azure Data Box Gateway is a virtual appliance deployed to an on-premises virtualized environment. You can write data locally using NFS and SMB protocols, and then this device uploads the data to Azure Storage.

Processing

In this phase, data is first stored in the data store. Next, it is prepared, modeled, and served. Once the data collection from multiple sources is complete, it moves to data storage.

The choice of the data store mostly depends on the data volume and variety. After that, it is prepared for analysis. The data preparation mostly involves data cleansing and transformation. Data cleaning and transformation can also be done while uploading to the data store. Once the data is prepared, it is then used for analysis (churn analysis, predictions, and so on). Let's look at the key business requirements of the data processing phase:

- Data storage should be cheaper.
- A solution should orchestrate and automate data movement and transformation.
- It should ensure regulatory compliance.
- It should allow real-time processing with a capacity to process millions of events per second.
- Data should be secure and encrypted.
- It should be a highly scalable solution to accommodate a high volume of data processing and future growth.

Microsoft offers the following services to meet the above business requirements:

- Azure Blob Storage
- Azure SQL Database
- Azure SQL Data Lake Store
- Azure Cosmos DB
- Azure Data Factory
- Azure Data Bricks
- Azure Data Lake Analytics
- Azure Synapse Analytics
- Azure Stream Analytics

Of these services, Azure Storage, Azure SQL Database, and Azure Cosmos DB were covered in Skill 3-1; the remaining services are covered next.

Archiving

Once the data completes its active life, it goes into the next phase—archiving. In this phase, data is moved from all production environments and stored in centralized storage. Following are the crucial business requirements of the data archiving phase:

- Data storage should be cheaper.
- Data should be secure and encrypted.
- Ease of moving data from a production environment to archive storage.
- Ensure regulatory compliance.

Azure Blob Storage is an ideal solution for archiving data. You can effortlessly move data from the Hot and Cool Access tiers to the Archive Access tier to save enormous costs. This data movement can be easily achieved by applying the Azure Blob Storage lifecycle policy.

Destruction

Once the data is no longer required, you can simply purge it. The key requirements of the data destruction phase are as follows:

- Ease of purging data.
- Cost of data purging should be significantly less.
- Ensure regulatory compliance.

Azure Blob Storage is an ideal solution for purging data. The destruction of data can be easily achieved by applying the Azure Blob Storage lifecycle policy.

Azure Data Factory

Azure Data Factory (ADF) is Microsoft's cloud-based, fully managed, serverless, and cost-effective data integration and data transformation service that allows you to create data-driven workflows and orchestrate, move, and transform data. It is designed for complex hybrid extract-transform-load (ETL) and extract-load-transform (ELT) patterns. ADF does not store any data; it ingests data from various sources, transforms it, and publishes it to data stores called *sinks*. You can also run SSIS packages in Azure Data Factory. It also provides assistance in migrating existing SSIS packages.

Azure Data Factory pipeline can be created by using these tools or APIs:

- Azure portal
- Visual Studio
- PowerShell
- .NET API
- REST API
- Azure Resource Manager template

Azure Data Factory supports the following file formats:

- Avro format
- Binary format
- Common Data Model format
- Delimited text format
- Delta format
- Excel format
- JSON format
- ORC format
- Parquet format
- XML format

Let's look at the Azure Data Factory components before delving into how ADF works:

- **Linked services (connectors)** Linked services contain configuration settings required for ADF to connect to various external resources outside ADF. This information can include a server name, database name, credentials, and the like. This is similar to the connection string used to connect to the SQL server database. Depending on an external resource, it can represent data stores such as SQL server oracle, and so on, or it can represent compute resources such as HDInsight to perform execution of an activity. For example, an Azure Storage–linked service represents a connection string to connect to the Azure Storage Account.

- **Dataset** This component represents structures of data within data stores and provides more granular information about the data from linked sources you will use. For example, an Azure Storage–linked service represents a connection string to connect to the Azure Storage Account, and the Azure Blob dataset represents the blob container, the folder and path, and the blob's file name.

- **Activities** This component represents the action taken on the data. A pipeline can contain one or more activities. Azure Data Factory currently provides three types of activities—data-movement activities, control activities, and data transformation activities.

- **Pipeline** Pipelines are a logical grouping of activities that perform a task together.

- **Triggers** This component is a unit of processing that decides when a pipeline execution should be commenced. Azure Data Factory supports the following three types of triggers:

  - **Schedule trigger** This trigger invokes a pipeline at a scheduled time.

  - **Tumbling window trigger** This trigger invokes a pipeline at a periodic interval, while retaining its state.

  - **Event-based trigger** This trigger invokes a pipeline to respond to an event.

- **Integration Runtime (IR)** This component is a compute infrastructure used by ADF to carry out integration activities such as data movement, data flow, activity dispatch, and SSIS package execution. There are three types of integration runtimes:

  - **Azure IR** This is a fully managed, serverless compute used to perform data flow, data movement, and activity dispatch on a public and private network.

  - **Self-hosted IR** You can install a self-hosted IR inside on-premises networks secured by the Azure Storage Firewall or inside a virtual network. It only makes outbound HTTPS calls to the Internet. Currently, it is supported only on Windows.

  - **Azure-SSIS IR** This is used to natively execute SQL server integration services (SSIS) packages.

Figure 3-5 shows how Azure Data Factory works.

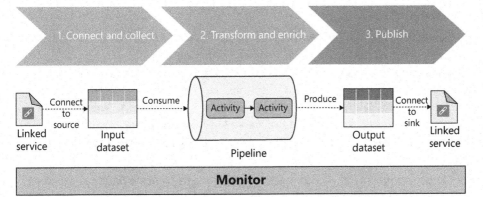

FIGURE 3-5 Azure Data Factory

The pipeline in Azure Data Factory is executed based on the schedule (for example, hourly, daily, or weekly), or it is triggered by an external event. In the execution, the pipeline performs the following steps, which are shown in Figure 3-5:

1. **Connect and collect**   The first step in the process is to connect to the source system and get the required data, as mentioned in the source linked service and input dataset. You can connect to various source systems in Azure, on-premises, and SaaS services. These systems can be used as a source, sink, or both, depending on the type of activity.

> **NEED MORE INFO?   AZURE DATA FACTORY CONNECTORS**
>
> For supported data stores, see *https://docs.microsoft.com/en-us/azure/data-factory/connector-overview.*

---

2. **Transform and enrich**   After collecting data, it is transformed and enriched using the data flow activity that is executed on Spark internally without any knowledge of the Spark cluster and its programming. If you would like to code the transformation, you can use external activities for the execution of transformation on compute services such as Data Lake Analytics, HDInsight, Spark, and Machine Learning.

3. **Publish**   After transforming or enriching data, it can be published to target systems such as Azure SQL Database, Azure Cosmos DB, and so on.

Azure Data Factory provides the **Monitor & Manage** tile on the **Data Factory** blade, where you can monitor pipeline runs. You can also monitor the pipeline programmatically using SDKs (.NET and Python), REST API, and PowerShell. The **Azure Monitor** and the **Health** panels in the Azure portal are additional ways to monitor the pipeline. You can view active pipeline executions, as well as the executions history.

Azure Data Factory is useful when we need to ingest data from a multi-cloud and on-premises environment. ADF is a highly scalable service to handle gigabytes and petabytes of data.

Azure Databricks

Azure Databricks is a fully managed, fast, and easy analytics platform that is based on Apache Spark on Azure. It provides flexibility to do a one-click setup, and you can use streamlined workflows and shared collaborative and interactive workspaces. Workspace enables data science teams consisting of data engineers, data scientists, and business analysts to collaborate and build data products. It is natively integrated with Azure services such as Blob Storage, Azure Data Lake Storage, Cosmos DB, Azure Synapse Analytics, and the like. It supports popular BI tools, such as Alteryx, Looker, Power BI, Tableau, and so on, to connect Azure Databricks clusters to query data.

Azure Databricks supports the following sources, either directly in the Databricks Runtime or by using small shell commands to enable access:

- Avro file
- Binary file
- CSV file
- Hive table
- Image
- JSON file
- LZO compressed file
- MLflow experiment
- Parquet file
- Zip file
- XML file

Let's look at Azure Databricks' key components:

- **Databricks Workspace**   The workspace is an environment for accessing all Azure Databricks assets. A workspace folder contains:

  - **Notebook**   A web-based user interface to documents that contain runnable code, narrative text, and visualizations.

  - **Dashboards**   A user interface that provides organized access to visualizations.

  - **Library**   A collection of code available to the notebook or job running on a cluster. Databricks provides many ready-made libraries, and you can add your own.

  - **Experiment**   A collection of MLflow runs for training a machine learning model.

- **Data Management**   Following are the objects that hold the data and are used to perform analytics and feed into the machine learning algorithm:

  - **Databricks File System (DBFS)**   This is a file system abstraction layer over a blob store.

- **Database**   This is a systematic collection of information that can be easily accessed, managed, and updated.
- **Table**   This is structured data that can be queried using Apache Spark SQL and Apache Spark APIs.
- **Metastore**   This stores structured information from the various tables and partitions.
- **Compute Management**   Following are the components that you need to know to run a computation in Azure Databricks:
    - **Cluster**   A computing resource to run notebooks and jobs. There are two types of clusters: all-purpose cluster and job cluster. An all-purpose cluster is created manually using UI, REST API, or CLI. A job cluster is created by Databricks when you trigger a job.
    - **Pool**   A collection of ready-to-use idle instances that reduce cluster start and autoscaling times.
    - **Databricks Runtime**   This is a set of core components that run on the cluster.
    - **Job**   This is an execution of a notebook or JAR at a scheduled time or instantly.

You can easily integrate and read data from Azure services such as Azure Blob Storage, Azure Data Lake Storage, Azure Synapse Analytics (formally Azure SQL Data Warehouse), and so on. You can also connect to Kafka, Event Hub, or IoT Hub and stream millions of events per second to Azure Databricks. You can integrate with Azure Key Vaults to store and manage secrets such as keys, tokens, and passwords. Azure Databricks integrates closely with Power BI for interactive visualization. You can create build and release pipelines for Azure Databricks with Azure DevOps for Continuous Integration (CI) and Continuous Deployment (CD).

The Azure Databricks Runtime is a set of components that run on the Databricks cluster. Azure Databricks offers several runtime variants such as runtime for ML, runtime for Genomics, and the like. These versions are updated and released regularly to improve the usability, performance, and security of big data analytics. It also offers a serverless option that helps data scientists iterate quickly.

Azure Databricks easily integrates with Azure Active Directory and provides role-based access control and fine-grained user permissions for notebooks, jobs, clusters, and data.

Azure Data Lake

Azure Data Lake is a fully managed, highly scalable data lake service on the Azure Cloud platform. It provides an enormous amount of storage to store structured, semi-structured, and unstructured data and perform analytics to gain business insights quickly. Figure 3.6 shows that the Azure Data Lake platform primarily consists of Azure Data Lake Analytics, Azure Data Lake Store, and Azure HDInsight.

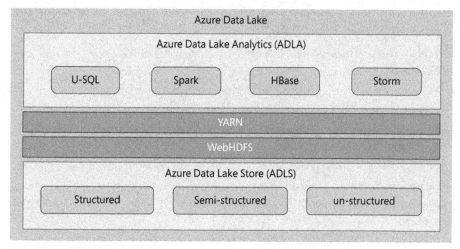

FIGURE 3-6 Azure Data Lake

Azure Data Lake includes three services: Azure Data Lake Storage, Azure Data Lake Analytics, and Azure HDInsight.

Azure Data Lake Storage (ADLS)

Azure Data Lake Storage is a fully managed, hyper-scale, redundant, and cost-effective data repository solution for big data analytics. This repository provides storage with no limits, without any restrictions on the file size or the type of data (structured, semi-structured, unstructured, or total data volumes). You can store trillions of files, and one file can be petabytes in size if needed. This allows you to run massively parallel analytics. ADLS easily integrates with Azure services such as Azure Databricks and Azure Data Factory. To protect data, it uses Azure Active Directory for authentication and role-based access control, and it uses Azure Storage Firewall to restrict access and encryption of data at rest.

Azure Data Lake Storage comes in two variants—Generation 1 and Generation 2:

- **Azure Data Lake Storage Generation 1** Azure Data Lake Storage Generation 1 uses a Hadoop file system that is compatible with Hadoop Distributed File System (HDFS). It also exposes a WebHDFS-compatible REST API that can be easily used by an existing HDInsight service. Also, Azure Data Lake Storage Gen1 is accessible using the new AzureDataLakeFilesystem (adl://) file system. This file system provides performance optimization that is currently not available in WebHDFS. ADLS Generation 1 can be easily integrated with Azure services such as Azure Data Factory, Azure HDInsight, Azure Stream Analytics, Power BI, Azure Event Hubs, and the like.

- **Azure Data Lake Storage Generation 2** Azure Data Lake Storage Generation 2 is built on Azure Blob Storage. Azure Storage brings its power like geo-redundancy, Hot, Cold, and Archive tiers, additional metadata, and regional availability. Azure Data Lake Storage Generation 2 combines all the features of Gen1 with the power of Azure Storage, which greatly enriches performance, management, and security. Generation 2 uses hierarchical namespace (HNS) to Azure Blob Storage, which allows the collection of objects within an account to be arranged into a hierarchy of directories and subdirectories like a file system on a desktop computer.

Azure Data Lake Analytics (ADLA)

Azure Data Lake Analytics is a fully managed and on-demand data analytics service for the Azure Cloud platform. It is a real-time analytic service built on Apache's Hadoop Yet Another Resource Negotiator (YARN). It allows the parallel processing of very large data (structured, semi-structured, unstructured), which eliminates the need to provision the underlying infrastructure. It easily integrates with Azure Data Lake Storage and Azure Storage Blobs, Azure SQL Database and Azure Synapse Analytics (formerly SQL Data Warehouse).

In Azure Data Lake Analytics, you can perform data transformation and processing tasks using a program developed in U-SQL, R, Python, and .NET. This U-SQL is new query language, which is a blend of SQL and C# that processes both structured and unstructured data of any size. You can also use a visual studio as your integrated development environment (IDE) to develop a U-SQL script. Performing analytics is quite easy with Azure Data Lake Analytics. As a developer, you simply need to write a script using U-SQL or your choice of language and submit it as a job.

Azure Data Lake Analytics pricing is based on ADLAU (Azure Data Lake Analytics Unit), also known as an analytics unit (AU). AU is a unit of compute resource (CPU cores and memory) provided to run your job. Currently, an AU is the equivalent of 2 cores and 6 GB of RAM. A job is executed in four phases—preparation, queuing, execution, and finalization. You need to pay for the duration of the job's execution and finalization phase.

Azure HDInsight

Azure Data Lake brings integration with an existing Azure HDInsight service. It is a fully managed, open-source Hadoop-based analytics service on the Azure Cloud platform. Azure HD Insight uses the Hortonworks Data Platform (HDP) Hadoop distribution. It is designed to process a massive amount of streaming and historical data. It enables you to build big data applications using open-source frameworks such as Apache Hadoop, Apache Spark, Apache Hive, Apache Kafka, and Apache Storm. You can also easily integrate Azure HDInsight with a range of Azure services, such as Azure Cosmos DB, Azure Data Factory, Azure Blob Storage, Azure Event Hubs, and so on.

Azure Synapse Analytics

Azure Synapse Analytics is an evolution of Azure SQL Data warehouse that brings the SQL data warehouse and big data analytics into one single service. It provides a unified experience to ingest, prepare, manage, and serve data for business intelligence and machine-learning needs.

Azure Synapse has four components:

- Synapse SQL
- Spark: (Preview)

- Data Integration: (Preview)
- Studio: (Preview)

Azure Synapse SQL uses a nodes-based architecture that separates compute and storage. This separation enables you to scale compute independently of the data. You can pause the service to free up compute resources. You will be charged only for storage when you pause the service. The data remains intact in storage during this pause period. Figure 3-7 illustrates the Azure Synapse SQL architecture.

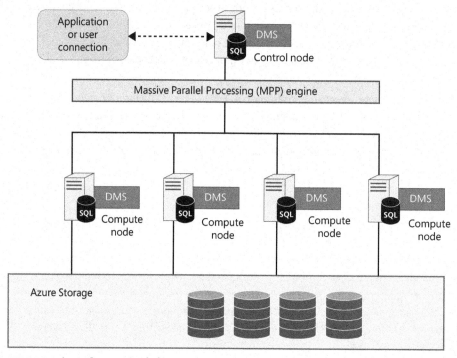

FIGURE 3-7 Azure Synapse Analytics

Control node

A user or an application connects to control nodes and gives T-SQL commands to the control node for execution. A control node optimizes queries using the Massive Parallel Processing (MPP) engine and then distributes it to multiple compute nodes to run in parallel.

Compute node

The Azure Synapse SQL pool distributes the processing on multiple compute nodes. It can use a maximum of 60 compute nodes for processing, which is determined by the service level for Azure Synapse SQL. A unit of compute power is called a data warehouse unit (DWU), and all the compute nodes run queries in parallel. The data movement service (DMS) manages data movement across compute nodes to run queries in parallel.

Azure Storage

Azure synapse SQL uses Azure Storage to store data. The data is horizontally partitioned and stored in a shard to optimize the performance of the system. In this sharding process, data is split up across 60 distributions. There are three methods of distribution—round robin, replicated, and hash. These distribution methods decide how rows in the table are split across nodes.

- **Round Robin**   This is the default method of distribution. In this method, data is distributed evenly across the nodes. It is quick and straightforward to create, but it is not optimized for query performance.
- **Replicated**   In this method, a complete table is replicated across nodes. This method is suitable for small tables and provides faster query performance.
- **Hash**   In this method, a hash function is used to distribute data. One of the columns in the table is used as a distribution key column. Azure Synapse SQL automatically spreads the rows across all 60 distributions based on distribution key column value.

Azure synapse provides end-to-end analytic solutions, which combine the power of a data warehouse, Azure Data Lake, and machine learning to offer a complete analytic solution at an immense scale on the Azure Cloud platform.

Skill 3.3: Select an appropriate storage account

As you know, in today's online world, data is getting generated at an unprecedented rate. Organizations are looking for a cheaper, faster, and better way to store, protect, and manage data. Microsoft Azure helps organizations address these challenges with the right set of services provided on the Azure Cloud platform.

In this skill, you will learn how to securely store data in Azure, how to access it, and how you can efficiently manage data in the storage.

> **This skill covers how to:**
> - Choose between storage tiers
> - Storage access solutions
> - Storage management tools

Choose between storage tiers

Azure Storage is Microsoft's cloud storage service on the Azure Cloud platform. The Azure Storage service is a highly available, scalable, durable, secure, fully managed, and widely accessible service. You can access Azure Storage over HTTP and HTTPS. It is also accessible using client libraries that are available for various languages, including .NET, PHP, Node.js, Java, Python, and Ruby.

As an Azure Solutions Architect, it is imperative to use storage capacity optimally, meeting the performance requirements of the workload and keeping costs low. Azure Storage provides the following three storage access tiers:

- **Hot Access Tier** This storage access tier is designed for frequently accessed data. The cost for data storage is higher as compared to the Cool and Archive tiers, whereas the cost of access is lowest. This storage access tier provides 99.99 percent SLA for RA-GRS storage and 99.9 percent for other redundant storage accounts. Use Hot Access Tier for production workloads or any other workloads in which data is accessed frequently.

- **Cool Access Tier** This storage access tier is designed for data that is accessed less often and remains stored for at least 30 days. Also, it is designed optimally for data that is accessed less frequently but that needs to be available instantly. The cost of data storage is lower, whereas the cost of access is higher. This tier has slightly lower SLA as compared to the Hot Access tier. It provides 99.9 percent SLA for RA-GRS storage and 99 percent for other redundant storage accounts. Use the Cool Access tier for older backups that still need to be accessed quickly. You also would use this tier for old media and documents that are not accessed frequently but that still need to be available instantly when required.

- **Archive Access Tier** This storage access tier is designed for data that is accessed very rarely and for data that remains stored for at least 180 days. The cost of data storage is the lowest, whereas the cost of access is the highest. The data stored in this tier is offline and cannot be read or modified directly. Before reading, updating, or downloading the data from the Archive Access Tier, the data needs to be first brought online This process is called blob rehydration. The metadata of blobs stored in this tier always remains online, and you can get metadata from the blob without rehydrating. The data stored in this tier takes several hours for retrieval, depending on the priority of rehydration (see Table 3-6). Use the Archive Access tier for old data that is rarely accessed, such as old backups, raw data, and so forth. You also would use this tier for data that must be maintained for compliance purposes but that is rarely accessed.

TABLE 3-6 Hot, Cool, and Archive Tiers

	Hot	Cool	Archive
Storage cost	High	Lower	Lowest
Access cost	Low	Higher	Highest

	Hot	Cool	Archive
Early deletion period	NA	30 days	180 days
Early deletion fee	No	Yes	Yes
SLA	99.99 percent for RA-GRS and 99.9 percent for others.	99.9 percent for RA-GRS and 99. percent for others.	Offline: Data needs to be moved to an online tier (Hot or Cool) before read/write.

Along with above access tiers, Azure Storage Accounts are also classified into the following performance tiers, which are further detailed in Table 3-7.

- **Standard Performance tier** The Azure Standard Performance tier account is the first storage account performance tier introduced by Microsoft. Later, Microsoft introduced the Premium Performance tier, which is used for storing blobs, files, tables, queues, and VMs' unmanaged and managed disks. The Premium Performance tier is available in General-Purpose V1, General-Purpose V2, and Blob Storage account types. The Hot, Cool, and Archive Access tiers are available in the Standard Performance tier only. Also, Hot, Cool, and Archive tiers are available only on General Purpose V2 storage account types. In Standard Performance tier, an unmanaged disk is charged based on the amount of storage consumed. For example, if you attached 128 GB as a standard unmanaged disk (page blob), and if you are consuming 50 GB only, then you will be charged for 50 GB only. This tier supports the following kinds of storage:

  - Locally redundant (LRS)
  - Geographically redundant storage (GRS)
  - Zone redundant storage (ZRS)
  - Read access geographically redundant storage (RA-GRS)
  - Zone-redundant storage (ZRS)
  - Geo-zone-redundant storage (GZRS/RA-GZRS) redundancy

- **Premium Performance tier** The Azure Premium Performance tier is a high-performance, low-latency tier. This tier stores data in a solid-state drive, so this tier's performance is better as compared to the Standard Performance tier. This performance tier is available in General-Purpose V1, General-Purpose V2, File Storage, and Block Blob Storage account types. This tier supports the following kinds of storage:

  - Locally redundant (LRS)
  - Zone redundant storage (ZRS) (in Block Blob Storage)

EXAM TIP

Data in Archive storage is not readily available for immediate read. You would need to copy or change the tier to Hot or Cool for instant read. To learn more, visit the Microsoft documentation at *https://docs.microsoft.com/en-us/azure/storage/blobs/storage-blob-rehydration?tabs=azure-portal.*

TABLE 3-7 Azure storage—Standard and Premium Performance tiers

	Standard Performance tier	Premium Performance tier
Account Kind	General-Purpose V1, General-Purpose V2, and Blob Storage	General-Purpose V1, General-Purpose V2, File Storage, and Block Blob Storage
Underlying hardware	HDD	SSD
Cost	Low	High
Read-write latency	Relatively high	Low
Throughput	Relatively low	High
Redundancy	LRS, ZRS, GRS, RA-GRS, ZRS, and RA-GZRS	LRS, ZRS (in Block Blob Storage)
Recommended for	All non-latency and throughput workloads	For all critical applications that require low latency and high throughput
Core storage services	Blob, File, Queue, Table	Blob

Storage access solutions

There are various ways to access Azure Storage Accounts based on the type of Azure Storage service and your needs. This section covers the various aspects of accessing Azure Storage, such as accessing storage with different authorization methods, securing Azure Storage using Azure Storage Firewall for limited access, programmatically accessing Azure Storage, and the tools to access your storage.

Authorization while Accessing Azure Storage:

When you provision an Azure Storage Account, it creates the following endpoints for each service:

- **Blob** *http://<<StorageAccountName>>.blob.core.windows.net*
- **File** *http://<<StorageAccountName>>.file.core.windows.net*
- **Table** *http://<<StorageAccountName>>.table.core.windows.net*
- **Queue** *http://<<StorageAccountName>>.queue.core.windows.net*

These endpoints can be accessed using the following authorization options:

- **Account key (Primary/Secondary)** The account key is also referred as a *shared key*. When you provision a storage account, two 512-bit storage account access keys are automatically generated—primary and secondary. A client who is accessing storage can pass one of these keys in the Authorization header to successfully authorize it for the storage account and access the content.
- **Shared Access Signature (SAS)** SAS is a granular method of providing access to resources in the storage accounts. With SAS, you can grant limited access to containers and blobs in a storage account. SAS is a URI that contains an SAS token and that grants

restricted access rights to the Azure Storage resource. This access includes specific permissions and a time period.

- **Azure Active Directory Integration** With this option, a client is authenticated using his or her AD credentials like a user, group, or application service principal and is given the appropriate Azure RBAC access. A client needs to authenticate against Azure AD, get a security token, and pass that token to access the Azure Blob or Queue service. Azure Table Storage does not support Azure Active Directory–based authorization.

- **Azure Active Directory Domain Services (Azure AD DS) authentication** This authorization option is applicable only for the Azure Files service using the Server Message Block (SMB) protocol. This option supports identity-based access to Azure file shares over SMB.

- **On-premises Active Directory Domain Services** Again, this authorization option is for Azure Files only. This is an identity-based authorization that either uses AD DS that has been set up on an Azure virtual machine or that goes through an on-premises server.

- **Anonymous public read access** When the **Allow Blob Public Access** setting on the Azure Storage **Configuration** blade is set to **Enabled**, then all Azure Blobs and containers can be accessed anonymously without any authorization. Anonymous public access should be avoided and allowed only when there is an absolute need.

Securing Azure Storage access

Using any of the authorization options discussed in the previous section, you can access Azure Storage endpoints publicly from the Internet. You can restrict this public access by configuring Azure Storage Firewall. By turning on a firewall rule, incoming requests to a storage account are blocked, and only selected VMs and public IP addresses can access the Azure Storage Account.

Accessing Azure Storage programmatically

Azure Storage offers different services like Blob, Files, Table, Queue, and Disk. Azure Disk is attached to the virtual machine and accessed using the SMB protocol. Similarly, Azure Files can be mounted on the Azure virtual machine and accessed using the SMB protocol. The Blob, Queue, and Table services can be access programmatically using client libraries that are available for various languages, such as .Net, PHP, Node.js, Java, Python, Ruby, and so on.

Accessing Azure Storage from Azure Virtual Network (VNet) using a service endpoint

The service endpoint method allows you to connect securely and directly to Azure Storage. In this method, routes to Azure Storage are optimized, and traffic is routed through the Microsoft Azure backbone to reach the Azure Storage service endpoint. Azure Storage can be accessed using a public endpoint, and traffic will go from the VNet to access Azure Storage. With a service endpoints configuration, Azure Storage service will be able to identify that the traffic is coming from Azure VNet and see the private IP address of the VNet. You can approve the private IP address of a VNet in Azure Storage Firewall to allow connections from a VNet. With service endpoints, you cannot connect storage from peered VNETs and on-premises networks.

Accessing Azure Storage from Azure Virtual Network (VNet) using the private link

The private endpoint is a method of securely and privately accessing Azure Storage from an Azure VNet using a private endpoint. With a private endpoint, traffic between clients inside the VNet and Azure Storage travels via the Microsoft Azure backbone instead traversing over the public Internet. The private endpoint uses a dedicated IP address assigned from the VNet IP address range. With a private endpoint, a client can use the same connection string and authorization method. No changes are required in either the connection string or authorization methods.

Table 3-8 shows comparison of service endpoint and private link for accessing Azure storage from Azure Virtual Network.

TABLE 3-8 Service endpoints versus private links

	Service Endpoint	Private Link
Service description	Extends a VNet to Azure Storage and allows Azure Storage to see whether the request is coming from client's (such as a VM) private IP address.	It enables you to access an Azure Storage service inside a VNet.
Connection method	Connects to an Azure Storage public IP using optimized routes.	Connects to a private IP address assigned to Azure Storage.
Connection from peered VNets and on-premises	Cannot connect from peered VNets and on-premises networks using service endpoints.	It enables connectivity from regionally and globally peered VNets and from on-premises using VPN or ExpressRoute.
Connectivity to Azure Blob, Files, Tables, Data Lake Storage Gen2, and Static Website.	No need to set up a separate service endpoint for each service. Once enabled on a subnet, you can access all Azure Storage services.	A separate private endpoint is required for each type of service.
Private IP address needed?	No	Yes. Per the Azure Storage Service (Blob, Files, Table, and so on) and per storage account.
Azure Storage Firewall configuration	Required because Azure Storage Firewall is controlling access through a public endpoint, and service endpoints connect to the public endpoint.	No specific Azure Storage Firewall configuration is required on an Azure Storage Account.
NSG	Because the destination is still a public IP, NSG needs to be opened.	No additional NSG rule is required because traffic is within the VNet only.
Exfiltration	Needs to be managed.	Built in.
Implementation	Simple.	Complex as compared to a service endpoint.
Cost	No cost.	Yes, at an additional cost.

Accessing Azure Storage through the Azure portal

The Azure portal provides flexibility to access Azure Storage services quickly. The Azure portal is also having Azure Storage explorer online UI to access Azure Storage services.

Accessing Azure Storage through Azure Storage Explorer

Azure Storage Explorer is a desktop application that you can install on Windows, macOS, and Linux. With this tool, you can access all Azure Storage services like Blob, Files, Queue, and Tables, as well as Azure Data Lake Storage and Cosmos DB.

Accessing Azure Storage through Microsoft Visual Studio Cloud Explorer

Accessing Azure Storage through Microsoft Visual Studio Cloud Explorer allows you to quickly view Azure resources by resource type or resource group. A developer can use this tool to see the properties of the Azure resources and to manage Azure resources. Only the Azure Resource Manager (ARM) model is supported.

Accessing Azure Storage using AzCopy.exe

AzCopy is a command-line utility that is used to copy Azure Storage Blob and Azure Storage Files to and from Azure Storage.

Storage management tools

In this skill, we discuss the various tools available for accessing and managing Azure Storage. We also cover the benefits of these tools and cover key management activities of Azure Storage and how we can perform the management activities using these tools.

All storage management activities can be done through the Azure portal. Following are a few scenarios in which you might need to access Azure Storage using these tools:

- Providing access to third-party organization to upload a file to Azure Storage using Azure Storage Explorer.
- Scripting file movement between an on-premises system to Azure Storage or copying data from AWS S3 buckets to Azure Storage using Azcopy.exe.
- A developer needs to quickly access storage from an integrated development environment (IDE) using Visual Studio Cloud Explorer.

Microsoft offers the following free tools for using and accessing Azure Storage.

- **Azure Storage Explorer** It is a standalone GUI based application, which helps us to easily access, visualize, manage, edit, and delete resources in Azure Storage. Along with Azure Storage services, you can also play with Azure Data Lake storage and Cosmos DB. This tool is available for Windows, macOS, and Linux. Using Azure Storage, you can easily manage multiple storage accounts from one or more Azure subscriptions. You can also attach a local storage emulator to work locally without any storage account.

- **AzCopy.exe** It is a command-line utility provided by Microsoft for copying data to/from Azure Storage and a file system. You can also use the AzCopy utility to copy data from Amazon S3 buckets to Azure Storage and for copying data to and from Azure Stack Hub. AzCopy is a simple executable file and does not require installation. It is available for Windows, Linux, and the macOS operating systems and supports Azure Active Directory and shared access signature–based authorization. Azure AD and SAS are supported for accessing Blob Storage. Currently, File Storage supports SAS only. The current version of AzCopy (version 10) does not support Azure Table Storage. If Azure Table Storage is required, then you need to use AzCopy version 7.3.

- **Microsoft Visual Studio Cloud Explorer** This tool is part of Visual Studio version 2017 and later. It gives a hierarchical view of Azure resources. You can see resources by resource group or resource type. Once you select a resource in Cloud Explorer, you can see its properties on the **Properties** tab, and you can take various actions on resources using the **Action** tab. You can also search for resources using the **Search** box. Visual Studio Cloud Explorer is not just limited to Azure Storage services; you can also manage other Azure services.

All the above tools support common management activities, such as creating, updating, reading, and deleting. Along with these activities, let's look at some critical management activities for Azure Storage and its services.

Azure Storage Account key rotation

Azure Storage Account keys (primary and secondary) are automatically generated when you create an Azure Storage Account. These keys serve as a root password to the Azure Storage Account. It is very crucial to keep these keys safe and only share them with intended users.

The best practice is to generate a shared access signature (SAS) instead of Azure account keys. With SAS, we can control what storage services to expose, what permissions (such as Read, Write, Delete, and the like) have been granted on SAS, and how long the SAS is valid.

Sometimes, a primary or secondary account key is used in the application instead of SAS, and sometimes these keys are shared with many people. These problems lead to leakage of these keys, which is followed by security issues.

To avoid such problems, it is recommended that you regenerate (rotate) these account keys periodically. You can regenerate keys manually or automatically using Key Vault. If possible, use Key Vault to regenerate keys because doing so removes manual dependency, and it also eliminates the possibility of missing the predefined key rotation schedule.

Azure Blob Storage Lifecycle Management

In the previous section, we looked at the **Hot**, **Cool**, **and Archive** storage access tiers. We also looked at how we benefit from using the appropriate access tier. Let's look at the nature of the data access pattern to optimize storage costs. These access patterns can be broadly categories as shown here:

- **Constant access pattern** In this pattern, data is accessed in the same pattern, and it does not change over the period. For example:
  - Data is accessed very rarely (such as data that is being maintained for compliance purposes).
  - Application data that is accessed regularly.
- **Variable access pattern** In this pattern, the data access pattern varies based on the lifecycle of the data, as shown here:
  - Data is accessed frequently in the early-stages, and it is accessed rarely in later stages.
  - Some data is accessed frequently for the first few days, but afterward, it is no longer needed and can be deleted.

With the variable access patten, it is advisable that you change the appropriate data access tier to match the lifecycle of the blob. If you do not modify the access tier, then you will be paying unnecessary Azure costs. Azure Blob Lifecycle Management helps you change the blob access tier to match the lifecycle of the blob and save costs, and it offers a simple rule-based policy to move the blob into an appropriate tier. You can create one of the following rules to change the blob access tier based on the schedule:

- Move the blob to Cool storage.
- Move the blob to Archive storage.
- Delete the blob.
- Delete the snapshot.

For example, you could move the blob to Cool storage after 30 days from the last modification.

Table 3-9 lists each Azure Storage access tool and its management capabilities.

TABLE 3-9 Azure Storage access tools

Azure Service	Azure portal	Azure Storage Explorer	Visual Studio Cloud Explorer	AzCopy
Blob	Yes	Yes	Yes	Yes
Table	Yes	Yes	Yes	Not in the current version (v10). Available in v7.3.
Queue	Yes	Yes	Yes	No
Files	Yes	Yes	Yes	Yes
Rotate Storage Account Key	Yes	No	No	No
Azure Blob Lifecycle Management	Yes	No	No	No

Azure Service	Azure portal	Azure Storage Explorer	Visual Studio Cloud Explorer	AzCopy
Generate a shared access signature	Yes	Yes	No	No
Storage network and firewall configuration	Yes	No	No	No

Chapter summary

- It is recommended that you use both the partition key and row key to query Azure Table Storage. Using the partition key and the row key, data retrieval is very fast; otherwise, a table scan operation is performed to search for the data in Azure Table Storage. Select the partition key and the row key wisely so that all data retrieval queries include both.

- A query executed against Azure Table Storage can return a maximum of 1,000 records. A query execution timeout is five seconds.

- The selection of database tier in a DTU-based purchasing model is mostly based on the CPU requirement, database size, IO throughput, latency, and backup retention period.

- Cosmos DB can be deployed into multiple regions, which helps to implement disaster recovery quickly, and it also helps to keep data closer to the user to improve network latency.

- All the databases deployed in elastic pools share DTUs.

- Horizontal scaling (scale-out) can be implemented by using the Elastic Database Tool.

- Azure SQL Managed Instance is suitable when you need to efficiently migrate databases from on-premises to Azure and leverage most of the SQL Server database engine, including the SQL Agent, cross-database queries, and offloading management work to Microsoft.

- Read scale-out is the best match for an analytics workload that only reads data.

- The Always Encrypt feature protects data at rest, in motion, and in use.

- SSL is the predecessor of TLS. Always try to use the latest version of TLS.

- By default, managed disks are encrypted using platform-managed keys. You can choose to manage your own keys.

- A modern data platform consists of data ingestion, data storage, data preparation, data modeling, and data serving.

- Azure Blob Storage Lifecycle Management can be used to save significant cost by applying a simple rule to move blobs to the Cool and Archive tiers and deleting blobs.

- Azure Table Storage does not support Azure Active Directory–based authorization.

- Azure Storage can be accessed programmatically using .Net, PHP, Node.js, Java, Python, Ruby, and so on. It can also be accessed using tools such as Azure Storage Explorer, AzCopy, and Visual Studio Cloud Explorer.

- It is recommended that you rotate Azure Storage keys either manually or automatically using Key Vault.

- Always try to use SAS tokens to delegate access to Azure Storage instead of sharing the account key.

Thought experiment

Now it is time to validate your skills and knowledge of the concepts you learned in this chapter. Answers are found in the "Thought experiment answers" section at the end of this chapter.

As an Azure Solutions Architect working for Contoso, you are responsible for architecting and designing applications and making the correct technical decisions to meet Contoso's business goals. Contoso has decided to adopt a cloud environment and migrate all its applications from an on-premises environment to the Microsoft Azure Cloud platform. Some of the business stakeholders are against this migration, though you support this cloud adoption initiative. Contoso has permitted the migration of only one LOB application. As an Azure Solutions Architect, you need to successfully migrate this application and prove yourself by accomplishing all the business requirements, as well as showing all the benefits of the cloud adoption.

The details of the current application are as follows:

- Develop a web application using the Microsoft .Net technology stack and deploy it to the IIS server.

- Deploy the database to SQL Server 2012 Standard Edition. The current size of the database is 5 TB.

- Use SQL Server Integration Services (SSIS) packages to connect to the business partners' SFTP server and retrieve business data.

- Archive and maintain old unstructured data in the local storage system. This data needs to be stored for three years to meet the company's compliance needs. The total size of the old data is 70 TB.

- Store the application users' uploaded images and videos in a local file system. These videos and images are used very frequently in the first six months and are very rarely used after six months.

After consulting with business users and other stakeholders, you have identified the following business requirements:

- Data stored in an SQL Server database, as well as all videos and images uploaded by the user should be encrypted at rest and in motion.

- Customer Social Security Numbers (SSN) that are stored in the database should be encrypted. Even database administrators and cloud security operation people should not be able to read it. The keys required to encrypt this data should not be stored in the cloud.

- A database should provide 99.99 percent availability.

- Archived data needs to be stored in Azure. The data migration solution should not depend on the network bandwidth because Contoso has low network bandwidth. The cost of storage should be lower. An easy solution is to require the purging of data older than three years.

- Your solution should be cost-effective.

- Your solution should leverage the Platform as a Service (PaaS) services as far as possible so that Contoso will offload management work.

- Migration should be smooth with fewer code changes.

With this information in mind, answer the following questions:

1. What database tier will you use for the SQL server database?

2. How will you address encryption requirements?

3. What solution would you implement for collecting data from the partners' SFTP server?

4. What solution would you implement to transfer archived data to Azure Cloud storage?

5. What would you recommend for purging old data without any manual intervention?

Thought experiment answers

This section contains the solution to the thought experiment. Each answer explains why the answer choice is correct.

1. Because the size of the current database is 5 TB, the most suitable option is to deploy this database into the Serverless tier of the vCore purchasing model. You can also use SQL Server on a virtual machine. However, Contoso would like to leverage PaaS services, so SQL server on a VM is not recommended. This option also provides auto-scaling with the Auto-pause feature to save compute cost. The serverless tier offers 99.99 percent of availability, which meets another business requirement.

2. The data stored in the Serverless database tier will be encrypted at rest by enabling transparent data encryption (TDE). It also always enforces (a TLS/SSL connection), irrespective of the Encrypt or TrustServerCertificate setting in the connection string.

   The Always Encrypted feature can be used to encrypt data in use. Azure Storage service, by default, encrypts data stored in Azure Storage with Microsoft-managed keys. You can encrypt data using your own keys also. Data encryption in transmission can be enforced by enabling the **Secure Transfer Required** setting in the Azure Storage Account configuration. Thus, you can fulfill all the business requirements of the encryptions.

3. Azure Data Factory can be used to collect data from the business partners. The existing SSIS package can be executed into SSIS runtime in the Azure Data Factory.

4. Because Contoso has low network bandwidth, it is advisable to use the Azure Data Box solution to ship data offline to the Microsoft Azure datacenter. The size of the archived data is 70 TB, which can easily fit into Azure Data Box. The Azure Import/Export service will require the creation of multiple jobs and investment to procure the required Azure Data Box disks.

5. Azure Blob Storage Lifecycle Management is the recommended solution for purging old data. A simple rule can be created to delete data after three years. Similarly, videos and images uploaded by customers should be kept in a Hot Access tier for the first six months. An Azure Blob Storage Lifecycle Management policy rule can be created to move it to the Cool Access tier and to automatically delete it after three years.

EXAM TIP

On the exam, always be aware that questions will often provide more information than is needed to answer use-case-style questions.

CHAPTER 4

Design business continuity

Cloud Solutions Architects understand the importance and need to design a business continuity solution. Most enterprises have a well-established business continuity and disaster recovery plan, also known as BCP/DR plan. Typically, the best starting while defining and choosing a business continuity solution is to perform a business criticality assessment. A criticality assessment will help you determine the criticality of systems and their impacts on the business if an outage occurs. This assessment should further guide you in developing the right business continuity strategy for the company. Once you perform the criticality assessment and identify critical applications, the next step is to figure out your backup and disaster recovery strategy.

The AZ-304 certification exam expects you to demonstrate a solid understanding of designing business continuity and disaster recovery using Azure Site Recovery, redundancy, and backup options that the Microsoft Azure platform provides. The Azure Solution Architect certification is an expert-level exam, so you are expected to have advanced-level knowledge of each of the domain objectives in this chapter.

Skills covered in this chapter:

- Skill 4.1: Design a solution for backup and recovery
- Skill 4.2: Design for high availability

Skill 4.1: Design a solution for backup and recovery

The success of any endeavor starts with preparing for failure. Successful architects typically follow the same approach while designing backup and recovery solutions. This approach is also known as design for failure. When design a solution for backup and recovery, you should first identify failure situations and their potential impacts on your organization. Then you should perform analysis along with a criticality assessment and a business continuity strategy. Also, you should document your data protection requirements. Finally, you should develop backup and recovery designs and plans to address the data protection requirements identified by your analysis.

Recommend a recovery solution for Azure hybrid and on-premises workloads that meet recovery objectives (RTO, RLO, RPO)

Large-scale outages or disasters can disrupt your business, staff, and users. When your systems are unavailable, your company could directly or indirectly lose value. Also, your company could face financial losses such as lost revenue or penalties for not meeting availability agreements for the services you provide.

Business continuity and disaster recovery (BCDR) plans are formal documents that organizations develop that cover the scope and actions to be taken when a disaster or large-scale outage happens. Each disruption is assessed on its merit.

For example, let's consider an example scenario in which an earthquake has damaged your datacenter's power and communication lines. This situation has made your corporate datacenter useless until power is restored and lines of communication are fixed. A fiasco of this size could take your organization's services down for weeks or days, not hours, so you need a full BCDR plan to get the services back online.

As part of your BCDR plan, you need to identify the recovery time objectives (RTOs) and recovery point objectives (RPOs) for your applications. Both objectives help you identify the maximum tolerable hours that your business can be without specified services, as well as what the data recovery process should be.

Before diving into the solutions, let's take a closer look at three widely used terms to define recovery objectives—RPO, RTO, and RLO.

- **Recovery point objective (RPO)**   The recovery point objective (RPO) is used to determine the maximum amount of time between the last available backup and a potential failure point. Also, the RPO helps determine the amount of data, in terms of time, that a business can afford to lose in a failure. For example, if your backup occurred every 24 hours at 4 AM and a disaster happened at 1 PM the following day, then 9 hours of data would be lost. If your company's RPO is 12 hours, then no data would be lost because only 9 hours has passed, and you have a better recovery point backup available from which you can recover. However, if the RPO is 4 hours, then your backup strategy is not meeting your RPO requirement, and damage would occur to the business.

- **Recovery time objective (RTO)**   The recovery time objective (RTO) is used to determine the maximum time a data recovery process can take. It is defined by the amount of time the business can afford for the site or service to be unavailable. For example, let's say one of your application has an RTO of 12 hours. This means your business can manage for 12 hours if this application is unavailable. However, if the downtime is longer than 12 hours, your business would be seriously harmed.

- **Recovery-level objective (RLO)**   Recovery level objective (RLO) is the objective that defines the granularity with which you must be able to recover data—regardless of whether you must be able to recover the whole application stack.

Figure 4-1 explains the recovery point and recovery time concepts. The recovery time is the amount of time needed to recover the data, while the recovery point is the last point a successful backup was made.

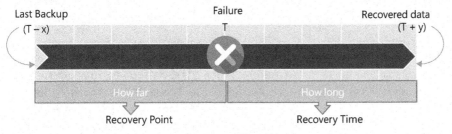

FIGURE 4-1 Recovery Point objective and Recovery Time objective

To meet your business continuity and disaster recovery strategy, it is recommended that you use Azure Site Recovery. Using Azure Site Recovery, you can perform application-aware replication to Azure or to a secondary site. You can use Azure Site Recovery to manage replication, perform a DR drill, and run failover and failback. Azure Site Recovery supports apps running on Windows- or Linux-based physical servers, VMware, or Hyper-V.

Azure Site Recovery (ASR) is recommended for application-level protection and recovery:

- ASR can be used to replicate workloads running on a supported machine.
- ASR offers near-real-time replication with recovery point objectives (RPO) as low as 30 seconds. Typically, this meets the needs of most critical business apps.

- ASR can take app-consistent snapshots for single- or multi-tier applications.

- ASR also offers an integration with SQL Server AlwaysOn and other application-level replication technologies such as Active Directory replication and Exchange Database Availability Groups (DAGs).

- ASR recovery plans are very flexible and enable you to recover the entire application stack with a single click and include external scripts and manual actions in the plan.

- ASR also offers advanced network management capabilities to simplify app network requirements, such as the ability to reserve IP addresses, configure load-balancing, and integrate with Azure Traffic Manager for low-recovery-time objective (RTO) network switchovers.

- Lastly, a rich automation library is available, which provides production-ready, application-specific scripts that can be downloaded and integrated with recovery plans.

Design an Azure Site Recovery solution

Let's learn how to design a business continuity and disaster recovery (BCDR) plan to keep your workloads running and your data safe. You can use tools like Azure Site Recovery and Azure Backup to design a site recovery solution.

Azure Site Recovery (ASR) is a managed service that provides BCDR features for your applications. Azure Site Recovery can protect workloads running in Azure, on-premises, and in other cloud providers. Azure Site Recovery helps to automate disaster recovery by allowing you to define how machines are failed over, as well as the order in which they should be turned on after being successfully failed over. In this way, Azure Site Recovery also helps automate manual tasks, thereby helping reduce recovery time objectives. We advise you to use Azure Site Recovery to periodically test failover to ensure that the recovery process will work when it is needed.

Azure Site Recovery (ASR) offers the best-in-class RTO and RPO and is one of the prime disaster recovery solutions on the Azure platform. ASR is a first-class solution that gives Azure the edge over other solutions. With just a few clicks, you can enable, test, and perform disaster recovery for customers. The availability of integrations with other resources to achieve parity between the source and target is one of the critical differentiators when choosing a disaster recovery solution. This also reduces recovery time because it eliminates the number of manual steps required once the virtual machine is brought online in the target.

Following are some notable features of Azure Site Recovery:

- **Central management** Replication can be set up and managed from Azure portal. Also, failover and failback can be invoked from within the Azure portal.

- **On-premises virtual machine replication** On-premises virtual machines can be replicated to Azure or a secondary on-premises datacenter if necessary.

- **Azure virtual machine replication** Azure virtual machines can be replicated from one region to another.

- **App consistency during failover**   By using recovery points and application-consistent snapshots, the virtual machine and the application state are consistent after the failover.

- **Flexible failover**   Failover can be run on-demand as a test, or they can be triggered during an actual disaster. Tests can be run to simulate a disaster recovery scenario without interrupting your live service. When the primary site becomes available again, ASR's failback capabilities can be used to move the service back from the secondary site to the primary site.

- **Network integration**   Site Recovery can manage network management during a replication and disaster recovery scenario. Reserved IP addresses and load balancers are configured so that the virtual machines can work in the new location.

> *NEED MORE REVIEW?*   **AZURE SITE RECOVERY DOCUMENTATION**
>
> You can find comprehensive guidance about learning what's new in Azure Site Recovery service, as well as quick-start instructions and a how-to guide in the Azure Site Recovery documentation at *https://docs.microsoft.com/en-us/azure/site-recovery*.

Recommend a site recovery replication policy

A site recovery replication policy defines three essential aspects for your recovery solution:

- RPO threshold (in minutes): ASR will generate alerts if the RPO for a replication, associated with a specific policy, exceeds this threshold.
- The settings for the recovery points retention history
- The frequency of app-consistent snapshots

By default, Azure Site Recovery creates a new replication policy with these default settings:

- 24 hours for the recovery points retention history
- 60 minutes for the frequency of app-consistent snapshots

Recommend a solution for site recovery capacity

The Azure Site Recovery Deployment Planner tool is one of the essential tools for your site recovery solution. This tool helps you analyze source workloads, estimate bandwidth needs, identify resources you will need at the source location, and identify VMs and storage you will need at the target location. The ASR deployment planner tool provides the following details:

- **Compatibility assessment**
  - VM eligibility assessment, based on the number of disks, disk size, IOPS, churn, and a few VM characteristics.
  - Network bandwidth need versus RPO assessment
  - The estimated network bandwidth required for delta replication

- The throughput that Azure Site Recovery can get from on-premises to Azure
- RPO that can be achieved for a given bandwidth
- Impact on the desired RPO if lower bandwidth is provisioned.

- **Azure infrastructure requirements**
  - The storage type (standard or premium storage account) requirement for each VM
  - The total number of standard and premium storage accounts to be set up for replication
  - Storage-account naming suggestions based on Azure Storage guidance
  - The storage-account placement for all VMs
  - The number of Azure cores to be set up before test failover or failover on the subscription
  - The Azure VM-recommended size for each on-premises VM

- **On-premises infrastructure requirements**
  - The required free storage space on each volume of Hyper-V storage for successful initial replication and delta replication to ensure that VM replication will not cause any undesirable downtime for your production applications
  - Maximum copy frequency to be set for Hyper-V replication

- **Initial replication batching guidance**
  - Number of VM batches to be used for protection
  - List of VMs in each batch
  - Order in which each batch is to be protected
  - Estimated time to complete initial replication of each batch

- **Estimated DR cost to Azure**
  - Estimated total DR cost to Azure: compute, storage, network, and Azure Site Recovery license cost
  - Detailed cost analysis per VM

The Azure Site Recovery deployment planner is a command-line tool for both Hyper-V to Azure and VMware to Azure disaster recovery scenarios. You can run the Site Recovery deployment planner command-line tool (ASRDeploymentPlanner.exe) in any of these four modes:

- Get the virtual machine (VM) list
- Profile
- Generate a report
- Get throughput

First, run the tool to get the list of VMs from a single or multiple Hyper-V hosts. Then run the tool in profiling mode to gather VM data churn and IOPS. Next, run the tool to generate the report to find the network bandwidth and storage requirements.

Recommend a solution for site failover and failback (planned/unplanned)

A failover is when the disaster recovery plan for the business is invoked. Failover happens when the current live environment, which is protected by using Azure Site Recovery, is moved over to the replica environment. This target replica environment takes the place of the live environment and becomes the primary infrastructure.

A failback is the reverse of a failover. The previous live environment (which is now the replica environment because a failover has taken place) takes back its original role and becomes the live environment again. After the failover has happened in the first instance, a reprotection phase needs to occur. In this phase, you bring the original environment back in sync with the new live environment. This process allows the failover and failback to happen without any data loss. The reprotection phase is likely to be a lengthy process because you need to determine whether the old live environment works correctly after the disaster.

Azure Site Recovery gives you the flexibility to failover to Azure if a disaster occurs and fails back to on-premises machines after the event is over. Following are the four stages of failover and failback actions:

- **Failover to Azure**   If the on-premises primary site goes down, the decision to failover to Azure (or your secondary site) is made, which creates virtual machines from the primary replicated data.
- **Re-protect Azure virtual machines**   After the failover occurs, the Azure virtual machines must be re-protected so that they can replicate changes back to the on-premises environment after the disaster is averted. To ensure data consistency, virtual machines are powered off.
- **Failback to on-premises**   When the on-premises site is back up and running, it's possible to failover back to that environment. It then becomes the live environment again. You can't failback to physical servers. All systems must failback to virtual machines.
- **Re-protect on-premises virtual machines**   Reprotection of the on-premises virtual machines takes place so that they start replicating to Azure after the failback has happened successfully.

Recommend a solution for the site recovery network

In this section, we will learn about networking considerations as they relate to Azure Site Recovery.

Figure 4-2 depicts the typical scenario of an on-premises and replicated Azure environment. In this scenario, you replicate on-premises, physical/VMware or Hyper-V virtual machines to Azure VMs.

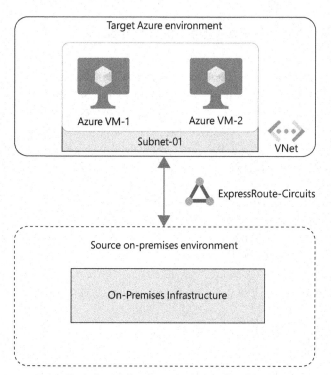

FIGURE 4-2 Typical scenario of on-premises and replicated Azure environment

ExpressRoute service enables you to connect on-premises networks with the Microsoft Azure cloud over a private connection, typically through a telecommunication or networking service provider. Once you have ExpressRoute configured, Azure Site Recovery leverages ExpressRoute as follows:

- **During replication between Azure regions** ExpressRoute is not required for replication between Azure regions because traffic for Azure VM disaster recovery, in this case, stays within Azure. However, if users are coming in from an on-premises site to the Azure VMs in the primary Azure site, there are several issues to be aware of when you're setting up disaster recovery for Azure VMs.

- **Failover between Azure regions** If you have configured failover from one region to another, then if outages occur, you will be able to initiate a failover for Azure Virtual machines from the primary region to the secondary Azure region. Once you have failed over to a secondary region, you have to consider several measures (covered next) to access the Azure virtual machines in the secondary region from on-premises using ExpressRoute. Following are some best practices to consider when you set up Azure Site Recovery to integrate with ExpressRoute:

We recommend that you provision networking components before you failover to a secondary region, with the following caveats:

- When you enable replication for Azure VMs, Azure Site Recovery can deploy networking resources such as virtual networks, subnets, and gateways in the target Azure region, based on source network settings.

- Azure Site Recovery, however, cannot automatically set up networking resources such as virtual network gateways. That is why we recommend that you manually pre-create these additional networking resources before failover.

- Outbound connectivity from target virtual machines deployed in the Azure virtual network requires you to consider the following aspects:

  - **Service Tags**   The service tags are the group of IP address prefixes from a given Azure service. Using services tags in your network security groups (NSGs), you can have a controlled outbound connection with network isolation to Azure services (typically PaaS services) with a public endpoint such as an Azure SQL Database, Service Bus, Azure Storage, and the like.

  - **Virtual Network service endpoints**   Virtual Network (VNet) service endpoint provides secure and direct connectivity to Azure services (typically PaaS services) with a public endpoint such as an Azure SQL Database, Service Bus, Azure Storage, and so on. When you use a VNet service endpoint, the outbound traffic toward Azure services remains in the Microsoft backbone network. Plan to execute regular disaster recovery drills:

- It is a best practice that you plan for a regular disaster recovery (DR) drill because it helps you validate your replication strategy and avoid data loss or downtime. The best part is that doing a DR drill should not affect your production environment during the drill, but it helps you avoid last-minute configuration issues that can adversely impact RTO.

- The IP address for each NIC on a target virtual machine is configured as follows:

  - **DHCP**   If the NIC of the source VM is using DHCP, the NIC of the target VM would also use DHCP.

  - **Static IP address**   If the NIC of the source VM has a static IP address, the target VM NIC would also use a static IP address.

- Use a different IP address space for the virtual target network if you have a single ExpressRoute circuit. This avoids issues when establishing connections during regional outages.

- If you can't use separate address space, be sure to run the disaster recovery drill and test the failover on an isolated separate test network with different IP addresses. You can't connect two VNets with overlapping IP address spaces to the same ExpressRoute circuit.

Recommend a solution for recovery in different regions

The Site Recovery solution addresses the need to replicate Azure VM data from one region to another or from on-premises to Azure. Keep the following points in mind if you are using an Azure-to-Azure recovery scenario from one region to another:

- If Azure VMs use Azure managed disks, VM data is replicated to a replicated managed disk in the secondary region.

- If Azure VMs don't use managed disks, VM data is replicated to an Azure Storage Account.

- Replication endpoints are public, but replication traffic for Azure VMs doesn't cross the Internet.

Azure Site Recovery (ASR) can replicate workloads from a primary site to a secondary site. If an issue occurs at the primary site, ASR can be used to initiate failover of the protected virtual machines to another location. The purpose of the Azure Site Recovery service is to failover to another region and get your workloads running again as quickly as possible in the event of a disaster or failure. Azure Site Recovery not only supports protection for Azure servers but also supports your on-premises servers.

ASR supports three failover scenarios: Azure to Azure, on-premises to Azure, and on-premises to a secondary site. These scenarios can be further subclassified depending on what you are replicating, such as virtual servers, VMware, Hyper-V, or physical servers. If you want to protect physical or VMware servers, you will need a configuration server that will help you manage replication. A process server sends the replication data from the source server to Azure and to a master target server that manages replication data during failback. To enable site recovery replication, we will have to install the mobility service on every server that is being replicated. If you are replicating to another Azure region, then you need the same components. You will still keep the process server in the primary site, though the configuration and master target servers are kept in the secondary site.

The architecture for Hyper-V replication is straightforward. You will have to install the Azure Site Recovery Provider and the Recovery Services agent on every Hyper-V host or cluster node. For System Center Virtual Machine Manager (SCVMM), we have to install the Site Recovery Provider in SCVMM.

Figure 4-3 shows a screenshot of the Add Server pop-up window that shows the links to download Azure Site Recovery Provider and the vault registration key to register the host in a Hyper-V site.

FIGURE 4-3 Hyper-V site configuration in ASR

Please refer to Microsoft's documentation, where there's a list of supported operating systems available in each of these scenarios. For physical servers, the prerequisite is that the replicated machines must be running a minimum of Windows Server 2008 R2 SP1. If you have VMware servers, the minimum requirement is vSphere 5.5 or vCenter 5.5. For Hyper-V, the minimum requirement is Windows Server 2012 R2. For Hyper-V, guest VMs running Windows Server 2008 R2 or higher are supported.

> **NEED MORE REVIEW? AZURE SITE RECOVERY**
>
> To learn more about supported components and settings for disaster recovery of VMware VMs and physical servers to Azure using Azure Site Recovery, see the Microsoft documentation at *https://docs.microsoft.com/en-us/azure/site-recovery/vmware-physical-azure-support-matrix*.

When you use ASR for protection, there are six different options to choose from in the event of an outage.

- **Latest**   Using this option, you get the lowest Recovery Point Objective because the VM created after failover has all the data replicated to Site Recovery when failover was triggered.
- **Latest Processed**   Using this option to failover, you can replicate VMs to the latest recovery point already processed by Site Recovery. When you need a low RTO, this is a good choice because no time is spent processing unprocessed data.
- **Latest App-Consistent**   You can use this option to failover VMs over to the latest application-consistent recovery point that has been processed by Site Recovery.
- **Latest Multi-VM Processed**   When you use this option, VMs that are part of a replication group failover to the latest common multi-VM consistent recovery point. All other VMs (not part of replication group) failover to their latest processed recovery point. Please note that this option is only for recovery plans with at least one VM with multi-VM consistency enabled.
- **Latest Multi-VM App-Consistent**   When you use this option, VMs that are part of a replication group failover to the latest common multi-VM application-consistent recovery point. All other VMs (not part of the replication group) failover to their latest application-consistent recovery point. Please note that this option is only for recovery plans with at least one VM with multi-VM consistency enabled.
- **Custom**   This option is only for failover of individual VMs.

Using these options, you can tell ASR which recovery point you would like to failover. The default option is **Latest**. This option is usually preferred. After all, it will give you the best recovery point objective because it's the most recent recovery point available. One of the disadvantages of this option is that it will delay the failover because ASR needs to process all the latest data received and turn it into a recovery point.

An alternative is to choose **Latest Processed**, which ignores all the unprocessed data, so the failover happens very quickly. This option gives you a better recovery time objective, though the recovery point objective will be higher than if you had chosen **Latest**. The **Latest Processed** option does not use the latest recovery point. Choose this option based on your RTO/RPO requirements.

The **Latest Application-Consistent**, **Latest Multi-VM Processed**, and **Latest Multi-VM Application-Consistent** options are variations of the **Latest Processed** option. All three ignore unprocessed data.

Recommend a solution for Azure Backup management

You can use the Azure Backup service to back up data to the Microsoft Azure Cloud platform. Azure backup comprehensively protects your assets in Azure through a simple, secure, and cost-effective solution that requires zero infrastructure. Azure Backup is Microsoft's built-in data protection solution for a wide range of workloads. It helps protect your mission critical workloads, and ensures your backups are always available and managed at scale across your entire backup estate.

Azure Backup backs up the data, machine state, and workloads running on both on-premises VMs and Azure virtual machine (VM) instances. Let's look at these two scenarios:

- **Back up on-premises machines** You can back up on-premises Windows machines directly to Azure by using the Azure Backup Microsoft Azure Recovery Services (MARS) agent. Linux machines are not supported yet. You can back up on-premises machines to a backup server—either System Center Data Protection Manager (DPM) or Microsoft Azure Backup Server (MABS). You can then back up the backup server to a Recovery Services vault in Azure.

- **Back up Azure VMs** You can back up Azure VMs directly. Azure Backup installs a backup extension to the Azure VM agent that is running on the VM. This extension backs up the entire VM.
  - You can back up specific files and folders on the Azure VM by running the MARS agent.
  - You can back up Azure VMs to the MABS that is running in Azure, and you can then back up the MABS to a Recovery Services vault.

Azure Backup provides different backup agents, depending on what type of machine is being backed up:

- **Azure Backup Microsoft Azure Recovery Services (MARS) agent** MARS runs on individual on-premises Windows Server machines to back up files, folders, and the system state. Also, MARS runs on Azure VMs to back up files, folders, and the system state. Lastly, MARS runs on DPM/MABS servers to back up the DPM/MABS local storage disk to Azure.

- **Azure VM extension** The Azure VM extension runs on Azure VMs to back them up to a vault.

> **IMPORTANT AZURE BACKUP AGENT**
>
> The Azure Backup Agent does not just back up Azure VMs. It also backs up on-premises VMs and servers.

Azure Backup stores backed-up data in vaults—recovery services vaults and backup vaults. A vault is an online-storage entity in Azure that is used to hold data, such as backup copies, recovery points, and backup policies.

EXAM TIP

Azure Site Recovery and Azure Backup are two different services designed to address two separate scenarios. Azure Site Recovery service is designed to ensure business continuity by keeping business apps and workloads running during outages. Azure Backup service is designed to prevent data loss and helps to restore data from any point in time based upon your backup strategy.

Azure Backup service can seamlessly scale its protection across multiple workloads without any management overhead for you. Figure 4-4 shows the Azure Backup Service Architecture, which shows various components that come into play, such as workloads, the data plane, and the management plane.

Following are more details about some of the components shown in Figure 4-4:

- **Workloads** Azure Backup provides native integration with Azure Workloads (VMs, SAP HANA, SQL in Azure VMs, and even Azure Files) without requiring you to manage automation or infrastructure to deploy agents, write new scripts or provision storage.

- **Scalable, durable, and secure storage** Azure Backup uses reliable Blob storage with in-built security and high availability features. You can choose LRS, GRS, or RA-GRS storages for your backup data.

- **Data plane** Azure Backup automates provisioning and managing storage accounts for the backup data to ensure it scales as the backup data grows. Moreover, Azure Backup automatically cleans up older backup data to comply with the retention policies. You can also tier your data from operational storage to vault storage.

- **Management plane** Recovery Services and Backup vaults provide the management capabilities and are accessible via the Azure portal, Backup Center, Vault dashboards, SDK, CLI, and even REST APIs. These vaults are also an Azure RBAC boundary, which provide you with the option to restrict access to backups only to authorized Backup Admins. Azure Backup integrates with Log Analytics and allows you to see reports via workbooks for monitoring and reporting. Azure Backup takes snapshots for some Azure native workloads (VMs and Azure Files), manages these snapshots, and allows fast restores from them. This option drastically reduces the time to recover your data to the original storage.

Design a solution for data archiving and retention

Generally, data archiving is confused with data backups, so this section explores the differences between these two concepts.

Data backups are useful to restore data if it is lost, corrupted, or destroyed. In contrast, data archives protect older information that is not needed for everyday business operations but might occasionally need to be accessed. Backups are used for operational recoveries and to quickly recover an overwritten file or a corrupted database. The focus is usually on speed— both on the backup and the recovery and the data integrity. On the other hand, archives typically store a version of files that are unlikely to change.

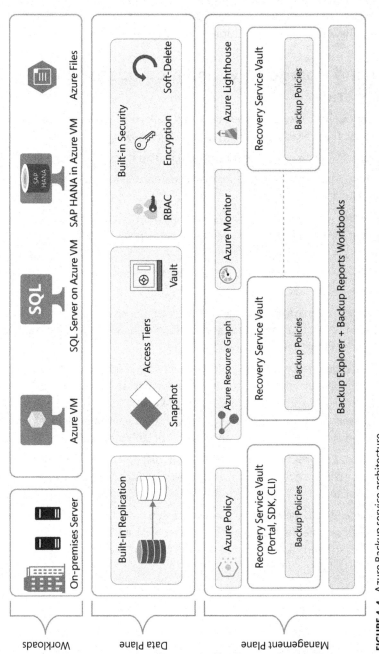

FIGURE 4-4 Azure Backup service architecture

An efficient data archiving strategy is a necessary part of every enterprise. Archiving is the practice of moving data that is no longer used to a separate storage device. Besides, data archives consist of older data that might still be important and necessary for future reference, or it could be data that must be retained for regulatory compliance. Sometimes, data archives are indexed and have search capabilities to locate and retrieve files and parts of files quickly.

Recommend storage types and methodology for data archiving

Azure offers various Azure Storage access tiers, which allows you to store blob object data in a cost-efficient way. The available access tiers include the following:

- **Hot tier**   This tier is optimized for storing data that is accessed frequently.
- **Cool tier**   This tier is optimized for storing data that is infrequently accessed and that is stored for at least 30 days.
- **Archive tier**   This tier is optimized for storing data that is rarely accessed and stored for at least 180 days with flexible latency requirements.

The Hot tier is optimized for storing frequently accessed data and is designed to read and modify data actively. When compared with the other tiers, Hot tier incurs a higher storage cost, but it has the lowest access cost.

The cool access tier has a lower storage cost when compared with the Hot tier, but it has a higher access cost. The cool access tier is designed for data that will remain in storage for at least 30 days, such as short-term backups.

The Archive tier has the lowest storage cost, but it has the highest access cost. The Archive tier is intended for data that needs to stay in the tier for at least 180 days. Note that when you retrieve data, you might experience several hours of latency. Data in this tier is offline and cannot be copied, overwritten, or modified. Snapshots cannot be taken of blobs in this tier. Blob metadata remains available, allowing for the retrieval of blob properties, metadata, and lists.

When you want to access the data from the Archive tier, the blob must be rehydrated. This activity is done by changing the tier for the blob to either Cool or Hot. Rehydration might take 15 hours to complete.

It is a recommended to move less frequently accessed blobs to lower-cost storage tiers. You can change the storage tier for blobs from the Azure portal at the blob level by accessing the properties of the blob and choosing the desired tier from the drop-down menu. Below are the considerations for different storage access tiers:

- Hot, Cool, and Archive tiers can be set at the blob level during or after upload.
- The Archive access tier is not available at the account level.
- Hot and Cool access tiers can be set at the account level.
- Data in the Cool access tier can tolerate slightly lower availability, but it still requires high durability, retrieval latency, and throughput characteristics like Hot data. Cool data

has a slightly lower availability service-level agreement (SLA) and higher access costs, which are acceptable trade-offs for lower storage costs (when compared to the Hot tier).

- Archive storage stores data offline and offers the lowest storage costs, but it has the highest data re-hydration and access costs.

Identify business compliance requirements for data archiving

Typically, businesses require various forms of compliance, which means they need to comply with data archiving requirements or rules. Following are some examples when such practices might be necessary:

- Regulatory, where there is a need to adhere to specific laws such as retaining financial data
- Retain data for compliance audit required
- Legal hold process, where there is a need to hold data for e-discovery or other investigative reasons
- Other regulations apply to specific industries and business operations. These include federal, state, and municipal rules, and the like.

When you have a legal hold, you can use a legal hold policy option to place existing blobs in the container in a non-writable, non-deletable state until the legal hold is cleared. But this option would let you create blobs and read from the container. In such cases, legal holds are associated with a user-defined tag that you can use as an identifier.

For various compliance reasons, healthcare providers retain HIPAA-related documents for several years. Typically, there are high data storage requirements for patient data archives of high-resolution images and ultrasound content. Archive tier storage allows healthcare providers to save on their storage costs and provides them with secure, globally compliant storage for their sensitive data.

If you want a time-bound control, then time-based retention policies can be used to place the blobs in any container in a non-writable, non-deletable state for a specified period. Time-based retention policies should be locked in the blob to be in an immutable state.

Identify SLA(s) for data archiving

As we learned earlier in this chapter, Azure Storage offers different access tiers, allowing you to store blob object data most cost-effectively. There are three access tiers:

- **Hot**   Hot tier data is optimized for storing data that is accessed frequently.
- **Cool**   Cool tier data is optimized for storing data that is infrequently accessed and stored for at least 30 days.
- **Archive**   Archive tier data is optimized for storing data that is rarely accessed and that is stored for at least 180 days with flexible latency requirements on the order of hours.

Even though Archive tier storage is the cheapest in terms of data storage, its data retrieval costs are higher when compared with the Hot and Cool tiers. Data in the archive tier remain offline until you change the data tier using a hydration process. Rehydrating Archive tier data to either the Hot or Cool tiers can take hours depending on the data priority. Consequently, we recommend using the archive tier to store only the data for which you can afford such delay when you need to access archived data.

Note that Azure also does not provide availability SLAs for the Archive tier. However, resiliency of storage is assured by enabling replication at the storage level. Like other tiers, the Archive tier also supports locally redundant storage (LRS), geo-redundant storage (GRS), and RA-GRS storage types.

Recommend a data retention policy

Data retention refers to the length of time that data should be preserved by the organization that gathered it. Data archiving refers to the intentional long-term preservation of data to which you need access. Data disposal is the process of deleting data safely and responsibly. Data must remain in the Archive tier for at least 180 days or you will be subjected to an early deletion charge.

You can use the Lifecycle Management feature of Azure storage for implementing a retention and archive policy. This feature allows you to create rule-based policies to transition data to appropriate storage tiers and to expire data at the end of its lifecycle. You can manage Lifecycle Management policies using PowerShell, the Azure command-line interface, REST APIs, or programming client tools in .NET, Python, Node.js, and Ruby.

A policy consists of a version and a collection of rules. Each rule consists of a filter set and an action set. The filter set limits the rule actions to a filtered set of objects in a container or a specific object name. The action set defines the storage tier or the delete action for the objects to find in the filter set. Lifecycle Management can automate placing objects in the appropriate storage tier, such as for data that has not been accessed in the last 30 days to be moved to the cool tier. Data that has not been accessed for 180 days is moved to the Archive tier.

Immutable storage policies for Azure Blobs is an Azure storage setting that provides for two types of retention policies: time-based retention and legal holds. These two policies can be used for regulatory compliance and secure document retention, and they ensure that critical documents in litigation or criminal investigations are retained in a tamper-proof state.

- **Legal Hold** A legal hold policy places existing blobs in the container in a non-writable, non-deletable state until the legal hold is cleared. However, blobs can be created and read. Legal holds are associated with a user-defined tag that is used as an identifier string.

- **Time-Based** Time-based retention policies place the blobs in a container in a non-writable, non-deletable state for a specified interval. Time-based retention policies must be locked in the blob to be in an immutable state. To be SCC compliant, policies should be locked within 24 hours.

Immutable storage is usually configured. Simply navigate to the storage container and from the **Settings** blade choose **Access Policy**. Select **Add Policy** from the **Immutable Blob Storage** section and select the type of policy: **Time-Based** or **Legal Hold**.

Skill 4.2: Design for high availability

Resiliency, fault tolerance, and high availability are essential attributes of mission-critical systems. A system can recover from failures and continue to function. You should design systems for failure. Every system has its particular failure modes, which you must consider when designing and implementing your application.

High availability (HA) is the capability of any computing system to provide desired and consistent uptime even in the event of its underlying infrastructure failure. This requirement is vital for mission-critical systems that will not tolerate an interruption in service. It is also critical for any system for which any downtime would cause damage or financial loss. Highly available systems guarantee a percentage of uptime. For instance, a system that has 99.9 percent uptime can be down only 0.1 percent of the time, so in a year, to meet 99.9 percent SLA, you can only have 8.77 hours of downtime. The number of nines in the percentage is usually used to specify the degree of high availability that is offered. For instance, "five nines" indicates a system that is up 99.999 percent of the time.

Designing your apps for high availability and resiliency usually means running your applications in a healthy state without significant downtime. This design begins with gathering requirements. For example, how much downtime is acceptable? What will this potential downtime cost your business? What are your customer's availability requirements? How much can you invest in making your application highly available? How much risk versus the cost can you tolerate?

Following are three essential characteristics of a highly available system:

- **Redundancy** This means ensuring that any elements crucial to the system operations have an additional, redundant component that can take control in the unlikely event of failure.

- **Monitoring** This means gathering data from a running system and identifying when a component fails or fails to respond.

- **Failover** This refers to a mechanism that could automatically switch from the currently active component to a redundant component if monitoring shows a breakdown of the active component.

By design, Microsoft Azure services are designed and built at every layer to deliver the highest levels of redundancy and resilience to its customers. Azure infrastructure is comprised of geographies, regions, and Availability zones, which limit the blast radius of failure and therefore limit the potential impact on customer applications and data.

Microsoft defines its SLA for each Azure service. See the Azure documentation for the assured SLA for the services you are currently using. If you need to have a higher SLA than what is assured by Azure, you can set up redundant components with failover.

> **This skill covers how to:**
> - Recommend a solution for application and workload redundancy, including compute, database, and storage
> - Recommend a solution for autoscaling
> - Identify resources that require high availability
> - Identify storage types for high availability
> - Recommend a solution for geo-redundancy of workloads

Recommend a solution for application and workload redundancy, including compute, database, and storage

Azure offers many redundancy features at every level of failure, from an individual VM to an entire region.

- **Single VMs** Single VMs also have a service-level agreement (SLA) offered by Azure. If you use premium storage for all operating system disks and data disks, you can get 99.9 percent SLA. If you use Standard SSD, you could get 99.5 percent SLA and with Standard HDD, you will get only 95 percent SLA. For production workloads that need redundancy, it is recommended that you run two or more VMs to achieve a higher SLA. A single VM might only be reliable enough for some workloads.

- **Availability sets** Availability sets are a highly recommended feature that protects you from localized hardware failures, such as a disk, network switch, or hardware failures. As per Microsoft, VMs in an availability set are distributed across up to three fault domains and update domains. A fault domain is a group of VMs that share a common power source and network switch. If a hardware failure affects one fault domain, Microsoft will route network traffic to VMs in the other fault domains.

- **Availability zones** Availability zones are physically separate zones within an Azure region. As per Microsoft, each availability zone has a distinctive power source, network, and cooling. Deploying VMs across Availability zones will help you to protect your workload against datacenter-wide failures.

> **NEED MORE REVIEW? AVAILABILITY ZONES SUPPORTED REGIONS**
>
> Note that not every Azure region supports Availability Zones. You can find the list of supported Azure regions for Availability Zones in the Microsoft documentation at *https://docs.microsoft.com/en-us/azure/availability-zones/az-region#azure-regions-with-availability-zones.*

- **Proximity placement groups** As Microsoft continues to expand its Azure footprint across the globe, a single availability zone might span across more than one data center within Azure regions, resulting in increased latency for your deployed virtual machines. This is where the concept of proximity placement groups comes in. A proximity placement group is a logical grouping that ensures Azure compute resources are physically located close to each other for low network latency between virtual machines.

Every application scenario has its own high availability and redundancy requirements. See Figure 4-5 as starting point.

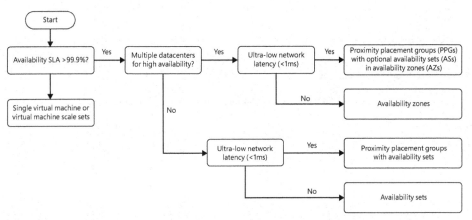

FIGURE 4-5 Decision tree deploying highly available and redundant applications

If you plan to use Availability zones in your deployment, first make sure that your application architecture and codebase support this configuration. If you deploy commercial software, consult with the software vendor and test the software adequately before deploying it into production. An application must maintain state and prevent loss of data during an outage within the configured zone. The application must support running in an elastic and distributed infrastructure with no hard-coded infrastructure components.

Azure Site Recovery can be used to replicate your Azure VMs to another Azure region to address business continuity (BC) and disaster recovery (DR) requirements. The VM is replicated with the specified settings to the selected region so you can recover your applications in the event of outages in the source region. During a DR drill exercise, you should verify that the recovery time objective (RTO) and recovery point objective (RPO) meet your BCP/DR requirements.

When you host your application workload in Azure multi regions for BCDR, you use Azure Traffic Manager to distribute Internet traffic to different regions, protecting an application against a regional outage. Each Azure region is paired with another region. Together, these regions form a *regional pair*. Note that to meet data residency requirements, regional pairs are typically within the same geography.

To improve application resiliency, Microsoft typically plans platform updates (planned maintenance) across each region pair in such a way that only one paired region is updated at a time.

EXAM TIP

You must add one or more virtual machines into availability sets to avoid a single point of failure within a datacenter and achieve 95.95 percent of Azure SLA on VMs. However, it is recommended that you use Availability zones to ensure high availability even in case of a datacenter failure. With Availability zones, you get 99.99 percent VM uptime Azure SLA.

Table 4-1 compares Azure redundancy features across these resiliency strategies:

TABLE 4-1 Azure redundancy features

	Availability set	Availability zone	Azure Site Recovery
Scope of failure	Rack	Datacenter	Region
Request routing	Azure Load Balancer	Cross-zone load balancer	Azure Traffic Manager
Network latency	Exceptionally low	Low	Mid to high
Virtual network	Azure virtual network	Azure virtual network	Cross-region virtual network peering

Out of the box, Azure Availability zones provide software and networking solutions to protect you from datacenter failures and to provide enhanced high availability (HA) to customers. Availability zones are distinctive physical locations within an Azure region. Each zone has been made up of one or more datacenters along with independent power, cooling, and networking. The physical separation of Availability zones within a region limits the impact from zone failures to applications and data. Failures can be caused by many reasons, such as large-scale flooding, major storms and superstorms, and other events that can disrupt site access, safe passage, extended utility uptime, and the accessibility of resources. Availability zones and their associated datacenters are specially designed such that if one zone is compromised, the services, capacity, and availability will be supported by the other Availability zones in the region.

Azure services supporting Availability zones can be divided into two categories: zonal and zone redundant. You can categorize your workloads to utilize architecture scenarios to meet an application's performance and durability needs.

With zonal architecture, a resource can be deployed to a self-selected availability zone to provide stricter latency or performance requirements. Resiliency is architected by replicating applications and data to one or more zones inside the region. You can select specific Availability zones for synchronous replication, offering high availability, asynchronous replication, delivering backup, or offering cost advantages. You can pin resources, such as virtual machines, managed disks, or standard IP addresses, to a specific zone, allowing for improved resilience by having one or more instances of resources spread over the zones.

Similarly, for zone-redundant architecture, the Azure platform automatically replicates the resource and data across zones. Microsoft is responsible for managing the delivery of high availability because Azure automatically replicates and distributes instances within the region.

In the event of a zone failure, the zonal services in the failed zone might no longer be available until the zone has recovered. If you architect your solutions to use replicated VMs in zones, you can protect your applications and data from a zone becoming unavailable. For example, if one zone becomes compromised because of a power outage, replicated apps and data are instantly available in another zone.

NEED MORE REVIEW? **AVAILABILITY ZONES**

To learn more, visit the Microsoft documentation at *https://docs.microsoft.com/en-us/azure/ architecture/high-availability/building-solutions-for-high-availability.*

As a standard practice for any well-architected highly available system, the following components are typically leveraged to implement the concepts of redundancy, monitoring, and failover:

- **Backup and recovery**   Automatically backs up data to a secondary location and recovers back to the source. This component can be used to set up redundancy and failover.

- **Load balancing**   A load balancer is configured to route traffic between more than one system that can serve inbound traffic. The load balancer could detect a failure in any of the target systems and redirect user traffic to the available system, thus implementing monitoring and failover.

- **Clustering**   A cluster contains multiple nodes that serve a similar purpose, and users typically access and see the whole cluster as one unit. Each node in the cluster could potentially failover to another node if a failure occurs. By setting up replication within the cluster, you can create redundancy between cluster nodes.

From a database perspective, there are four major potential disruption scenarios:

- **Local hardware or software failures affecting the database node**   For example, a disk-drive failure.

- **Data corruption or deletion typically caused by an application bug or by human error**   Such failures are application-specific and typically cannot be detected by the database service.

- **Datacenter-wide outage, possibly caused by a natural disaster**   This scenario requires some level of geo-redundancy with application failover to an alternate datacenter.

- **Upgrade or maintenance errors** Unanticipated issues that occur during planned infrastructure maintenance or upgrades might require rapid rollback to a prior database state.

To mitigate the local hardware and software failures, Azure SQL Database includes a high availability architecture, which guarantees automatic recovery from these failures with up to 99.995 percent availability SLA (for Azure SQL Database Business Critical or Premium tiers configured as Zone Redundant Deployments).

To protect your business from data loss, Azure SQL Database and Azure SQL Managed Instance automatically create full database backups weekly, differential database backups every 12–24 hours, and transaction log backups every 5–10 minutes. All automated backups for both Azure SQL Database and Managed Instance are stored in geo redundant Azure Blob storage for high availability and disaster recovery. All service tiers except Hyperscale and Basic tier, support a configurable backup retention period for a point-in-time restore, for up to 35 days.

Azure SQL Database and Azure SQL Managed Instance also provide several business continuity features that you can use to mitigate various unplanned scenarios.

- Temporal tables enable you to restore row versions from any point in time.

- Built-in automated backups and Point-in-Time Restore enable you to restore a complete database to some point in time within the configured retention period of up to 35 days.

- You can restore a deleted database to the point at which it was deleted if the server has not been deleted.

- Long-term backup retention allows you to keep the backups for up to 10 years. This is in limited public preview for SQL Managed Instance.

- Active geo-replication enables you to create readable replicas and manually failover to any replica in case of a datacenter outage or application upgrade.

- An auto-failover group allows for the recovery of a group of databases in a secondary region if a regional disaster occurs or if there is a full or partial loss of an Azure SQL Database or Azure SQL Managed Instance.

Recommend a solution for autoscaling

Autoscaling is the process of dynamically allocating resources to match performance requirements. There will be times when an application might require more resources to maintain the desired performance levels and to satisfy service-level agreements (SLAs) when demand grows. As demand loosens and the additional resources are no longer needed, they can be deallocated to reduce the costs. Autoscaling takes full advantage of the elasticity of cloud-hosted environments. The automation eliminates the need for human-centric maintenance to continually monitor the performance of a system and makes decisions automatically based on auto-scale rules for adding or removing resources.

Typically, when it comes to scaling any workload, there are two main ways:

- **Vertical scaling** Vertical scaling is also known as scaling up and down. It means changing the capacity of a resource. For example, you could move a workload to a larger VM size. Vertical scaling often involves making the system temporarily unavailable while it is being redeployed. Therefore, it is less common to automate vertical scaling.

- **Horizontal scaling** Horizontal scaling, also known as scaling out and in, means adding or removing instances of a resource. The application continues running without disruption as new resources are provisioned. When the provisioning process has been completed, the solution is deployed on additional resources. Similarly, when the demand drops, the additional resources can be shut down and deallocated.

Auto-scaling mostly applies to compute resources. While it is technically possible to scale a database or message queue horizontally, this usually involves data sharding or partitioning, which is generally not automated.

A typical scenario where auto-scaling is useful is when the load on a service varies over time. A typical autoscaling strategy consists of the following critical components:

- Monitoring at the application, service, and infrastructure levels, and monitoring to capture metrics, such as CPU and memory utilization and response times.

- Decision-making logic that checks these metrics against thresholds or that uses a schedule to decide whether to scale out or in.

- Components that are required to scale your system.

- Testing, monitoring, and tuning of the autoscaling strategy to ensure that it functions as expected.

Azure provides built-in autoscaling mechanisms that address common scenarios, and it provides the option of using custom implementations. You may need a custom solution if the service you plan to use does not provide built-in autoscaling functionality. Sometimes you have specific requirements that warrant a custom implementation. You can use a custom implementation that would first collect operational and system metrics, analyze the metrics, and then auto-scale resources. Azure offers built-in autoscaling for most compute options:

- Azure VMs provide auto-scale capabilities via virtual machine scale sets, which manage a set of Azure virtual machines as a group. When you configure your workload to run on Azure virtual machine scale sets, it could automatically scale-out/in by increasing or decreasing the number of instances that run your application. This automated and elastic behavior lowers the management overhead to monitor and optimize the performance of your application. You create rules that define acceptable performance for favorable user experience. When predefined thresholds are met, auto-scale rules trigger and take steps to increase/decrease your scale set's capacity. Auto-scale rules can also be created for schedules. Schedule-based rules allow you to automatically increase or decrease your scale set's capacity as per a predefined schedule.

- Service Fabric also supports autoscaling by using virtual machine scale sets. A Service Fabric cluster consists of multiple nodes that are set up as a separate virtual machine scale set. This helps each node type to be scaled in or out independently. Autoscaling is supported for both containers and regular Service Fabric services. To use auto-scaling, you need to be running on version 6.2 or above of the Service Fabric runtime. Supported Service Fabric scaling triggers work with logical load metrics or with physical metrics like CPU or memory usage. Service Fabric can monitor the reported load for each metric and evaluate the trigger periodically to determine if there is a need to scale.

- Azure App Service also has built-in autoscaling. Broadly, there are two options for auto-scaling any App Service plan. Either you can scale out or scale in based on a schedule, or you can use various metrics in an auto-scale rule. Once you configure auto-scale settings for an App Service it will apply to all of the apps within that App Service plan. The out-of-box settings do not allow you to scale up automatically; instead, you can only scale-out. Scaling up/down for an App Service can be configured manually. However, if you want to implement an auto-scale for scaling up/down, you can implement custom solutions that leverage REST APIs.

- Azure Cloud Services offers a built-in autoscaling feature at the role level. For this feature, the trigger is based on a metric for the cloud service, such as CPU usage, disk activity, or network activity. You can also include a conditional value. Moreover, you can have the trigger based on a message queue length or the metric of some other Azure resource in your subscription. Like Azure App Service, the legacy Cloud Services offering also allows you to scale out or scale in based on a schedule.

Azure Functions work a little differently as compared to other compute options because you do not need to configure any auto-scale rules. Instead, Azure Functions automatically allocates compute power when your code is running, scaling out as necessary to handle the load. For more information, see Skill 5-1 "Design a compute solution" in Chapter 5, "Design infrastructure."

All these compute options use Azure Monitor to provide a standard set of autoscaling functionality.

NEED MORE REVIEW? **HOW TO GET STARTED WITH AUTOSCALE IN AZURE**

To learn more about how to set up your auto-scale settings for your resource in the Microsoft Azure portal, see the Microsoft documentation at *https://docs.microsoft.com/en-us/azure/ azure-monitor/autoscale/autoscale-get-started*.

IMPORTANT **SCALE-OUT AND SCALE-IN RULE COMBINATIONS**

When configuring auto-scale, always use both a scale-out and scale-in rule combination that performs an increase and decrease.

EXAM TIP

Using Azure virtual machine scale sets, you create a group of load balanced VMs. The number of VM instances can automatically increase or decrease in response to demand or a defined schedule. Scale sets are different from availability sets in the sense that availability sets are logical groupings of two or more VMs to avoid a single point of failure. Availability sets ensure at least one VM is always available in case of planned or unplanned maintenance. However, VM scale sets provide redundancy and improved performance and workloads are typically distributed across multiple virtual machines.

Identify resources that require high availability

To identify resources that require high availability, our typical recommendation is that you perform the failure mode analysis process. Failure mode analysis (FMA) is a process in which you build resiliency into a system by identifying possible failure points in the system. A best practice is that FMA should be done during the architecture and design phases itself so that you can identify resources that require high availability from the beginning.

- Identify all the components within the system, including external dependencies, such as identity providers and third-party services.

- For each such component, identify potential failures. Note that a single component can have more than one single point of failure. For example, consider read failures and write failures separately because the effect and possible mitigation steps are going to be different.

- Rate each failure mode according to its overall risk. Consider these factors:

  - What is the likelihood of failure? Is it relatively common? Extremely rare? You do not need exact numbers; the purpose is to help rank the priority.

  - What is the impact on the application in terms of availability, data loss, monetary cost, and business disruption?

- For each failure mode, determine how the application will respond and recover. Consider trade-offs in cost and application complexity.

Identify storage types for high availability

Azure always stores multiple copies of your data stored in Azure storage to ensure that it is protected against planned and unplanned incidents, including transient hardware failures, network or power outages, and substantial natural disasters. Redundancy ensures that your storage account fulfills the Service-Level Agreement (SLA) for Azure Storage.

While thinking about which redundancy option is best, you should consider the trade-offs between costs and durability. The factors that help determine which storage type you should choose include:

- How do you replicate your data in the primary site?

- If your data needs to be replicated to a second site is it geographically distant from the primary site to protect against any regional disasters?

- Does your application need read access to the replicated data in the secondary region if the primary region is no longer available for any reason?

As noted earlier, Azure maintains multiple copies of your data that is stored in Azure Storage. Azure offers two options for Azure Storage, based on how data will be replicated throughout the primary region:

- **Locally redundant storage (LRS)**   Data is replicated synchronously three times within a single physical location in the primary region. Because LRS provides local redundancy, it is the least expensive option, but it is not recommended for mission-critical applications that require better availability.

- **Zone-redundant storage (ZRS)**   Data is replicated synchronously across three Azure Availability zones in the primary region. For applications requiring high availability, Microsoft recommends using ZRS in the primary region, and you also should replicate to a secondary region as well.

For mission-critical applications requiring the best availability, you can choose to additionally replicate the data in your storage account to another region that is at least hundreds of miles away from the primary region. When your storage account is replicated to a secondary region, your data is more durable. You are covered even in the case of a complete regional outage or a disaster (even if the primary region is not recoverable).

Microsoft offers two options for Azure Storage that offer redundancy for your data to another region:

- **Geo-redundant storage (GRS)**   Data is synchronously replicated three times within a single physical location in the primary region using LRS. Then your data is copied asynchronously to a single physical location in the secondary region.

- **Geo-zone-redundant storage (GZRS)**   Data is replicated synchronously across three Azure Availability zones in the primary region using ZRS. Azure then copies your data asynchronously to a single physical location in a secondary region.

If you compare GRS and GZRS, you will find that the only difference is how data is copied in the primary region. There is no difference in replication to the secondary region. For both alternatives, within the secondary region, data is always replicated three times using LRS. This LRS redundancy in the secondary region protects your data against any hardware failures.

Note that for both GRS or GZRS, the secondary location data will not be available for read or write access unless you do a failover to the secondary region. If you need read access to data in the secondary location, you should go for read-access geo-redundant storage (RA-GRS). If you also need zone redundancy as well, go for read-access geo-zone-redundant storage (RA-GZRS).

When the primary region is unavailable, you can choose to failover to the secondary region. Once the failover is completed, the secondary region will become a new primary region, and you will again be allowed to read and write data.

> **NEED MORE REVIEW?**
>
> For more information on to failover to the secondary region. see the Microsoft documentation at *https://docs.microsoft.com/en-us/azure/storage/common/storage-disaster-recovery-guidance*.

Table 4-2 describes critical parameters for each redundancy option:

TABLE 4-2 Redundancy parameters

Parameter	LRS	ZRS	GRS/RA-GRS	GZRS/RA-GZRS
Percent durability of objects over a given year	At least 99.999999999 percent (eleven 9s)	At least 99.9999999999 percent (twelve 9s)	At least 99.99999999999999 percent (sixteen 9s)	At least 99.99999999999999 percent (sixteen 9s)
Availability SLA for read requests	At least 99.9 percent (99 percent for Cool access tier)	At least 99.9 percent (99 percent for Cool access tier)	At least 99.9 percent (99 percent for Cool access tier) for GRS At least 99.99 percent (99.9 percent for Cool access tier) for RA-GRS	At least 99.9 percent (99 percent for Cool access tier) for GZRS At least 99.99 percent (99.9 percent for Cool access tier) for RA-GZRS
Availability SLA for write requests	At least 99.9 percent (99 percent for Cool access tier)	At least 99.9 percent (99 percent for Cool access tier)	At least 99.9 percent (99 percent for Cool access tier)	At least 99.9 percent (99 percent for Cool access tier)

> **NEED MORE INFO?**
>
> For more information about Azure Storage guarantees for durability and availability, see *https://azure.microsoft.com/support/legal/sla/storage/.*

Table 4-3 depicts the durability and availability of data in various scenarios, depending on which type of redundancy is in effect for your storage account.

TABLE 4-3 Durability and availability of data

Outage scenario	LRS	ZRS	GRS/RA-GRS	GZRS/RA-GZRS
A node within a datacenter becomes unavailable.	Yes	Yes	Yes	Yes
An entire datacenter (zonal or non-zonal) becomes unavailable.	No	Yes	Yes	Yes
A region-wide outage occurs in the primary region.	No	No	Yes	Yes
Read access to the secondary region is available if the primary region becomes unavailable.	No	No	Yes (with RA-GRS)	Yes (with RA-GZRS)

> **NOTE   ACCOUNT FAILOVER**
>
> Account failover is required to restore write availability if the primary region becomes unavailable. For more information, see *https://docs.microsoft.com/en-us/azure/storage/common/storage-disaster-recovery-guidance.*

Recommend a solution for geo-redundancy of workloads

Azure Storage offers a durable platform and multiple geo-redundant storage options to ensure high availability. Storage Account options with geo-redundant replication such as GRS and GZRS first synchronously replicate data in the primary region and then asynchronously replicate data to a secondary region that is at least a few hundred miles apart.

Microsoft offers two options for geo-redundant Azure Storage types. Depending on how exactly you want your data to be replicated in the primary region, these are your options:

- **Geo-zone-redundant storage (GZRS)** Microsoft will replicate your data synchronously across three Azure Availability zones in the primary region using zone-redundant storage (ZRS), and then it will replicate the data asynchronously to another region. If you need to allow read access to data in the secondary region, you can choose read-access geo-zone-redundant storage (RA-GRS).

- **Geo-redundant storage (GRS)** Microsoft will replicate your data synchronously three times in the primary region using locally redundant storage (LRS), and then it will replicate asynchronously to the secondary region. If you need to allow read access to data in the secondary region, you can choose read-access geo-zone-redundant storage (RA-GRS).

> **IMPORTANT   MAXIMUM AVAILABILITY**
>
> If your budget permits, then GZRS/RA-GZRS will provide you with a maximum availability and durability solution.

> **NEED MORE REVIEW?**
>
> For more information about application design considerations when reading from the secondary, see the Microsoft documentation at *https://docs.microsoft.com/en-us/azure/storage/common/geo-redundant-design#application-design-considerations-when-reading-from-the-secondary.*

Chapter summary

- As part of your BCDR plan, identify the recovery time objectives (RTOs) and recovery point objectives (RPOs) for your applications.
- Azure Site Recovery Deployment Planner tool helps you analyze source workloads, estimate bandwidth needs, identify resources you will need at the source location, and identify VMs and storage you will need at the target location.

- Azure Site Recovery gives you the flexibility to failover to Azure if a disaster occurs and fails back to on-premises machines after the event is over.
- Azure Site Recovery can replicate workloads from a primary site to a secondary site. If an issue occurs at the primary site, ASR can be used to replicate the protected virtual machines to another location.
- Azure Site Recovery can protect workloads running in Azure, on-premises, and in other cloud providers.
- Azure Site Recovery (ASR) is recommended for application-level protection and recovery.
- Data backups are helpful to restore data if it is lost, corrupted, or destroyed. Data archives protect older information that is not needed for everyday business operations but may occasionally need to be accessed.
- Backups are used for operational recoveries to recover an overwritten file or corrupted database quickly. The focus is usually on the speed (backup and recovery) and on data integrity. On the other hand, the Archive tier typically stores a version of no longer accessed files that need long-term retention.
- An efficient data archiving strategy is a necessary part of every enterprise.
- Microsoft offers Hot, Cool, and Archive Azure Storage access tiers that allow you to store blob object data.
- When you want to access the data from the Archive tier, the blob must be rehydrated.
- Availability zones are distinctive physical locations within an Azure region made up of one or more data centers, along with independent power, cooling, and networking. The physical separation of Availability zones within a region limits the impact to applications and data from zone failures.
- Autoscaling is a process of dynamically allocating computing resources to match performance requirements.
- Azure always stores multiple copies of your Azure Storage data to ensure that it is protected against planned and unplanned incidents, including transient hardware failures, network or power outages, and substantial natural disasters.
- Azure Storage offers a durable platform and multiple geo-redundant storage options to ensure high availability. Storage Account options with geo-redundant replication such as GRS and GZRS first synchronously replicate data in the primary region and then asynchronously replicate data to a secondary region that is at least a few hundred miles away.
- If your budget permits, then GZRS/RA-GZRS will provide you with a maximum availability and durability solution.

Thought experiment

Now it is time to validate your skills and knowledge of the concepts you have learned in this chapter. Answers to these questions can be found in the "Thought experiment answers" section at the end of this chapter.

You have been hired to work as a Cloud Solutions Architect for Contoso. You need to design a disaster recovery and high availability strategy for your internally hosted applications, database, and storage. Your company has a primary office in Seattle and branch offices in New York, Chicago, and Dallas. As part of this project, you plan to move three on-premises applications that belong to different departments. Each application has a different requirement for business continuity, as given below:

- **Sales Department** The application must be able to failover to a secondary datacenter.
- **HR Department** The application data needs to be retained for three years and from disaster recovery perspective, the application needs to run from a different Azure region with a recovery time objective (RTO) of 15 minutes.
- **Supply Chain Department** You need to ensure that the application must be able to restore data at a granular level. The recovery time objective requirement is six hours.

You must recommend which services should be used by each department. While there could be multiple answers, choose the options that will help minimize cost.

1. Which of the following would you use for the sales department?
   A. Azure Backup only
   B. Azure Site Recovery only
   C. Azure Site Recovery and Azure Migrate
   D. Azure Site Recovery and Azure Backup

2. Which of the following services would you recommend for the HR department?
   A. Azure Backup only
   B. Azure Site Recovery only
   C. Azure Site Recovery and Azure Migrate
   D. Azure Site Recovery and Azure Backup

3. Which of the following services would you recommend for the supply chain department?
   A. Azure Backup only
   B. Azure Site Recovery only
   C. Azure Site Recovery and Azure Migrate
   D. Azure Site Recovery and Azure Backup

Thought experiment answers

This section contains the answers to the "Thought experiment" questions. Below, you will find the answers and an explanation for why each answer is the best answer.

1. **Which of the following would you use for the sales department?**

    B: Azure Site Recovery Only

    Explanation   You can use the Azure site Recovery services to ensure that you can failover your application to a secondary region. The other options are not correct because you just need Azure Site Recovery services to address the sales department's requirement for the failover,. You don't need Azure Migrate because it should be used in scenarios where you want to migrate VMs from, say, VMWare VMs to Azure VMs.

2. **Which of the following services would you recommend for the HR department?**

    Azure Site Recovery and Azure Backup

    Explanation   As stated in the requirements, you need to retain backups for three years, so you need to use Azure Backup. You will also need Azure Site Recovery service to ensure that the application can run in another datacenter in case of a disaster, so you will need both Azure Backup and the Azure Site Recovery service. The other options are not adequate to meet the stated requirements.

3. **Which of the following services would you recommend for the Supply Chain Department?**

    A: Azure Backup only

    Explanation   As stated in the requirements, you need to be able restore from any point in time in the past. Azure Backup is what you use. Azure Backup automatically creates recovery points when subsequent backups are taken so that you run the restore operations from any point in time.

CHAPTER 5

Design infrastructure

Azure provides a wide range of infrastructure services such as compute, network, and application services. These infrastructure services are among the most consumed services by Azure customers around the globe. As AZ-304 is an advanced level exam, you need to understand Microsoft's infrastructure services thoroughly, use your design skills, and your experience designing solutions on the Azure platform.

This chapter looks at various ways to design solutions on the Azure platform using compute, network, application, and migration services.

Skills covered in this chapter:

- Skill 5.1: Design a compute solution
- Skill 5.2: Design a network solution
- Skill 5.3: Design an application architecture
- Skill 5.4: Design migration

Skill 5.1: Design a compute solution

A compute service is a hosting model to host and run your application on the cloud. This service provides processing power, memory, and local storage. Compute is one of the fundamental building blocks of your workload. Microsoft Azure offers various compute services such as VMs, Azure App Service, function apps, Service Fabric, and so forth to cater to your needs.

As an Azure Solutions Architect, you need to be mindful of choosing the right compute service to balance your business needs and Azure spend optimally. In this skill, you learn the various Azure compute offerings available to host your application and the differences between them to make the right choice for your application scenario.

> **This skill covers how to:**
> - Recommend a solution for compute provisioning
> - Determine appropriate compute technologies
> - Recommend a solution for containers
> - Recommend a solution for automating compute management

Recommend a solution for compute provisioning

The first step in using Azure compute services is to provision it. Imagine an on-premises world, and you need a high-end server with 64 core 128 GB memory. For such a high-end machine, you need to go through several steps such as procurement and installation. This typically takes days to get you a required server. In Azure, you can provision the same server in a few clicks. This is the beauty of the Azure Cloud platform.

Now suppose you need hundreds of Azure VMs, all the virtual machines need an antivirus agent, a few of them need Internet Information Server (IIS), and so forth. You can do it manually, but that is going to be time consuming and error prone. The Azure platform offers multiple solution options to automate the provisioning process. In this section, you learn the various options available to provision compute on the Azure Cloud platform.

Table 5-1 shows a high-level comparison of the automation tools:

TABLE 5-1 Automation tools

	ARM Templates	Ansible	Chef	Puppet	Terraform
Agent/agentless	No	No	Yes	Yes	No
Need extra infrastructure	No	No	Yes	Yes	No
Need master server	No	No	Yes	Yes	No
Declarative	Declarative	Procedural	Procedural	Declarative	Declarative
Immutable infrastructure	Mutable	Mutable	Mutable	Mutable	Immutable
Open source	Microsoft Automation Tool	Yes	Yes	Yes	Yes
Supported cloud providers	Azure Only	All	All	All	All

Azure Resource Manager (ARM) template

An ARM template is Microsoft's native solution to provision resources quickly in Microsoft Azure. The template is a JavaScript Object Notion (JSON) file, which you can use to write code for Azure infrastructure. In the ARM template JSON file, you use a declarative syntax to define what resources you want to provision, their names, properties, and dependencies. In a single template, you can deploy multiple Azure resources with their dependencies.

Let's look at the basic structure of the ARM template shown in the following code snippet, which is broken down in Table 5-2:

```
{
"$schema": "https://schema.management.azure.com/schemas/2019-04-01/
deploymentTemplate.json#",
"contentVersion": "",
"apiProfile": "",
```

```
"parameters": { },
"variables": { },
"functions": [ ],
"resources": [ ],
"outputs": { }
}
```

TABLE 5-2 ARM template syntax

Element Name	Description
schema	This is the location of the JSON schema file. This field is mandatory.
content version	This is a version of the template defined by you to manage your templates. This field is mandatory.
parameters	List of values that you need to provide while deploying a template, such as the name of the VM, username, and password.
apiProfile	This is a collection of API versions for resource types.
variables	These are like programming language variables used to store a value.
functions	These are user-defined functions that are available within the template.
resources	This is the actual collection of resources that you are going to provision.
Outputs	This is used to assign the output value of the deployment such as the IP address, which can be passed to another deployment.

ARM templates and their parameter files can be developed using Visual Studio Code or your choice of any JSON file editor. Visual Studio Code's key features are code snippets, Azure schema completion and validation, the ability to create and validate parameter files, and template navigation.

NEED MORE REVIEW? **DEVELOP AN ARM TEMPLATE WITH VISUAL STUDIO CODE**

For more information about developing an ARM template with Visual Studio, see *https:// docs.microsoft.com/en-us/Azure/Azure-resource-manager/templates/quickstart-create- templates-use-visual-studio-code?tabs=CLI.*

NEED MORE REVIEW? **QUICKSTART TEMPLATES**

A library of QuickStart Azure ARM templates with templates developed by the community is available at *https://github.com/Azure/Azure-quickstart-templates.*

ARM templates can be deployed using the Azure portal, Azure PowerShell, Azure CLI, and VS Code or Visual Studio. You can also use Azure Pipelines to deploy ARM templates. When you deploy ARM templates using either of the above methods, they are submitted to Azure Resource Manager. Azure Resource Manager parses the JSON file, fills in the parameter values, validates, sorts, and calls REST APIs of the respective resources defined in the ARM templates. Key features of Azure Resource Manager templates:

- You can quickly develop ARM templates using familiar tools such as Visual Studio, and Visual Studio Code, using declarative syntax in JSON file format.

- You can quickly deploy ARM templates using your familiar tools such as Azure Power-Shell, Azure CLI, the Azure portal, Azure Pipelines, Visual Studio, and Visual Studio code.

- Integration with Azure DevOps and Azure Pipelines for CI/CD, and the Azure portal to track your deployments. You can also deploy ARM templates directly from GitHub to your Azure subscription using the **"Deploy to Azure"** or **"Deploy to Azure Gov"** action.

- A library of ARM templates which contains hundreds of commonly used ARM templates to expedite your environment provisioning.

Ansible

Ansible is an open-source automation tool designed for provisioning, configuration management, deployment, orchestration, continuous delivery, and security automation. It is an agentless tool that manages remote machines using SSH (Linux and UNIX) or WinRM (Windows). It performs automation using playbooks. Playbooks contain automation tasks. You can author playbooks using YAML (Yet Another Markup Language). Key features of Ansible are:

- Ansible is easy to set up and use.

- Ansible is an agentless tool; no software or client is required to be installed on a remote machine. It manages remote machines using SSH (Linux and UNIX) or WinRM (Windows).

- Ansible is simple and easy to learn with a low learning curve for developers, IT managers, and administrators.

- Ansible provides more than 450 modules for day-to-day tasks.

- Ansible allows you to deploy multi-tier applications easily and quickly.

- Ansible provides simple, consistent, and reliable configuration management.

Chef

Chef is an open-source infrastructure automation tool for configuration management, deployment, and compliance. Chef uses Ruby, a domain-specific language (DSL) for writing system configuration called a recipe and cookbook. It provides a multi-cloud solution, multi-OS (operating system), or hybrid (cloud and on-premises) environments.

Chef uses a client-server architecture, and it also includes workstations. The workstation is the system in which cookbooks are created and tested. The workstation sends the cookbook to the Chef server using Chef Knife. The Chef server stores all the cookbooks, recipes, and metadata. The Chef client pulls the configuration from the server and updates nodes with the configuration present on the server. Key features of Chef are:

- It provides support for multiple operating systems such as Windows, RHEL/CentOS, FreeBSD, macOS, AIX, Solaris, and Ubuntu.

- It supports all major public cloud providers.
- With Chef, you can manage hundreds of servers with few employees.
- Chef has broad and growing community support.

Puppet

Puppet is an open-source automation tool for configuration management and continuous delivery. Puppet implementation is based on the master-slave architecture. The master and slave securely communicate with each other using SSL/TLS.

The Puppet agent sends a slave state in a key-value pair to the master. The Puppet master uses the client state information and compiles a catalog, which is a desired state of the slave. The Puppet slave implements the required configuration and reports back to the master. Key features of Puppet:

- Puppet has a large community of developers and hence better documentation and pre-built modules.
- Puppet also provides commercial support.
- It is scalable, reliable, consistent, and deploys faster.

Terraform

Terraform is an open-source automation tool by HashiCorp for provisioning and configuration management. Terraform uses a declarative language called the HashiCorp configuration language (HCL) to safely and efficiently manage the environment.

Terraform can manage infrastructure deployed on-premises or in the public cloud, such as Microsoft Azure, Google Cloud Platform, or Amazon Web Services. Key features of Terraform are:

- Terraform is platform agnostic.
- The planning step of Terraform allows you to generate an execution plan which shows what Terraform is going to change and in what order.
- You can implement complex automation with minimal human interaction.
- Terraform creates resources in parallel, based on the dependency of resources, and thus improves efficiency.

Determine appropriate compute technologies

Microsoft Azure Cloud platform offers many flavors of compute services. Each compute service has its own capabilities such as manageability, scalability, flexibility, control, and cost. The AZ-304 exam expects you to have deep insights into the various compute services to make the right decision when designing and architecting Azure compute solutions.

Let's look at each Azure compute service, its capabilities, and reasons to choose it in your solution design.

Azure virtual machines

Azure VMs are fully Infrastructure as a Service (IaaS), which provides a virtual processor, memory, storage, and network interfaces, along with the operating system of your choice. You can connect to VM by using the Remote Desktop Protocol (RDP) connection for Windows and SSH for Linux VMs, and you can take full control of a VM. You can install the required software and all the necessary configuration of the server for your application. While you get full control of the VM, the VM's manageability is your responsibility, so you need to take care of backup and OS-patching activities.

When to use an Azure VM:

- When you need to quickly migrate servers/applications from on-premises to Azure; this is also called a "lift-and-shift" or rehost of the server from on-premises to Azure.

- For migrating legacy applications that you think would be challenging to redesign/remediate and deploy them into Azure PaaS services.

- For deploying databases with features not supported in Azure PaaS, such as SQL Server database with the full database engine, SQL Server Integration Services (SSIS), SQL Server Reporting Services (SSRS), and SQL Server Analysis Services (SSAS).

- For deploying custom off the shelf (COTS) applications that you cannot remediate and deploy into Azure PaaS services.

- When you need full control over the application server, including the operating system and services.

- When you quickly need a development and test environment for your applications, you can provision an Azure VM quickly and use the VM's auto-shutdown feature to save costs. Once your development is complete, you can delete the VMs that are no longer required.

- When you need a secondary site for your disaster recovery, you can configure the Azure region as your secondary site using Azure Site recovery. If the primary datacenter fails, you can quickly provision VMs in the secondary region for your critical workloads and delete the VM when your primary datacenter becomes available again.

Azure App Service

Azure App Service is a fully managed platform (PaaS) to deploy enterprise-grade web applications and you need to focus on the application functionality. The load balancing, high availability, backup, security, and OS patching is taken care of by the Azure platform. Azure App Service also provides features that allow you to configure scalability of your application. You can manually scale up your Azure App Service Plan from, say, basic to standard tier, and then behind the scenes, the platform scales the infrastructure as per the plan and vice versa.

Azure App Service is useful for hosting web applications, REST APIs, and mobile backends. It provides Windows and Linux operating systems. You can develop applications using your choice of languages such as .NET, .Net Core, PHP, Ruby, Java, Python, and Node.js. You can also develop and deploy background tasks as web jobs in Azure App Service. You can run executables developed using a programming language such as .NET, Java, PHP, Python, or Node.js, or scripts such as .cmd, .bat, PowerShell, or Bash. The web jobs can be scheduled or triggered by a specific action.

Let's look at the key features of Azure App Service:

- **Manageability**   Automatic patching of the operating system and language framework.
- **Scalability**   You can scale up or scale out manually, or you can also configure auto-scaling.
- **Availability**   Microsoft provides 99.95 percent availability for Azure App Service excluding applications deployed in the free and shared tiers.
- **Security**   You can protect your application by configuring Active Directory authentication, IP address restriction, encryption, and managed identity.
- **Compliance**   App services are PCI-, ISO-, and SOC-compliant.
- **Ease of development**   Microsoft provides a dedicated tool for rapid application development. It also offers ready-made templates in the Azure Marketplace, such as WordPress. You can also easily deploy other CMS solutions such as Drupal to Azure App Service using Web App for Containers service offering. This is a standard offering by Microsoft. Maybe we can provide a link for more info for readers - https://azure.microsoft.com/en-us/services/app-service/containers/.
- **Continuous Integration and Continuous Delivery (CI/CD)**   It provides CI/CD support with Azure Pipelines, BitBucket, GitHub, Azure Container Registry, and Docker Hub.
- **Backup**   Azure App Service provides manual as well as automatic backup at scheduled times. You can restore the app or create another app from the backup.

When to use Azure App Service:

- When you would like to offload manageability of your application's underlying operating system and infrastructure to the Microsoft Azure Cloud platform and configure management aspects with ease such as automatic patching of OS and language framework, backup, security, and compliance
- When your application needs infrastructure to handle fluctuating traffic
- When migrating web applications from on-premises to Azure with the luxury of time and effort to remediate application code to fit the application into PaaS to get the most benefit of the cloud

Azure Service Fabric

Azure Service Fabric is a Platform as a Service (PaaS) offering, facilitating the development, packaging, deployment, and management of highly scalable microservices and containers. It is a distributed system that provides infrastructure designed to run stateless and stateful microservices across the Service Fabric cluster of machines. You could create a Service Fabric cluster using Windows or Linux operating systems in Azure, on-premises, or other cloud providers.

Let's look at the key features of the Service Fabric:

- **Development and management**   Simple and quick microservices development and application lifecycle management.
- **Near-real-time analysis**   Service Fabric allows you to perform near-real-time data analysis, event processing, parallel transaction, and in-memory computation in your application.
- **Compliance**   Azure Service Fabric is ISO-, PCI DSS-, SOC-, GDPR-, and HIPAA-compliant.

- **Ease of development** You could easily build a Service Fabric application using Visual studio or your choice of Integrated Development Environment (IDE). You could also use Service Fabric Explorer to visualize the node health and application state, such as warnings and errors.

- **Continuous integration and continuous delivery (CI/CD)** Azure Service Fabric provides CI/CD support with Azure DevOps, BitBucket, and GitHub.

When to use Azure Service Fabric:

- When you are developing a new application based on microservices architecture or event-driven architecture to develop highly available and scalable microservices

- For developing applications that require low-latency reads and writes, such as gaming and session-based integrative applications

- For IoT applications to collect and process data from millions of devices

- For data analytics and workflow processing applications that require optimized reads and writes to process events or streams reliably.

Azure Functions

Azure Functions is a Function as a Service (FaaS), which abstracts underlying infrastructure and operating systems and allows you to execute smaller tasks at a scheduled time or when triggered by external events.

You can develop Azure Functions in various languages, such as C#, F#, Java, JavaScript, Python, PowerShell, and TypeScript. You can write code and execute the function without worrying about the infrastructure to run the application.

Azure also provides the following templates to help you quickly get started with function development:

- `TimerTrigger` Schedule your code to execute at predefined times.

- `QueueTrigger` Run your function code when a new message arrives in the Azure Storage queue.

- `HTTPTrigger` Trigger the execution of code based on the HTTP request.

- `CosmosDBTrigger` Run your function code to process new or modified Azure Cosmos DB documents.

- `EventGridTrigger` Run your function code to respond to Azure Event Grid events.

- `EventHubTrigger` Respond to events delivered to an Azure Event Hub.

- `ServiceBusQueueTrigger` Run your function code when a new message arrives in the Azure bus queue.

- `ServiceBusTopicTrigger` Run your function code to respond to the service bus topic message.

Triggers can invoke Azure Functions. Triggers define how a function is called. Many triggers are available for Azure Functions such as `TimerTrigger`, which runs a function at a predefined time. Triggers have associated data that is passed as the payload to the function. An Azure function should have only one trigger and optional bindings. Bindings are a way of connecting other resources to the function. Bindings are optional, and a function can have one or more input/output bindings.

There are two types of binding:

- **Input bindings**   The data that your function receives.
- **Output bindings**   The data that your function sends.

Azure Functions has three hosting plans:

- **Consumption plan**   As the name implies, you only pay for the consumption when your functions are running. Instances are dynamically added or removed based on the number of events. The Consumption plan's billing is based on the number of executions, execution time, and memory used.
- **Premium plan**   Like a Consumption plan, Azure Functions dynamically adds or removes the host based on incoming events. The Premium plan's billing is based on the number of core seconds and memory allocated across instances. The Premium plan comes with additional features such as virtual network connectivity, pre-warmed instances, unlimited execution duration, and higher compute (up to 4 cores and 14 GB RAM).
- **Dedicated (App Service) plan**   This is the same App Service plan that is mostly used with Azure App Service. The benefit of using the App Service plan is that you are using the existing underutilized App Service plan (running some other app services) for Azure Functions at no additional cost.

EXAM TIP

The AZ-304 exam typically includes one or more scenario questions to choose an appropriate answer to the given scenario. The following tips should help you select the right Azure Functions hosting plan:

- The Premium and Dedicated plans offer virtual network integration.
- With the Consumption plan, you have the option to save costs because you do not need to pay for the idle compute or reserve capacity.
- The Premium plan is more costly than the Consumption plan.

Let's look at the key features of the Azure Functions:

- You can build Azure Functions using various languages such as C#, F#, Java, JavaScript, Python, PowerShell, TypeScript, and Node.js. You can use NuGet and NPM libraries.
- It provides CI/CD support with Azure Pipelines, BitBucket, and GitHub.
- It is developed once and deployed into various hosting plans, Kubernetes clusters, or IoT devices for edge computing.
- You pay only when your code is running.
- It allows serverless development of serverless applications on Microsoft Azure.

- HTTP triggers can be protected using Azure Active Directory, Microsoft accounts, and Google, Facebook, and Twitter accounts.

- The Azure Functions runtime is open source and is available on GitHub.

- Integration with other Azure services such as blobs, queues, databases, Event Hub, and Event Grid.

- Auto-scaling based on the number of events/loads.

- Monitoring using Application Insights.

When to use Azure Functions:

- For infrequent tasks such as DB clean up and monthly archive.

- For the processing of service bus messages. For example, processing orders by reading messages from the service bus queue and storing the result into the database.

- For the processing of files (CSV, Images) when uploaded to Azure Storage.

- For big data processing with serverless MapReduce.

- For developing APIs with unpredictable traffic during events such as a concert/conference.

- IoT data processing where usage is high during the day and very low or nonexistent at night.

- Execution of small tasks/code using an event-driven serverless architecture.

Windows Virtual Desktop

Windows Virtual Desktop (WVD) is a desktop virtualization service on Microsoft's cloud platform. This WVD service can be accessed by your choice of a device such as Windows, Mac, Android, iOS, or any device having an HTML5 web client.

Let's look at the key features of Windows Virtual Desktop:

- A complete desktop virtualization environment in Azure without any additional gateway servers.

- Cost-efficient solution. Windows Virtual Desktop service is a cost-efficient service as you don't have to pay for this service separately; you use your existing Microsoft 365 or Windows per-user licenses. You can further optimize costs by leveraging Windows 10's multi-session capability.

- You can use your own operating system image.

- Publish multiple host pools for your workload.

- End users can use Teams and Microsoft Office and OneDrive, and get a local desktop experience.

Azure Batch

Azure Batch is a managed service designed to run large-scale parallel and high-performance computing (HPC) batch jobs in Microsoft's Azure Cloud platform.

In a typical workflow, you need to perform the following steps to run a parallel workload:

1. The client uploads files into Azure Storage. These files can include scripts or applications that process data.

2. You create a pool of compute nodes—which can be Windows or Linux VM images—and you define the size of the pool and a job to run on the workload.

3. You create a job and tasks. (A job is a collection of tasks. You associate your job with a specific pool.)

4. Azure Batch downloads input files and applications. After downloading, Azure Batch executes tasks on assigned nodes.

5. Your client application will monitor tasks that are being executed on the compute nodes.

6. Azure Batch uploads task output to Azure Storage.

7. Your client application downloads output files/data.

You don't have to pay for the Azure Batch service separately. You only need to pay for the underlying compute, network, and storage resources. An organization can use Azure Batch to deliver on-demand and high-end processing for their applications.

Let's look at the key features of the Azure Batch:

- It provides flexibility to run large-scale parallel workloads by using low-priority VMs.

- Integration with Azure Storage to upload/download data.

- Auto-scaling of the nodes allows you to add nodes, install applications, identify failures, and re-queue work.

- Monitoring using Batch Explorer and Azure Monitor's Application Insights feature.

When to use Windows Azure Batch:

- You need massive computing capacities, such as image processing and analysis, weather forecasting, and engineering simulations.

- For running intrinsically parallel workloads such as:

  - Financial risk modeling using Monte Carlo simulations

  - Data ingestion, processing, and ETL operations

  - VFX and 3D image rendering

  - Image analysis and processing

  - Media transcoding

  - Genetic sequence analysis

  - Optical character recognition (OCR)

  - Software test execution

High-performance computing (HPC)

High-performance computing (HPC)—also called "big compute"—uses many CPU- or GPU-based computers to solve complex mathematical tasks. With Azure HPC services, you get access to vast computing resources geared explicitly toward HPC workloads. For example, Azure provides various high-performance computing resources such as H-series virtual machines for memory-bound applications, N-series virtual machines for graphic intensive and CUDA/OpenCL based applications, and Cray fully dedicated and customized supercomputer delivered as a managed service.

With Azure HPC, you also have a choice to burst your HPC applications into Azure using data stored in on-premises NAS devices with HPC cache or using Azure NetApp files to access large amounts of I/O with sub-millisecond latency. You have an option to use a high-throughput storage solution, such as Cray ClusterSor, which is a Lustre-based, bare-metal HPC storage solution that is fully integrated with Azure.

Many industries use HPC to solve some of their most challenging problems, such as

- Genomics
- Oil and gas simulations
- Finance
- Semiconductor design
- Engineering
- Weather modeling

There are multiple ways to design and implement HPC in Azure. Typically, it includes the following components:

- **HPC head node**   A VM that acts as a managing server and takes care of scheduling workload and jobs to a worker node.
- **Virtual machine scale sets**   These are the worker nodes that execute the allocated tasks.
  - **Virtual network**   This provides connectivity between the head node, compute node, and storage nodes.
  - **Storage**   This node allows the storage of structured, unstructured, and executable files. This can be Azure Blob Storage, Azure Data Lake Storage Gen 2, Disk Storage, and Azure Files.
  - **Azure Resource Manager**   Azure Resource Manager templates and script files used to deploy the application.

***NEED MORE REVIEW?* COMMON SCENARIO TO BUILD HPC SOLUTION**

To learn more about common scenarios to build an HPC solution, see *https://docs.microsoft.com/ en-us/azure/architecture/example-scenario.*

Let's look at the key features of the HPC solution on Azure:

- A highly scalable solution on the Azure Cloud platform.
- A high-end CPU and GPU virtual machine and supercomputers from Cray.

- Azure's InfiniBand-enabled H-series and N-series VMs communicate over low latency and high bandwidth and provide the best HPC performance.

- Support for most common MPI libraries, including Intel MPI, OpenMPI, MPICH, MVAPICH2, Platform MPI, and all remote direct memory access (RDMA) verbs.

- Easily extends an on-premises HPC environment to Azure Cloud.

You should use HPC on Azure for all applications that require very intensive compute power, such as:

- Reservoir simulation in the oil and gas industry

- Market modeling in the finance industry

- Weather modeling in meteorology

- Gene sequencing in genetic science

- GPU-accelerated graphics applications such as 3D CAD modeling, 3D rendering, and scientific visualization

Containers

Containers provide immutable infrastructure for your application. It allows you to bundle your application code, libraries, dependencies, configuration as a container image. You can seamlessly deploy images into Azure, other cloud providers, and on-premises.

Let's look at the key features of Containers:

- Containers make your application deployment platform agnostic.

- Containers help with consistency across the environment by bundling application code and its dependencies.

- Containers are small, lightweight, and scalable.

- Containers are resilient; allow spinning up or down rapidly.

- You can run multiple applications on isolated containers on a single VM host.

> **NEED MORE REVIEW?** **GUIDE TO CHOOSING AN AZURE COMPUTE SERVICE**
>
> Microsoft Azure offers a variety of compute services to deploy your application. Microsoft's guidance for choosing the right compute service to meet the business needs of your application can be found at *https://docs.microsoft.com/en-us/azure/architecture/guide/technology-choices/compute-decision-tree*.

Recommend a solution for containers

Over the past few years, containerization has gained much traction. It has completely changed the IT industry, especially with organizations moving to the cloud with a multi-cloud strategy.

With that vision in mind, the Azure platform has made it incredibly simple to develop and deploy containerized applications, leveraging industry-leading container technologies.

In this section, you learn the following compute choices available in Azure to run containerized applications on Azure and understand when you would choose one over the other.

- **Azure Container Instances (ACI)**   The Azure Container Instances service offering gives you the ability to spin up containers on demand without worrying about existing infrastructure such as Azure VMs. Azure manages all the underlying infrastructure mechanics transparently, and you just focus on building applications and deploying them in a readily available containerized environment. Azure Container Instances is best suited for scenarios that can operate in isolated containers and do not need orchestration. You can deploy and run small event-driven applications, simple web apps, and small batch processing jobs using Azure Container Instances, and you have the advantage of only paying for those containers. ACI is a managed service, and you get rid of infrastructure management and operational overhead, such as upgrading/patching the underlying operating system or Azure VMs.

- **Azure Kubernetes Services (AKS)**   AKS is also a fully managed Kubernetes service that allows you to deploy and manage containerized applications with full-fledged container orchestration capabilities. AKS eliminates the operational and maintenance overhead, just as if you were to manage your Kubernetes deployments. As part of managed servers, Azure handles critical Kubernetes tasks such as health monitoring of underlying infrastructure, and it handles the desired state and lifecycle of containerized applications, including autoscaling, health monitoring of individual services, auto-discovery for interservice communication, and load balancing. The best part is that AKS is free, and you only pay for the agent nodes within your clusters; you do not pay for the masters controlling the AKS cluster.

EXAM TIP

Azure Kubernetes Service (AKS) provides different ways to expose your services running within the AKS cluster. To learn more about these options, see *https://docs.microsoft.com/en-us/azure/aks/ingress-basic*.

Recommend a solution for automating compute management

The first step in automating compute is provisioning. We have already seen automation of compute provisioning in the previous section. Now, we will look at the other computation automation aspects, such as configuration, update management, continuous delivery, and automation for compliance purposes. We can easily automate these jobs using Microsoft's native solutions such as Azure Automation, PowerShell desired state configuration, ARM templates, custom script extension, and Azure Pipelines. Also, there are multiple third-party solutions available in the market, such as Ansible, Chef, Puppet, Terraform, and Jenkin.

In the following sections, we'll look at Microsoft's native solution for compute automation.

Azure Automation

Azure Automation is a Cloud-based, cost-effective automation service on Microsoft's Azure Cloud platform. Azure Automation allows you to automate time-consuming, repetitive, and error-prone tasks across Azure and non-Azure environments. Following are the key features of Azure Automation:

- **Process automation** Azure Automation allows you to automate your day-to-day manual, repetitive, time-consuming, error-prone tasks. You can simply build your process logic into a PowerShell script or Python, or you can develop graphically (based on PowerShell) as a serverless runbook and schedule it as a job. It also offers hundreds of built-in PowerShell modules for everyday tasks that you can reuse in your runbook. You can also integrate easily with other systems by using these modules. You can also set up the Hybrid Runbook Worker at your on-premises location. Hybrid Runbook Worker allows you to run a runbook and connect to on-premises resources. An Automation runbook can also be exposed as a webhook and can be triggered by a monitoring system, DevOps, and ITSM.

- **Configuration management** Configuration management has two features:

  - **Change tracking and inventory** This allows you to track your infrastructure, including virtual machine states such as files, software, and registry, and you can generate alerts for unwelcome changes.

  - **Azure Automation state configuration** This allows you to manage the desired state configuration of virtual and physical machines.

- **Update management** This feature allows you to see the current compliance state of Windows and Linux VMs, create a deployment schedule, and install patches on the scheduled window.

- **Source control integration** Azure Automation supports GitHub, Azure Repos (Git), and Azure Repos Team Foundation Version Control (TFVC).

- **Heterogeneous support** Azure Automation supports Windows as well as Linux systems across a hybrid cloud environment.

- **Role-based access control** Azure Automation supports role-based access control (RBAC) to an Azure Automation account and its resources.

- **Integration** Azure Automation easily integrates with Azure services or other public systems.

Custom Script Extension

Azure custom script extension allows you to download and run a script on an Azure VM. The extension is useful for configuring the VM after provisioning. For example, you can install software, set up services, configure the server, automate the job, and so forth. The custom script can be applied using the Azure portal, Azure PowerShell, the REST API, or ARM templates. The script file can be downloaded from Azure Storage, GitHub, a local share using SMB protocol, or any other location (such as a public URL accessible from a VM). You need to ensure that Network Security Group (NSG) and firewalls are correctly configured to access the script location.

Key features of the Custom Script Extension include:

- This is a simple and easy way to run a script on a VM and configure it. You can apply custom script extensions on a VM with few clicks using the Azure portal.
- The custom script extension can be applied using Azure CLI, Azure PowerShell, ARM template, or the REST API.

Packer

Packer is HashiCorp's open-source automation tool for the creation of VM images. Packer helps automate the entire VM image creation process. You can install the necessary software/tools and customize a VM using a post-configuration script and then capture the VM as a managed disk.

Following are the key features of Packer:

- Use Packer when you need to build a hardened VM image.
- You can quickly set up an environment and use easy-to-understand JSON templates to build images.
- You can employ easy-to-use automation to create VM images that are supported on multiple clouds such as Azure, AWS, and Oracle Cloud.
- Packer works well with Terraform to create an image and install and deploy it with Terraform.
- Packer can create multiple images in parallel targeted for various platforms.
- Packer allows you to transform an artifact from the builder (AMI or VMWare image) into a Vagrant box file.

We covered other automation-related topics such as Ansible, ARM, Chef, Puppet, and Terraform earlier in this chapter. (See "Recommend a solution for compute provisioning.")

Skill 5.2: Design a network solution

With a spaghetti of cable running through the datacenter and the massive amount of networking gear such as ports, connectors, plugs, routers, and switches to manage, understanding a traditional datacenter network can be a daunting topic. Fortunately, the basic principles of cloud networking architecture are relatively straightforward.

As an Azure Solutions Architect taking the AZ-304 exam, you need to understand Azure networking services to set the foundation right because it is the glue between most of the Azure resources you must deal with for your solutions. In this skill, we are looking at various Azure networking services and their capabilities, so that you can recommend the right solutions.

Recommend a network architecture

Azure Virtual Network is a foundational building block for your private network in Azure. Azure Virtual Network enables many Azure resources, such as VMs, VM scale sets, the App Service environment, App Service, and Azure Functions with virtual network integration and Kubernetes clusters, to communicate with each other securely via on-premises networks and on the Internet.

Azure provides virtual networks with the following capabilities:

- Secure communication for Azure resources to communicate with each other.
- You can configure endpoints on virtual networks for services that require Internet communication.
- A virtual network is a logical isolation that is dedicated to your Azure subscription.
- You can implement multiple virtual networks within Azure regions in your subscriptions.
- Isolation from other virtual networks.
- You can use private and public IP addresses defined in RFC 1918 and expressed in CIDR notation.
- If you use your public IP addresses as the virtual network's address space, those public IPs would not be routable from the Internet and are still private from an accessibility standpoint.
- You can connect two virtual networks by using virtual network peering. Once any two virtual networks peer, resources in one virtual network can connect to resources in other virtual networks.
- Peered virtual networks can be in the same or different regions.

By default, Azure learns routes from on-premises over ExpressRoute, routes for all peered virtual networks, and a default route to the Internet. Azure also allows customers to override these system routes with user-defined routes. You can assign user-defined routes at the subnet level.

Network topology is a critical element of enterprise-scale architecture because it defines how applications can communicate with each other. This section explores topology approaches for Azure enterprise deployments. There are three core approaches: Azure-only virtual networks, topologies based on the hub-and-spoke model, and topologies based on Azure virtual WAN.

Hub-and-spoke network topology

A hub-and-spoke network topology isolates workload while sharing services, such as identity, connectivity, and security. The hub virtual network, as the name suggests, is a central point of connectivity. Spoke virtual networks connect to the hub virtual network using virtual network peering or global virtual network peering. Typically, you would deploy network security gear, such as Azure Firewall or third-party firewall appliances in the hub. Shared services are typically deployed in the hub or as a separate spoke peered with the hub. In contrast, you would deploy individual production and non-production workloads as spoke virtual networks.

You can provision ExpressRoute gateway in the gateway subnet. Once you add an ExpressRoute gateway in the gateway subnet, you cannot deploy anything else in the gateway subnet.

In a hub-and-spoke topology, all the spoke-to-spoke communication transits through the hub. You also need to set your firewall (Azure Firewall or NVAs) as the next hop in your user-defined routes (UDR) attached to subnets in spoke virtual networks. With the UDR, you override system routes that would otherwise send all the traffic destined for an on-premises network through the gateway. With the UDR, you would set your virtual appliance as a next-hop address.

Figure 5-1 shows the implementation of the hub-and-spoke network topology. The spoke virtual networks typically host a management subnet and at least a workload subnet each. The hub virtual network hosts core networking and security solutions in subnets dedicated for gateway, management, firewalls, Active Directory, etc. You should use virtual network peering between hub-and-spoke virtual networks and express route circuit private peering connecting to an on-premises gateway and an Express Route gateway in the hub virtual network.

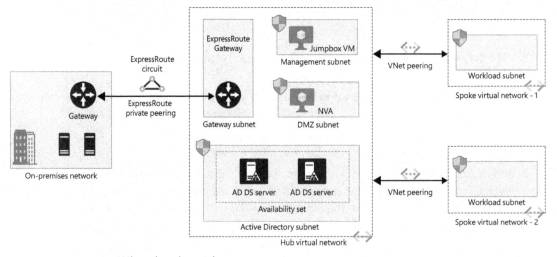

FIGURE 5-1 Hub-and-spoke topology

Following are the design considerations for the hub-and-spoke topology:

- Implementing a hub-and-spoke topology in Azure centralizes standard services, including connections to on-premises networks and firewalls.

- The hub virtual network acts as a central point of connectivity and hosts shared services used by workloads hosted in spoke virtual networks.

- Enterprises typically use a hub-and-spoke configuration.

- Spoke virtual networks isolate workloads; spoke-to-spoke communication goes through a hub; and a centralized firewall has visibility and can control traffic flow. Each workload can include multiple tiers.

- Azure lets you provision hub-and-spoke virtual networks in the same or different resource groups or subscriptions. You can also have spoke virtual networks in different subscriptions from that of the hub. Moreover, the subscriptions can be either associated with the same or different Azure Active Directory (Azure AD) tenants.

- This topology allows for decentralized management of each workload while sharing services maintained in the hub network.

You can use a virtual WAN to meet large-scale, multi-site interconnectivity requirements. Because a virtual WAN is a Microsoft-managed service, it reduces overall network complexity and modernizes your organization's network.

Use a traditional Azure network topology if these are your requirements:

- You intend to deploy resources across multiple Azure regions.

- You have a low number of branch locations per region.

- You need fewer than 30 IPSec tunnels.

- You require full control.

- You need granularity for configuring your Azure network.

Azure Virtual WAN topology

Azure Virtual WAN is a Microsoft-managed networking solution that provides end-to-end global transit connectivity. Virtual WAN hubs eliminate the need to configure network connectivity manually. For example, with Virtual WAN hubs, you are not required to configure user-defined routing (UDR) or network virtual appliances (NVAs) for hub-and-spoke connectivity. You can use NVAs with a virtual WAN if you require NVAs in your architecture.

Following are the design considerations for Azure Virtual WAN:

- Azure Virtual WAN simplifies end-to-end network connectivity in Azure and cross-premises by creating a hub-and-spoke network architecture with a Microsoft-managed

hub. The architecture can span multiple Azure regions and multiple on-premises locations (any-to-any connectivity) out of the box, as shown in Figure 5-2. This diagram
shows the global transit network with Azure Virtual WAN.

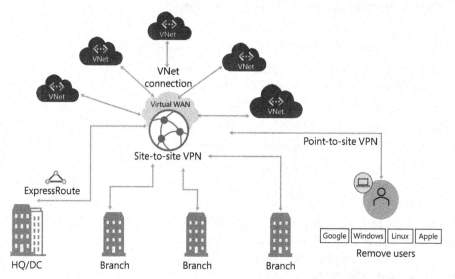

FIGURE 5-2 Global transit network with Azure Virtual WAN

- Virtual WAN hub virtual networks are locked down. You cannot deploy any resources
  in the WAN hub virtual network, except virtual network gateways (point-to-site VPN,
  site-to-site VPN, or Azure ExpressRoute); Azure Firewall through Firewall Manager; and
  route tables.

Azure Virtual WAN transitive connectivity supports the following:

- Virtual network to branch
- Branch to virtual network
- Branch to branch
- Virtual network to virtual network (same region and across regions)
- With Virtual WAN, you get an increased limit of prefixes advertised from Azure to
  on-premises via ExpressRoute private peering. The limit changes from 200 to 10,000
  prefixes per virtual WAN hub. The limit of 10,000 prefixes includes prefixes advertised
  over site-to-site VPN and point-to-site VPN as well.
- Microsoft recently announced the general availability (GA) for virtual WAN hub-to-
  hub connectivity and network-to-network transitive connectivity (within and across
  regions) features.
- Because of the router in every virtual hub, Azure enables transit connectivity
  between the virtual networks in a standard virtual WAN. Every virtual hub router
  supports up to 50 Gbps aggregate throughput.
- Virtual WAN integrates with a variety of SD-WAN providers.

- You must use ExpressRoute circuits with the premium add-on, and they should be from an ExpressRoute Global Reach location.

- You can scale VPN gateways in Virtual WAN up to 20 Gbps and 20,000 connections per virtual hub.

- Azure Firewall Manager allows the deployment of Azure Firewall in the virtual WAN hub.

Virtual WAN is a recommended solution for new global network deployments in Azure when you need global transit connectivity across multiple Azure regions and various on-premises locations. Figure 5-3 shows an example of global deployment with datacenters spread across Europe and the United States and many branch offices across regions. The environment is connected globally via a virtual WAN and ExpressRoute Global Reach.

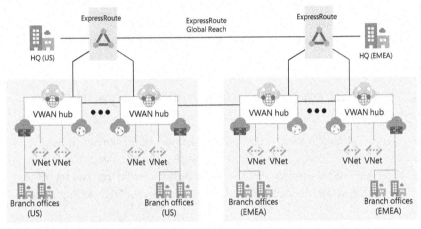

FIGURE 5-3 Global connectivity using a virtual WAN and ExpressRoute global reach

The recommended solution is to use Virtual WAN as a global connectivity resource. You can use one or many virtual WAN hubs per Azure region to connect multiple landing zones across Azure regions via local virtual WAN hubs.

Following are a few design recommendations that you should follow while implementing virtual WAN solutions:

- Connect virtual WAN hubs with on-premises datacenters using ExpressRoute.

- Deploy required shared services such as DNS or Active Directory domain controllers in a dedicated landing zone. Note that you cannot deploy such shared resources in the virtual WAN hub virtual network.

- You can connect branches and remote locations to the nearest virtual WAN hub using site-to-site VPN or branch connectivity to a virtual WAN through one of the SD-WAN partner solutions.

- You can connect users to the virtual WAN hub through a point-to-site VPN.

- We recommend that you follow the "traffic within Azure should stay in Azure" principle. With this solution, communication between Azure resources across regions occurs over the Microsoft backbone network.

- Azure Firewall in a virtual WAN hub helps with east-west and south-north traffic protection.

- Suppose you require third-party network virtual appliances for east-west or south-north traffic protection and filtering. In that case, you could choose to deploy the network virtual appliances in a separate virtual network, such as a shared virtual network. You can connect it to the regional virtual WAN hub and the landing zones that need access to NVAs.

- You do not need to build a transit network on top of an Azure Virtual WAN. The virtual WAN solution itself satisfies transitive network topology requirements. It would be redundant and increase complexity.

- Do not use existing on-premises networks such as multiprotocol label switching (MPLS) to connect Azure resources across Azure regions because Azure networking technologies support Azure resources' interconnection across regions through the Microsoft backbone.

Recommend a solution for network addressing and name resolution

You can use Azure Virtual Networks to provision and manage virtual private networks in Azure. Each Azure virtual network you create has its own CIDR block and can be linked to other virtual networks and on-premises networks if CIDR blocks do not overlap. You can segment the virtual network into subnets as needed. You can also configure your DNS setting for each virtual network.

You must provide a private IP address space using private (RFC 1918) addresses or public address space that your organization owns while provisioning an Azure virtual network. Azure assigns a private IP address to resources from the address space you assign to your virtual network. For example, when you deploy a VM in an Azure virtual network with an address space of 10.0.0.0/24, Azure assigns a VM's virtual network interface a private IP such as 10.0.0.4.

You can segment your virtual network into subnets so that you can allocate a portion of the virtual network's address space to each of those subnets. You can secure resources in subnets by associating network security groups to subnets and adding inbound and outbound NSG rules to allow or deny traffic as per your requirement.

Following are the design considerations for network addressing and name resolution:

Network addressing:
- Do not use overlapping IP address space across on-premises and Azure regions.

- You can add additional address spaces after you create a virtual network. However, when you are using virtual network peering, the process requires an outage. You are required to delete and re-create virtual network peering.

- Azure reserves five IP addresses for each subnet. You must factor in those addresses when you are sizing virtual networks and encompassed subnets.

- Azure allows you to delegate subnets to certain services to inject instances of such a service within that subnet.

Name resolution:

- Start with IP addresses from the address allocation for private networks (RFC 1918) for all your virtual network address spaces.
- Ensure that you are using non-overlapping IP address spaces across Azure regions and on-premises locations well in advance.
- In case you have limited availability of private IP addresses (RFC 1918), consider using IPv6.
- Avoid creating unnecessarily large virtual networks (for example, 10.1.0.0/16) to use available IP address spaces efficiently.
- Create virtual networks after planning the required address space and considering near-future expansion.
- Avoid using random public IP addresses for virtual networks unless those public IP addresses are owned by your organization and are not in use elsewhere on the network.
- The Domain Name System, or DNS, translates readable and easily memorable domain names or service names into its IP addresses. Azure DNS is a service for DNS domains that provides name resolution using the Microsoft Azure infrastructure.
- Resources that are deployed in virtual networks use one of the two methods to resolve domain names to internal IP addresses:
- Azure-provided name resolution (also includes Azure DNS private zones)
- Name resolution that uses a DNS server (which might forward queries to the Azure-provided DNS servers)

Azure-provided name resolution

Azure-provided name resolution provides only necessary authoritative DNS capabilities. If you use this option, Azure manages the DNS zone names and automatically records them, and you do not control the DNS zone names or the lifecycle of DNS records. If you need a fully featured DNS solution for your virtual networks, you must use Azure DNS private zones or customer-managed DNS servers.

Azure DNS supports private DNS zones in addition to supporting Internet-facing DNS domains. Azure Private DNS provides a reliable, secure DNS service to manage and resolve domain names in a virtual network without adding a custom DNS solution. By using private DNS zones, you can also use custom domain names rather than the Azure-provided names that are available by default.

You can also configure zone names with a split-horizon view, which allows a private and a public DNS zone to share the same name. To resolve DNS records of a private DNS zone from your virtual network, you must link a virtual network with that private DNS zone. Each linked virtual network can resolve all DNS records published in the private zone. You can also enable auto-registration on a virtual network link. When you enable auto-registration on a virtual network link, Azure registers VMs' DNS records on that virtual network in the private zone. When auto-registration is enabled, Azure DNS updates the zone records whenever a VM is created, changes its IP address, or is deleted.

Using your own DNS server

Domain Name System (DNS) is of the essential services in enterprise architecture. You can use your existing investments in DNS, or you can use cloud adoption as an opportunity to modernize your internal DNS infrastructure and use native Azure capabilities.

Typically, customers choose to use custom DNS servers when your name resolution needs to go beyond out-of-the-box features. Custom DNS servers within a virtual network can forward DNS queries to the Azure recursive resolvers to resolve hostnames within that virtual network. For example, a domain controller (DC) running in Azure or on-premises can respond to DNS queries for its domains and forward all other Azure queries. Forwarding queries allows VMs to see both your on-premises resources (via the DC) and Azure-provided hostnames (via the forwarder). Azure provides access to the recursive resolvers via the virtual IP 168.63.129.16.

The type of name resolution you use depends on how your resources need to communicate with each other. Below are the design considerations for a custom DNS:

- You might have a requirement to use your existing DNS solutions across both on-premises and Azure.
- You can only link just one private DNS zones to a virtual network with auto-registration enabled.
- You can link up to 1,000 private DNS zones to a virtual network without auto-registration enabled.
- You can use a DNS resolver along with Azure Private DNS for cross-premises name resolution.

Following are some design recommendations for DNS:

- If all you need is name resolution in Azure, then you can use Azure Private DNS. You can create a delegated zone for name resolution.
- If you need name resolution across Azure and on-premises, you can use the existing DNS solution (for example, Active Directory-integrated DNS) deployed on Azure VMs (two VMs for high availability). You would then configure DNS settings in virtual networks to use those custom DNS servers.
- Particular workloads such as OpenShift that require and deploy their own DNS should use their preferred DNS solution.
- You can enable auto-registration for Azure DNS to automatically manage the DNS records' lifecycle within a virtual network.
- Use a DNS on an Azure VM as a resolver for cross-premises DNS resolution with Azure Private DNS.

- Create the Azure Private DNS zone within a global connectivity subscription. You can create other Azure Private DNS zones (for example, `privatelink.database.windows.net` or `privatelink.blob.core.windows.net` for Azure Private Link) as needed.

Recommend a solution for network provisioning

Azure Virtual Network enables many Azure resources, such as Azure VMs, to securely communicate with each other, the Internet, and on-premises networks. All resources in an Azure virtual network can, by default, communicate outbound to the Internet. To communicate inbound from the Internet with a resource, you can provide a public IP address or a public Load Balancer.

When you plan to create your Azure landing zone, planning for virtual networks is usually in the first few steps. Network creation can be a daunting task in the physical world, but it is very straightforward in Azure. You can do it manually using various options such as the Azure portal, PowerShell, and CLI. However, the best practice is to use Infrastructure as Code (ARM templates or Terraform templates) to automate the provisioning process.

An ARM template is a JSON file that defines your project's Infrastructure as Code (IaC). The template uses declarative syntax, which lets you state what you intend to deploy without writing the sequence of programming commands to create it.

To create a `Microsoft.Network/virtualNetworks` resource, add the JSON shown in Listing 5-1 to the resources section of your template.

LISTING 5-1 ARM template for a virtual network

```
{
 "name": "string",
 "type": "Microsoft.Network/virtualNetworks",
 "apiVersion": "2020-06-01",
 "location": "string",
 "tags": {},
 "properties": {
  "addressSpace": {
   "addressPrefixes": [
    "string"
   ]
  },
  "dhcpOptions": {
   "dnsServers": [
    "string"
   ]
  },
  "subnets": [
   {
    "id": "string",
    "properties": {
     "addressPrefix": "string",
     "addressPrefixes": [
      "string"
     ],
```

```
      "networkSecurityGroup": {
       "id": "string",
       "location": "string",
       "tags": {},
       "properties": {
        "securityRules": [
         {
          "id": "string",
          "properties": {
           "description": "string",
           "protocol": "string",
           "sourcePortRange": "string",
           "destinationPortRange": "string",
           "sourceAddressPrefix": "string",
           "sourceAddressPrefixes": [
            "string"
           ],
           "sourceApplicationSecurityGroups": [
            {
             "id": "string",
             "location": "string",
             "tags": {},
             "properties": {}
            }
           ],
           "destinationAddressPrefix": "string",
           "destinationAddressPrefixes": [
            "string"
           ],
           "destinationApplicationSecurityGroups": [
            {
             "id": "string",
             "location": "string",
             "tags": {},
             "properties": {}
            }
           ],
           "sourcePortRanges": [
            "string"
           ],
           "destinationPortRanges": [
            "string"
           ],
           "access": "string",
           "priority": "integer",
           "direction": "string"
          },
          "name": "string"
         }
        ]
       }
      },
      "routeTable": {
       "id": "string",
       "location": "string",
```

```
   "tags": {},
   "properties": {
    "routes": [
     {
      "id": "string",
      "properties": {
       "addressPrefix": "string",
       "nextHopType": "string",
       "nextHopIpAddress": "string"
      },
      "name": "string"
     }
    ],
    "disableBgpRoutePropagation": "boolean"
   }
  },
  "natGateway": {
   "id": "string"
  },
  "serviceEndpoints": [
   {
    "service": "string",
    "locations": [
     "string"
    ]
   }
  ],
  "serviceEndpointPolicies": [
   {
    "id": "string",
    "location": "string",
    "tags": {},
    "properties": {
     "serviceEndpointPolicyDefinitions": [
      {
       "id": "string",
       "properties": {
        "description": "string",
        "service": "string",
        "serviceResources": [
         "string"
        ]
       },
       "name": "string"
      }
     ]
    }
   }
  ],
  "ipAllocations": [
   {
    "id": "string"
   }
  ],
```

```
      "delegations": [
       {
        "id": "string",
        "properties": {
         "serviceName": "string"
        },
        "name": "string"
       }
      ],
      "privateEndpointNetworkPolicies": "string",
      "privateLinkServiceNetworkPolicies": "string"
     },
     "name": "string"
    }
   ],
   "virtualNetworkPeerings": [
    {
     "id": "string",
     "properties": {
      "allowVirtualNetworkAccess": "boolean",
      "allowForwardedTraffic": "boolean",
      "allowGatewayTransit": "boolean",
      "useRemoteGateways": "boolean",
      "remoteVirtualNetwork": {
       "id": "string"
      },
      "remoteAddressSpace": {
       "addressPrefixes": [
        "string"
       ]
      },
      "remoteBgpCommunities": {
       "virtualNetworkCommunity": "string"
      },
      "peeringState": "string"
     },
     "name": "string"
    }
   ],
   "enableDdosProtection": "boolean",
   "enableVmProtection": "boolean",
   "ddosProtectionPlan": {
    "id": "string"
   },
   "bgpCommunities": {
    "virtualNetworkCommunity": "string"
   },
   "ipAllocations": [
    {
     "id": "string"
    }
   ]
  },
  "resources": []
}
```

Recommend a solution for network security

You can implement network security solutions using appliances on-premises, network virtual appliances (NVAs) running in the cloud, or a native offering. Azure provides various native network security services such as Azure Firewall, Azure Web Application Firewall (WAF), and Azure Front Door. These are fully managed platform services (PaaS). You can also use third-party network virtual appliances in the following situations:

- Your organization prefers to use network virtual appliances.
- Native services do not satisfy your organization's specific requirements.

Network virtual appliances (NVAs)

Third-party networking offerings play a critical role in Azure, allowing you to use brands and solutions you already know, trust, and have the skills to manage. Most third-party networking offerings are available as network virtual appliances in the Azure marketplace. These NVAs offer a diverse set of capabilities such as firewalls, WAN optimizers, application delivery controllers, routers, load balancers, proxies, and more. These third-party capabilities enable many hybrid solutions.

A virtual network appliance is often a full Linux VM image consisting of a Linux kernel and includes user-level applications and services.

Figure 5-4 shows an example of a reference architecture that uses a demilitarized zone (DMZ) as a perimeter network between on-premises and Azure, using network virtual appliances (NVAs).

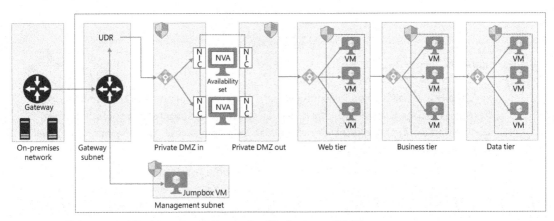

FIGURE 5-4 Reference architecture using NVAs as a demilitarized zone (DMZ)

Azure Firewall

Azure provides a cloud-native network security service (known as Azure Firewall) that is highly available by design. It auto-scales with usage, and you pay as you use it. Microsoft provides support for Azure Firewall with a published SLA. It fits into the DevOps model for deployment and uses cloud-native monitoring tools. Azure Firewall is a managed, stateful firewall as a service with built-in high availability and unrestricted cloud scalability (see Figure 5-5).

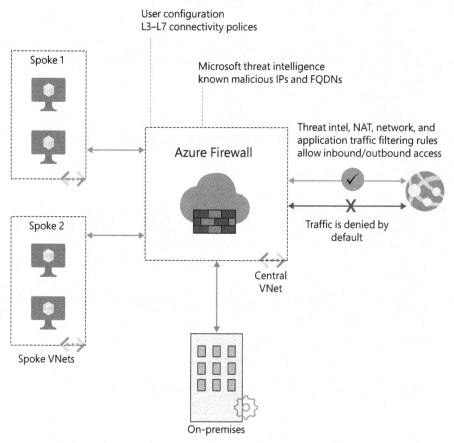

FIGURE 5-5 Azure Firewall

Azure Firewall allows you to centrally create, enforce, and log network connectivity policies across Azure virtual networks. Azure Firewall uses a static outbound public IP address to identify traffic originating from your virtual network. You can use Azure Monitor for firewall logs, metrics, and log analytics.

The Azure Firewall feature set has improved over time, and it provides the following advantages as a cloud-native managed service when compared with network virtual appliances (NVAs):

- Offers easy DevOps integration; quickly deployed using Infrastructure as Code (IaC), PowerShell, CLI, or REST.

- Built-in high availability with cloud-scale.
- Zero-maintenance service model.
- Unique Azure specialization with features such as service tags and FQDN tags.
- Lower total cost of ownership (TCO).

Organizations have diverse security needs. As mentioned earlier, third-party offerings often play a critical role in Azure. You can find most next-generation firewalls as network virtual appliances (NVA) on Azure Marketplace. NVAs typically provide a richer next-generation feature set that is a must-have for some organizations.

Table 5-3 provides a feature comparison between Azure Firewall and typical network virtual appliances:

TABLE 5-3 Azure Firewall and NVA feature comparison

Feature	Azure Firewall	Typical NVA
FQDN filtering and SSL Termination.	Yes	Yes
Inbound/outbound traffic filtering and 5-tuple rules (source IP, destination IP, source port, destination port, and protocol).	Yes	Yes
Network address translation (secure network address translation [SNAT] and destination network address translation [DNAT]).	Yes	Yes
Traffic filtering based on thread intelligence feed to identify high-risk sources/destinations.	Yes	Yes
Full logging, including SIEM integrations.	Yes	Yes
Built-in high availability with unrestricted cloud scalability.	Yes	Not all vendors provide this; some offer VM-based options.
Azure service tags and FQDN tags for easy policy management.	Yes	No
Integrated monitoring and management; zero maintenance.	Yes	No
Easy DevOps integration with Azure REST/PS/CLI/ARM/Terraform.	All	ARM and Terraform
SSL termination with deep packet inspection (DPI) to identify known threats.	Roadmap	Yes
Traffic filtering rules by target URI (full path, including SSL termination).	Roadmap	Yes
Central management.	Azure Firewall Manager and third-party solutions	Vendor-specific options.
Application and user-aware traffic filtering rules.	Roadmap	Yes

Feature	Azure Firewall	Typical NVA
IPSEC and SSL VPN gateway.	Azure VPN Gateway	Yes
Advanced, next-generation firewall; features for example sandboxing.	No	Yes

Azure Private Link

Azure Private Link is a service that lets you use a private endpoint in your network to access Azure platform services (such as an Azure Storage Account, Azure SQL Database, Cosmos DB, and so on) and Azure-hosted and customer-owned or partner services. With Azure Private Link, traffic between your Azure virtual network and such services travels over Microsoft's backbone network instead of the Internet (see Figure 5-6). Hence, you don't have to consume such services over the public Internet. Conversely, you can create your own private link service in your virtual network and deliver it to your customers to consume.

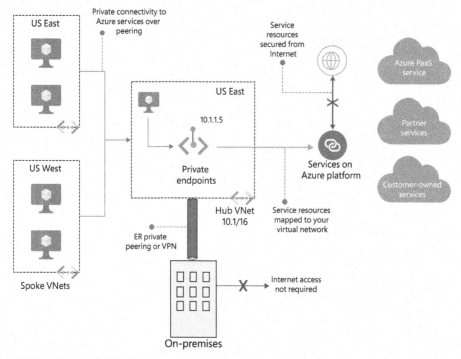

FIGURE 5-6 Azure Private Link

Application Gateway

Application Gateway is an application layer load balancer (OSI Layer 7) that allows you to manage traffic to your web applications. Azure load balancers operate at the transport layer (OSI layer 4) and route traffic based on IP address, protocol, and port to a destination IP address and port. Azure application gateway uses host-based bindings.

Application Gateway makes routing decisions based on URI path or host headers. For example, let's consider a scenario in which you need to route traffic based on the incoming URL. If the /images text appears in the incoming URL, you can route traffic to a specific set of servers (known as a pool) that are configured for images. If the /video text appears in the URL, the gateway routes traffic to another pool that is optimized for videos. This is known as application layer (OSI layer 7) load balancing. See Figure 5-7.

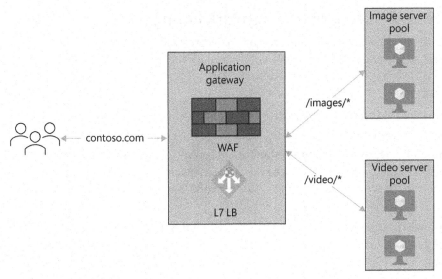

FIGURE 5-7 Application gateway

Web Application Firewall (WAF)

Web Application Firewall (WAF) provides centralized protection of your web applications from common exploits and vulnerabilities.

Increasingly, modern attackers are targeting web applications with malicious attacks that exploit commonly known vulnerabilities, such as SQL injection attacks and cross-site scripting attacks. Preventing such attacks in application code can sometimes be challenging and can require rigorous maintenance, patching, and monitoring at many of the application's layers. A centralized web application firewall helps make such security management much more straightforward and assures protection against such threats.

With a WAF solution in place, you can react to a security threat faster by remediating a known vulnerability centrally versus remediating multiple individual web applications. In Azure, you can easily convert existing application gateways to a Web Application Firewall–enabled application gateway.

Azure allows you to enable WAF features with Application Gateway, Azure Front Door, and Azure Content Delivery Network (CDN) service. WAF on Azure CDN is currently under public preview.

Recommend a solution for network connectivity

Azure provides various solutions for network connectivity such as virtual networks, ExpressRoute, VPN gateways, virtual WANs, virtual network NAT gateways, and Azure Bastion.

Virtual network

Azure VM is the basic building block for your private network in Azure. You can use a virtual network in the following ways:

- **Communicate between Azure resources** When you deploy VMs and other Azure resources such as Azure App Service environments, Azure Kubernetes Service (AKS), and Azure VM scale sets in an Azure virtual network, these resources can communicate using a virtual network connection.

- **Communicate between each other** When you connect two or more virtual networks using virtual network peering, it enables resources in either virtual network to communicate with each other. When two virtual networks you want to connect are in two different Azure regions, you can peer them using global virtual network peering to allow communication between them.

- **Communicate to the Internet** By default, all resources in each virtual network can communicate outbound to the Internet. When you assign a public IP or add an available load balancer in front of your VMs, you can manage your inbound communication as well.

- **Communicate with on-premises networks** You can connect your on-premises network to an Azure virtual network with VPN or Express Route connections.

EXAM TIP

Virtual network peering is the most secure and cost-efficient solution for establishing low-latency connectivity between Azure VMs deployed in different virtual networks in the same or different regions. The traffic between Azure VMs in the peered network remains in the Microsoft backbone infrastructure.

Azure Bastion

Azure Bastion is a native platform (PaaS) service that provides secure RDP/SSH connectivity to your VMs. With Bastion, you don't have to expose your VMs over the Internet by attaching a public IP and opening ports for RDP/SSH access. Users will access Bastion using browsers over the Internet using the SSL protocol and will be able to perform a remote login securely (see Figure 5-8).

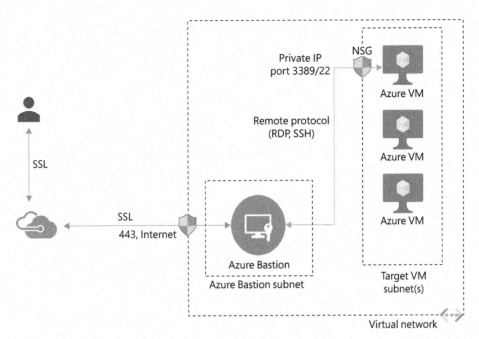

FIGURE 5-8 Azure Bastion

ExpressRoute

Most enterprise customers have hybrid connectivity needs. ExpressRoute service enables extensions of on-premises networks into Azure over a private connection that is facilitated by a connectivity provider. With ExpressRoute, you can expect better reliability and higher through-put with lower and predictable latencies than with typical connections over the Internet (see Figure 5-9).

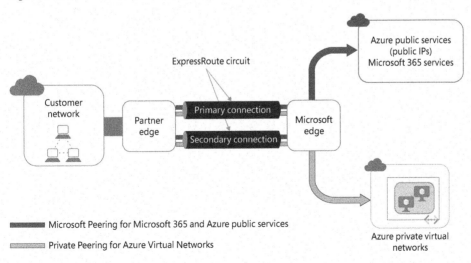

FIGURE 5-9 ExpressRoute

There are two types of connectivity available with ExpressRoute: private peering and Microsoft peering: With ExpressRoute Private Peering, you enable private connectivity between your Azure virtual network and the on-premises network. With Microsoft peering, you enable accessing Microsoft public endpoints from your on-premises network over a secure connection and not over the public Internet.

Leveraging your existing network provider that is already part of the ExpressRoute partner ecosystem can help reduce the time to get extensive bandwidth connections to Microsoft.

Microsoft also offers the ExpressRoute Direct service, which allows you to directly connect your on-premises network to the Microsoft backbone. ExpressRoute Direct offers two different line-rate options: dual 10 Gbps or 100 Gbps.

Azure VPN Gateway

Azure VPN Gateway is another networking service that helps you create encrypted cross-premises connections from your virtual network to on-premises locations or create encrypted connections between various virtual networks. There are different VPN Gateway connections available, such as site-to-site, point-to-site, or virtual network–to–virtual network.

Figure 5-10 depicts two site-to-site VPN connections from on-premises sites to the same Azure virtual network.

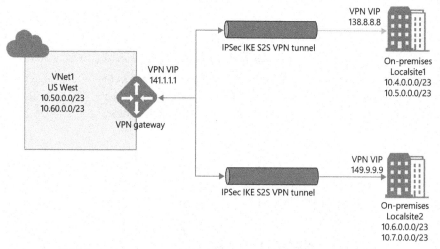

FIGURE 5-10 VPN Gateway

Azure Virtual WAN

Microsoft provides an optimized branch to the Azure virtual network connectivity service known as an Azure Virtual WAN. Azure regions act as hubs you can choose to connect your branches. You can leverage Microsoft's backbone to connect branches and branch-to-VM connectivity. Azure Virtual WAN consolidates many Azure Cloud connectivity solutions, such as site-to-site VPN, ExpressRoute, and point-to-site user VPN into a unified virtual WAN solution. You can establish connectivity to Azure virtual networks by using virtual network connections.

Virtual network NAT gateway

Virtual Network NAT (network address translation) is a service that simplifies outbound-only Internet connectivity for virtual networks. Virtual network NAT is a new service that Microsoft offers, which enables outbound connectivity even when you don't have a load balancer or public IP directly attached to your VMs. When you configure NAT on a subnet with this service, your partners see traffic from your specified static public IP addresses for your outbound connectivity (see Figure 5-11).

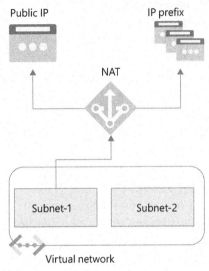

FIGURE 5-11 Virtual network NAT gateway

Service endpoints

With service endpoints, traffic from your virtual network to specific Azure PaaS services always remains on the Microsoft Azure backbone network. Virtual Network service endpoints extend your virtual network's identity to the Azure services, such as an Azure Storage Account, over a direct connection. Service Endpoints also allow you to secure your critical Azure service resources to only your virtual networks.

Recommend a solution for automating network management

Network management automation means automating the planning, deployment, operations, and optimization of network resources. At a basic level, network management automation solutions transform manual processes performed in each stage of the network lifecycle with automation solutions repeatably and reliably.

The Azure platform provides you with multiple options such as Azure DevOps, ARM templates, Azure Automation, GitHub Actions, or other CI/CD solutions to automate infrastructure deployments.

Azure Automation is a cloud-based automation platform service that supports consistent management across your Azure and non-Azure environments. Azure Automation provides complete control during the deployment and operation of resources.

Azure Automation also offers a Desired State Configuration (DSC) service that allows you to create definitions for your configuration. DSC ensures that the required configuration is applied and that the resources stay consistent. Azure Automation DSC can run on both Windows and Linux platforms.

You can use Azure Network Watcher tools to monitor, diagnose, manage metrics, alerts, and logs for resources in an Azure virtual network. By design, Azure Network monitors and repairs the network health of IaaS (Infrastructure as a Service) products, including VMs, virtual networks, application gateways, and load balancers.

For Network Watcher, an endpoint can be a virtual machine, a fully qualified domain name (FQDN), a uniform resource identifier (URI), or any IPv4 IP address.

This tool's connection monitor capability can monitor communication at a regular interval and let you observe reachability, latency, and network topology changes between the VM and the endpoint.

If an endpoint becomes unreachable, you can use the connection troubleshooter tool to figure out the reason. This tool is useful to triage typical issues, such as a DNS name resolution problem, high CPU utilization, high memory utilization, Guest OS firewall blocking traffic, mis-configured or missing routes, NSG rules blocking traffic, no servers listening on designated ports and inability to open a socket at specified source port.

With the connection monitor tool, you also get the minimum, average, and maximum latency observed for a connection over time. If you want to test a connection point in time and then monitor it over time, you should use Network Watcher.

Also, Microsoft offers the Network Performance Monitor (NPM) tool, a cloud-based hybrid network monitoring solution that helps you monitor network performance between various points in your network infrastructure and Azure ExpressRoute. NPM is good at detecting network issues such as traffic blackholing, routing errors, and issues that conventional network monitoring methods cannot detect.

As you add more and more Azure resources to your network, it can become very challenging to understand how various resources relate to each other. Network Watcher's topology capability enables you to generate a visual diagram of the resources in a virtual network and its relationships.

Network security groups (NSGs) are the network access control lists that let you allow or deny specific inbound or outbound traffic to a network interface or subnet. The NSG flow log capability in Network Watcher allows you to view the NSG logs that show the source IP, destination IP, port, protocol, and whether traffic was allowed or denied by an NSG. This comes in handy while troubleshooting because with NSG flow logs, you can analyze these entries using multiple tools, such as PowerBI and Traffic Analytics. Traffic Analytics provides rich visualizations of data written to NSG flow logs.

Recommend a solution for load balancing and traffic routing

In networking, the load balancing service is significant for any application architecture related to traffic distribution across multiple computing resources. You can use load balancing to make workloads redundant and highly available. Load balancing helps optimize resource use, maximize throughput, minimize response time, and avoid overloading any single resource.

Azure provides multiple services for managing how to distribute and load balance your network traffic. Azure allows you to use these load-balancing and traffic-routing services individually or together. Depending on your use cases, you can build optimal solutions by combining these services. Following are the primary load-balancing services currently available in Azure:

- **Azure Front Door** Azure Front Door is an application delivery network service that provides global load balancing and site acceleration for web applications. Azure Front Door service lets you manage global routing for your web traffic by optimizing the best performance and instant global failover. It also offers layer 7 capabilities for your applications, such as SSL offloading, path-based routing, fast failover, and caching to improve your applications' performance and high availability.

- **Traffic Manager** Traffic Manager is a DNS-based traffic load balancer that allows you to distribute traffic optimally to services across global Azure regions. Because Traffic Manager is a DNS-based load-balancing service, it works at the domain level.

- **Application Gateway** Microsoft Application Gateway offers several layer 7 load-balancing capabilities. For example, it lets you optimize web farm productivity by offloading SSL termination at the gateway.

- **Azure Load Balancer** This is a high-performance, ultra-low-latency layer for load-balancing services (inbound and outbound) for all UDP and TCP protocols. The Azure load balancer service is a highly scalable service that can handle millions of requests per second. Azure Load Balancer supports zone redundancy, ensuring high availability across Availability Zones.

However, every application has unique requirements, so that you can refer to the decision tree in Figure 5-12 as a starting point:

EXAM TIP

The AZ-304 exam typically includes one or more scenario questions to test this skill. The following tips should help arrive at your recommendations:

- Include Azure Front Door or Traffic Manager in your recommendation in case the requirement is a multi-region deployment.
- Determine which load-balancing option is more appropriate when SSL/TLS offloading, Web Application Firewall, cookie-based session affinity, and URL-path-based routing are the requirements.
- You might need more than one traffic routing or load-balancing service in your final design, such as Traffic Manager + Azure Load Balancer or Azure Front Door + Application Gateway. Refer to the decision tree in Figure 5-13 for various options based on your requirements.

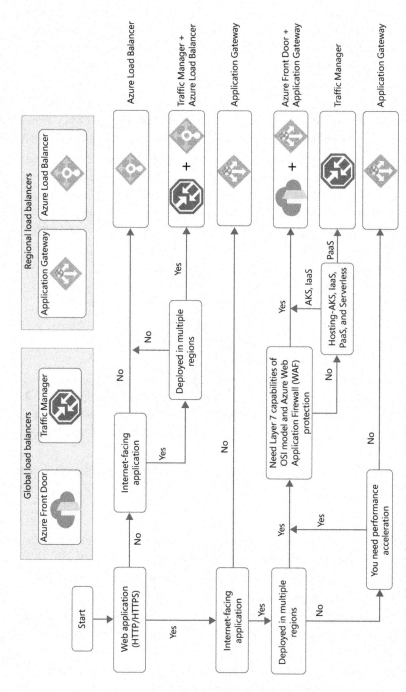

FIGURE 5-12 Decision tree for load balancing options in Azure

Skill 5.3: Design an application architecture

This domain objective focuses on key Azure services that are intended to design cloud-native applications. As an Azure Solutions Architect, you are expected to have insights into these services and understand why you would choose one over the other and how to select the appropriate service for a given use case.

> **This skill covers how to:**
> - Recommend a microservices architecture
> - Recommend an orchestration solution for deployment and maintenance of applications
> - Recommend a solution for API integration

Recommend a microservices architecture

One of the critical deciding factors for many organizations when considering moving to cloud architecture is the speed and agility for their enterprise-grade, mission-critical applications. With that in mind, you would need to move away from the traditional N-tier way of architecting applications and adapt to a modern architecture approach specifically designed for cloud-platforms.

The microservices architecture helps you gain the best-of-class benefits for cloud-based applications that are difficult to achieve with a traditional N-tier architecture style or a legacy monolithic approach. Microservices are self-contained and loosely coupled services, representing an end-to-end domain or business capability, and embrace development, deployment, and scale autonomy. When developing microservices-based applications on the cloud, you see the following key benefits:

- **Cost-efficient scaling**   Microservices allow you to scale part of the application instead of scaling the entire application.
- **Agility**   With a microservice, you can accelerate process efficiency and time to market. You can become more agile to analyze and fix defects faster and add new features to the application rapidly.
- **Fault isolation**   Microservices empower you to deploy and test application components independently without impacting or redeploying the entire application. This further increases the fault isolation between application components. If one service becomes unavailable, the entire application does not encounter a cascading effect—provided that the other components are designed to handle faults gracefully.

In the microservices architecture, you might face complexity in deployment, testing, and maintainability of the various subsystems when building large and complex applications. Additionally, because the microservices are loosely coupled, you need to think wisely about microservices interservice communication. You can substantially simplify these challenges and complexities by using specific Azure services designed for microservices-based architectures.

In the following sections, you will learn the microservices scenarios and appropriate Azure services to address them.

Communication between microservices

Microservices embrace data sovereignty and should not directly access the data store outside its domain boundary. In this case, you would need a way for microservices to communicate with other microservices. Real-time communication is usually done by REST API calls. In contrast, you would need some robust event and messaging services to orchestrate workflows between different microservices in the asynchronous communication method.

Azure provides several different asynchronous messaging services.

- **Event Grid**   Event Grid allows events to be published in real-time instead of using the standard message polling mechanism. In this scenario, the event subscribers (individual microservices) are automatically notified about the event. In the events you have leeway to define custom data relevant to the business domain. The Event Grid provides an ability to apply filters to subscriptions so that only relevant events are forwarded to registered subscribers or microservices. As the Event Grid service is a managed service, it seamlessly integrates with almost all Azure services. It provides a high SLA and automatically handles data integrity, and it retries failed deliveries.

- **Event Hubs**   Event Hubs is a big-data pipeline solution design for a massive real-time stream of event data from various event producers such as IoT devices and GPS systems. Unlike Event Grid, Event Hubs act as an "event ingestor" that accepts and stores event data and makes that event data available for faster retrieval.

- **Service Bus**   Azure Service Bus offers messaging capability at an enterprise scale, enabling the loosely coupled microservices to connect asynchronously and scale independently. Service Bus provides enterprise messaging capabilities, including queuing, publish/subscribe, and an advanced integration patterns model for cloud-native applications that require advanced queuing capabilities such as first-in-first-out (FIFO), batching/sessions, transactions, dead-lettering, temporal control, routing and filtering, and duplicate detection. Unlike Event Grid and Event Hubs, Service Bus works with messages, not events, and lets the receiver decide when to consume the message.

- **Storage Queue**   Storage Queue, which is part of the native Azure Storage infrastructure, provides a similar queuing capability as a Service bus but with a limited set of features.

EXAM TIP

You are very likely to get multiple-choice questions for the Azure messaging services discussed in the previous sections. To learn more about the specific scenarios that could help you choose the best fit, see *https://docs.microsoft.com/en-us/azure/event-grid/compare-messaging-services*.

Serverless microservices and workflow orchestration

When you build microservices-based applications, you may have microservices that only run on an as-needed basis. The microservices that do not run continuously are the best candidates to be deployed on serverless infrastructure to save on compute cost. Serverless microservices increase productivity and ease of development. Serverless microservices also simplify interoperability with other microservices through event-driven triggers.

Serverless microservices provide great potential to optimize cloud spend with the pay-per-use cloud model. You pay for the resources only while the code is running; however, it is automatic, so you don't have to be bogged down with infrastructure-management activities such as tearing down VMs and related services when not in use.

Furthermore, Azure provides you with better serverless workflow orchestration choices between microservices based on events and triggers to build features and functionalities with no or minimal code.

Azure Functions and Logic Apps are the two recommended services you should consider while designing serverless microservice architecture with automated workflow orchestration.

Figure 5-13 shows an example of serverless architecture and the serverless event-driven capabilities we have discussed so far. In this architecture, users shop on the eCommerce website and place orders for their products. They also can return the product if they do not like it and track their refunds.

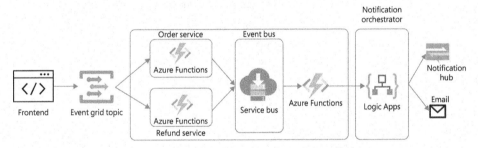

FIGURE 5-13 eCommerce sample architecture using serverless service offerings

At a high level, the architecture consists of the following key Azure services:

- **Event Grid** Native support for events from other Azure services and custom events (known as topics). Users from the front-end place new orders or request refunds for their purchased products by submitting a return request. These two separate events are then sent over to Event Grid topics so that appropriate event subscribers (microservices) can consume them. In Figure 5-13, the order events are consumed by the order service, and the return request events are taken over by the refund microservices, respectively.

- **Azure Functions** Azure Functions provides the event-driven, serverless compute capabilities in this architecture. Azure Functions runs the business logic for a given microservice based on the event it receives from Event Grid.

- **Azure Service Bus** You can use Azure Service Bus in this architecture for resiliency. You could queue the messages in the service bus queue to handle faults and transient errors. The Service Bus can further be used to handle the other automation tasks such as notifications.

- **Azure Logic Apps** Azure Logic Apps is used for workflow task automation without writing code for them. These tasks can easily be implemented using built-in connectors. Tasks can range from email notifications to integrating with external management applications. In the sample architecture shown earlier in this chapter in Figure 5-13, Logic Apps sends confirmation notifications to users and administrators when new requests are placed to alert the operations team when there are anomalies in the application code.

Container Orchestrators

The applications that are designed and developed using the microservices principle are recommended to deploy using containers. Unlike the traditional way of deploying containers using VMs, Containers empower you to adopt DevOps processes and tools, including the CI/CD deployment model. Using containers, you get better control over managing releases with reduced deployment time. Also, you minimize the risk for new deployments with deployment automation across different environments, while implementing a seamless rollback strategy and many more benefits. For small- or medium-sized applications where you do not need more than a few containers, infrastructure management is not that complex. However, for large enterprise-scale applications, you need a container orchestrator.

The container orchestrator handles tasks related to deploying and managing containerized applications. These tasks include deploying services as pods, managing interservice communication, monitoring the health of services, restarting unhealthy services, load balancing network traffic across different services, scaling the number of instances of a service, and automatically deploying desired-state configurations. Following are the two most popular container orchestrators provided by Azure:

- **Azure Kubernetes Service (AKS)** As you have learned previously in this chapter, AKS is a managed Kubernetes service in Azure. It is recommended for workloads that are intended to run on the Kubernetes cluster.

- **Service Fabric** As you learned previously, Service Fabric is another container orchestrator choice in Azure, which comes with native Microsoft .NET technology stack integration. Service Fabric is a better choice for your applications that are built on a .NET Microsoft technology stack. Like AKS, Service Fabric manages the lifetime of services, such as provisioning, deployment, health monitoring, and upgrades. Using Service Fabric, you can deploy both stateless and stateful microservices.

> *NEED MORE REVIEW?* **SERVICE FABRIC APPLICATION SCENARIOS**
>
> Microsoft has comprehensive design recommendations on building microservices using Service Fabric. To learn more, see the Microsoft documentation at *https://docs.microsoft.com/ en-us/azure/service-fabric/service-fabric-application-scenarios*.

Azure App Configuration

Microservices-based applications pose a significant challenge in maintaining application and environment-specific configurations in a distributed environment. There are several methodologies available that help developers deal with this complexity by design. For instance, the 12-factor app is a well-known architectural methodology for building cloud-ready applications. The best practice is to keep configuration settings in some external place separated from the code runtime environment. Azure App Configuration can help you address the challenges mentioned above for cloud-based applications.

The following examples are the types of applications that are a best-fit use case for using Azure App Configuration:

- **Containerized applications**   Including AKS or Service Fabric, it is recommended that you use Azure App Configuration values to manage environment-specific deployments.
- **Serverless applications**   Including Azure Functions and Event Grid, you should enable applications to react to configuration changes (key-values) to trigger a configuration-oriented workflow such as starting an Azure Automation runbook via a webhook.

> **NEED MORE REVIEW?   12-FACTOR APP**
>
> 12-factor app is a well-known collection of patterns that are related to microservices approaches, and it is also considered as a requirement for cloud-native application architectures. To learn more, see the documentation at *https://12factor.net/*.

Recommend an orchestration solution for deployment and maintenance of applications

The adoption of container and serverless technology over the past few years has further pushed organizations to adopt DevOps practices to expand the value to users and businesses by delivering features much faster than ever. Using DevOps empowers you to automate infrastructure deployment and build, test, deploy, and monitor applications without manual intervention. DevOps practices enable organizations to achieve continuous delivery and continuous deployment in the software development lifecycles.

With DevOps practices infrastructure becomes part of the iterative release cycles, so the operations and development teams must work together as one team to manage infrastructure and application code through a unified process. This is where you need to have some automation and orchestration solutions to get the best out of cloud and DevOps practices.

Figure 5-14 shows a sample DevOps automation architecture that uses Azure DevOps and a few other Azure services to build an orchestration solution for automated application deployment and maintenance.

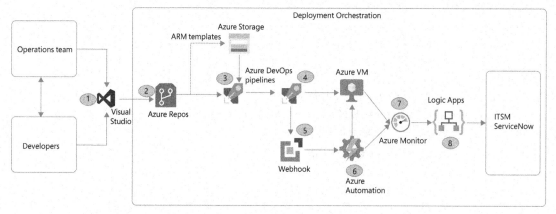

FIGURE 5-14 Automated orchestration solution for infrastructure and application deployment

At a high level, the architecture consists of the following key Azure services:

- **Visual Studio**   Developers and DevOps professionals use visual studio to develop application code and Azure Resource Manager (ARM) templates (Infrastructure as a Code) and commit their code into respective Azure Repos.

- **Azure Repos**   Azure Repos is a set of version control tools you can use to manage your application and infrastructure code.

- **Azure Pipelines**   Azure Pipelines combines continuous integration (CI) and continuous delivery (CD) to test and build your code and ship it to any target constantly and consistently. Azure Storage is used to stage the ARM templates.

- **Webhooks**   After the infrastructure is provisioned, the Azure pipeline's next task is to configure and validate the desired state.

- **Azure Automation**   Azure Automation runbooks kick in to deploy and run the PowerShell script for the VMs' desired state configuration.

- **Azure Pipelines**   Continuous deployment using a release pipeline triggers automated deployment of the application code on the configured environment.

- **Azure Monitor**   Azure Monitor is used as a standard monitoring solution for both infrastructure and application to collect and analyze health, performance, and usage data.

- **Logic Apps**   The Logic Apps with built-in ITSM connector is used to automate the operational task to notify the stakeholders of an anomaly in the application execution or infrastructure to automatically create tickets with the organization's IT service management tool such as ServiceNow.

Recommend a solution for API integration

With the emergence of cloud-based applications, microservices, and containerized applications, organizations adopt an API-first approach to reach the cloud platform's full potential.

Using the API-first approach, organizations become more agile by building applications rapidly and delivering value to business by exposing APIs to internal and external partners faster than ever. Additionally, the API approach empowers developers and accelerates development by giving them full insight into API internal implementation through API mocking and API documentation. Hence, it bridges the gap between the front-end and back-end teams.

Azure API Management (APIM) is a crucial solution for publishing and managing REST APIs for enterprise-grade applications. Figure 5-15 shows an example of an API gateway strategy in which an APIM is used to securely and efficiently manage APIs.

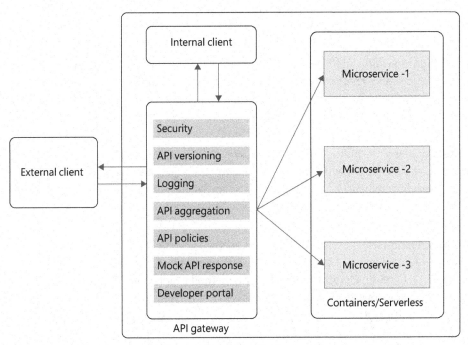

FIGURE 5-15 API gateway strategy for cloud-based applications

An API gateway acts as a reverse proxy between clients and services. It helps you address several cross-cutting concerns such as authentication, authorization, throttling, metering, caching, and monitoring. As you saw in Figure 5-15, Azure API Management acts as an API gateway. It provides you the following capabilities for your enterprise-grade, mission-critical cloud-based application.

- **Security** It is imperative to secure access to your APIs and ensure only authorized clients can access them. APIM supports the following mechanisms to secure published APIs without needing to do the custom development:
  - Subscriptions keys
  - OAuth2.0
  - Client certificates
  - IP Filtering (allow/deny)

- **API versioning**   When you use APIM as a single gateway for all back-end APIs, you get the leeway to publish a new version of the same feature/functionality without affecting the existing clients. APIM allows you to use revisions to publish a new version of an API, which may have breaking changes, and safely test and deploy them to QA/production without affecting existing consumers.

- **Logging and monitoring**   APIM has native integration with Azure Monitor and provides you with a unified monitoring experience of your published APIs in terms of the health and state of the API gateway. The activity logs help you determine how the APIs are being used by seeing the logs for write operations (PUT, POST, and DELETE) performed on your API Management services. The resource logs further provide deep insights into operations and errors necessary for auditing and troubleshooting purposes.

- **API Aggregation**   APIM helps you aggregate multiple individual requests into a single request to reduce chattiness between the client and the underlying APIs. The pattern is mostly used in microservices-based applications when a single operation needs to call multiple microservices. The APIM dispatches calls to several backend services, aggregates the results, and sends them back to the client.

- **API Policies**   The policies in APIM are a powerful capability of the system that allows you to change the behavior of the published API through custom configuration. The policies are automatically applied to the inbound request or outbound response of an API, so you have full control over how your APIs are exposed to internal and external customers.

- **Mock Responses**   This is one of the key capabilities of APIM that helps organizations accelerate development cycles. Using APIM, you can create a blank API and set a policy on an API to return a mocked response. This method enables developers to implement and test the APIM instance, even if the back-end API is still being developed.

- **Developer Portal**   Using APIM, you also get an automatically generated developer portal and a fully customizable website with your API's documentation, such as Swagger. The internal and external API consumers can discover your APIs, learn how to use them, request access, and try them out.

NEED MORE REVIEW?   **AZURE API MANAGEMENT POLICIES**

Microsoft has comprehensive documentation on setting policies and controlling ingress and egress behavior of your back-end APIs. To learn more, see the Microsoft documentation at *https://docs.microsoft.com/en-us/azure/api-management/api-management-policies.*

Skill 5.4: Design migration

With the acceleration of cloud adoption, it is vital to understand how to migrate on-premises servers to Azure. As a Cloud Solutions Architect, you are likely to face situations where you need to plan and execute such migrations. This section provides an overview of the design options for migrating to Azure.

Assess and interpret on-premises servers, data, and applications for migration

The effort required to migrate workloads such as servers, data, and applications generally falls into three phases: assess workloads, deploy workloads, and release workloads.

- **Assess workloads** Assess workloads to evaluate cost, modernization, and deployment tooling. This process focuses on validating or challenging the assumptions made during earlier discovery and assessments by looking more closely at rationalization options. You should also assess workloads to ensure technical success after migration.

- **Deploy workloads** After assessing the workloads, those workloads' existing functionality is replicated (or improved) in the cloud. Migration could involve a lift-and-shift or a rehosting to the cloud. However, many of the assets supporting these workloads are modernized to capitalize on the cloud's benefits.

- **Release workloads** Once you replicate the functionality, workloads can be tested, optimized, documented, and released for ongoing operations. It is critical to review the migrated workloads during this process and hand them off to governance, operations management, and security teams to support those workloads.

Azure Migrate

Azure Migrate is the native tool for assessing and migrating to Azure. Azure Migrate assesses on-premises infrastructure, applications, and data for migration to Azure.

- **Discover** You can use Azure Migrate for discovery from multiple vCenter servers. You can use a VMware VM running the Azure Migrate collector for discovery. You can use the same collector to discover VMs on different vCenter servers.

- **Assess readiness** Azure Migrate also allows you to perform a pre-migration assessment, regardless of whether your on-premises machines are suitable for running in Azure. Azure readiness assessment, besides doing feasibility analysis, also helps with:

  - **Sizing recommendations** Get sizing recommendations for Azure VMs, based on the performance and utilization history of on-premises VMs.

  - **Estimated monthly costs** Get an estimated Azure usage cost forecast for before migration to Azure.

- **Identify dependencies** Azure Migrate also offers visualization features that let you visualize the dependencies of VMs. This helps in creating optimal move groups for assessment and migration.

You can access the Azure Migrate service by logging in to the Azure portal. After you log in, search for **Azure Migrate** in the global search box and click **Azure Migrate** under the **Services** section. The screen, as shown in Figure 5-16, appears.

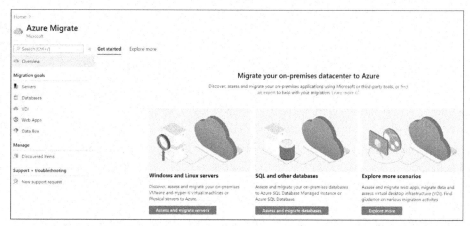

FIGURE 5-16 Azure Migrate

Azure Migrate is a native tool and a centralized hub for the assessment and migration of on-premises servers, infrastructure, applications, and data to Azure.

In the Azure Migrate hub, you can assess and migrate the following:

- **Servers** Assess on-premises servers and migrate them to Azure VMs or Azure VMware Solution (AVS).
- **Databases** Assess on-premises databases and migrate them to Azure SQL Database or SQL Managed Instance.
- **Web applications** Assess on-premises web applications and migrate them to Azure App Service using the Azure App Service Migration Assistant.
- **Virtual desktops** Assess your on-premises virtual desktop infrastructure (VDI) and migrate it to Windows Virtual Desktop in Azure.
- **Data** Migrate massive amounts of data to Azure quickly and cost-effectively using Azure Data Box products.

Azure Migrate: Server Assessment tool

The Azure Migrate Server Assessment tool can be used to assess on-premises VMware VMs, Hyper-V VMs, and physical servers for Azure migration.

This tool provides the following vital functions:

- **Azure readiness assessment** Checks whether on-premises machines are ready for migration to Azure.

- **Azure sizing** Estimates Azure VMs sizing or the number of Azure nodes after migration.
- **Azure cost estimation** This helps you get a cost estimate for Azure resources for the existing on-premises workload.
- **Dependency analysis** Identifies various server-to-server dependencies and optimization and grouping strategies for moving servers to Azure.

With the Azure Migrate tool, you can have greater confidence when you use the dependency analysis feature for assessing VM groups to migrate. Dependency analysis cross-checks various dependencies before you run the assessment, and it helps to avoid unexpected outages when you migrate to Azure. Azure Migrate behind the scenes leverages Service Map solution in Azure Monitor to enable dependency analysis.

Table 5-4 summarizes the differences between agentless visualization and agent-based visualization.

TABLE 5-4 Agentless versus agent-based visualization

Requirement	Agentless	Agent-based
Agent	No agents are needed on machines you want to analyze.	Agents are required on each on-premises machine that you want to analyze.
Log Analytics	Not required.	Azure Migrate uses the Service Map solution in Azure Monitor for dependency visualization.
Process	Captures TCP connection data on machines enabled for dependency visualization. After discovery, it gathers data at intervals of five minutes.	Service Map agents installed on a machine gather data about TCP processes and inbound/outbound connections for each process.
Data	Source machine server name, process, and application name. Destination machine server name, process, application name, and port.	Source machine server name, process, and application name. Destination machine server name, process, application name, and port. Azure Migrate uses the Service Map solution in Azure Monitor logs for dependency analysis.
Visualization	A dependency map of single server can be viewed for a duration of 30 days'.	You can view a single server or a group of servers' dependency maps for an hour's worth of data.
Data export	You can download the last 30 days' data in a CSV format.	You can query data with Log Analytics.
Support	When writing this chapter, this option was in preview and is only available for VMware VMs.	General availability (GA).

Movere

Movere is a Software as a Service (SaaS). Movere's agentless bots scan 1,000 servers per hour to capture everything in your IT environment and then surface that information into a dynamic and customizable dashboard. Additionally, it analyzes the data and then highlights the key insights IT administrators need to have visibility and control over in their environments.

Movere continues to learn your environment while eliminating duplicate data points to ensure that users can access the most accurate, reliable, and actionable data.

> **NOTE MOVERE**
>
> Microsoft acquired Movere and it is available through the Microsoft Solution Assessment and Microsoft Cloud Economics Program.

Recommend a solution for migrating applications and VMs

After using Azure Migrate for your assessment, you can decide which of your workloads are good candidates to be migrated to Azure. Azure Migrate can also perform a migration of VMWare VMs, Hyper-V VMs, and physical servers into Azure. Agentless replication options are available for VMware VMs and Hyper-V VMs. The agentless option orchestrates replication by integrating with the functionality provided by the virtualization provider.

Recommend a migration strategy

With the assessment complete, you need to identify tools to move applications, data, and Azure infrastructure.

When you start planning for migration and perform migration assessment, you typically perform a migration strategy known as the *cloud rationalization* process, which evaluates workloads to determine the best way to migrate or modernize each workload in the cloud. The five R's of migration dispositions are the most common options for cloud rationalization.

1. **Rehost** Also known as a lift-and-shift migration, a rehost effort is a no-code option for migrating existing applications to Azure quickly and with minimal change to the overall architecture. With the rehost strategy, you can migrate an application as-is with some of the benefits of the cloud IaaS and without the risks or costs associated with code changes.

2. **Refactor** Platform as a Service (PaaS) options can reduce the operational costs associated with many applications. It is a good idea to refactor an application to fit a PaaS-based model slightly. "Refactor" essentially ties to the application development process of restructuring code to enable an application to deliver new business opportunities.

3. **Rearchitect** In some cases, you might find a few aging applications that are not compatible with cloud providers because of some anti-patterns. In such cases, you might be better off rearchitecting before the transformation. In other cases, you could have a cloud-compatible application that is not cloud-native, and that might provide you with cost and operational efficiencies if you decide to rearchitect the solution into a cloud-native application. While rearchitecting, you can adopt resilient, independently deployable, highly scalable services in your architecture. Azure services can accelerate the process, scale applications with confidence, and manage applications with ease.

4. **Rebuild**   In some scenarios, the refactoring of an application can be too large to justify further investment. It is typical that an application has previously met a business's needs but is now unsupported or misaligned with the current business processes. In this case, you must create a new codebase to eliminate technical debt and align it with the cloud-native approach.

5. **Replace**   Typically, solutions are implemented by using the best technology and approach available at that time. However, as time passes, you could find a Software as a Service (SaaS) alternative to provide all the necessary functionality for the hosted application. With the "Replace" strategy, you replace legacy workloads with alternate solutions, effectively removing them from the transformation effort.

Migration tool

Azure Migrate is the native Azure service used for migration from within Azure and from on-premises sites to Azure. You can use Azure Migrate to orchestrate replication from an on-premises datacenter to Azure. When replication is set up and running, on-premises machines can be failed over to Azure, completing the migration.

As mentioned earlier, Azure Migrate provides a centralized hub to not only assess but also migrate to Azure from on-premises servers, infrastructure, applications, and data. The Azure Migrate hub includes the migration tools shown in Table 5-5 for migrating applications and VMs.

TABLE 5-5 Azure Migrate tools

Tool	Assess and migrate	Details
Azure Migrate: Server Migration	Migrate servers.	Migrate VMware VMs, Hyper-V VMs, physical servers, other virtualized machines, and public cloud VMs to Azure.
Web app migration assistant	Assess on-premises web apps and migrate them to Azure.	Use Azure App Service Migration Assistant to assess on-premises websites for migration to Azure App Service. Use Migration Assistant to migrate .NET and PHP web apps to Azure.

When you add the Azure Migrate: Server Migration tool to your Azure Migrate dashboard (which carries over machines and insights from the assessment), you can begin your replication by clicking **Replicate** in the tool window. Azure Migrate replicates up to 100 VMs simultaneously. If you need to do more, you can create multiple batches. Times for replication vary based on the number and size of VMs along with connection speeds between your datacenter and Azure. Figure 5-17 shows the Azure Migrate main screen, which shows discovered servers, replicating servers, tested migrated servers, and migrated servers.

Once all your targeted VMs are replicated to Azure, you can test your VMs to ensure everything works before migrating them into production. The process runs a prerequisite check, prepares for the test, creates a new test VM, and starts it.

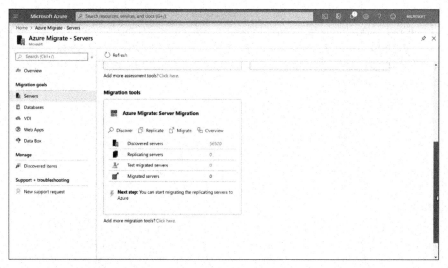

FIGURE 5-17 Azure Migrate

Once you are ready for the production migration, select **Migrate** from the replicating machine's window. That process prompts you to shut down the VM to avoid any data loss and perform a final replication. We recommended you do this during off-peak business hours because the VM would go down for a few minutes.

Figure 5-18 shows the **Replicating Machines** screen during a server migration. You can use this screen to see all the servers being replicated, and you can check the data sync status and replication health. For the servers that are ready to migrate, you can choose to test the migration (choose **Test**) or perform the migration (choose **Migrate**). Lastly, you can stop replication by choosing **Stop Replication**.

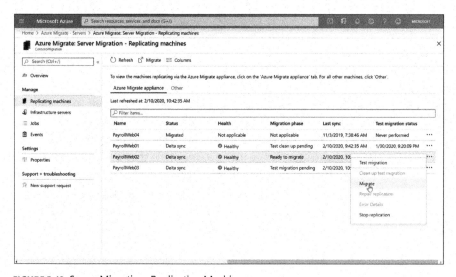

FIGURE 5-18 Server Migration–Replicating Machines

While it runs through the production migration process, you can check the status as it validates the prerequisites, prepares for migration, creates the Azure VM, and starts the Azure VM.

After the migration has taken place, review the security settings of the VM after the migration. Restrict network access for unused services by using network security groups. Deploy Azure Disk Encryption to secure the disks from data theft and unauthorized access. Consider improving the resilience of the migrated machines by doing the following:

- You should add a backup schedule that uses Azure Backup.
- You should consider replicating the machines to a secondary region using Azure Site Recovery.
- Complete clean-up tasks for the remaining on-premises servers. Such tasks may include removing the servers from local backups and removing their raw disk files from storage-area network (SAN) storage to free up space. Update documentation related to the migrated servers to reflect their new IP addresses and locations in Azure.

> **NEED MORE REVIEW?**   **AZURE MIGRATION BEST PRACTICES**
>
> Learn more about the best practices for migration to Azure at *https://docs.microsoft.com/ en-us/Azure/cloud-adoption-framework/migrate/Azure-best-practices/.*

Recommend a solution for migration of databases

Typically, any workload migration from on-premises to Azure involves one more database migration. Data is the heart of the application, and it is very critical to migrate databases with minimal downtime and without any loss of data. As a Cloud Solutions Architect, you must carefully choose a database migration strategy and solution to migrate databases from on-premises to Azure.

Typically, the migration process involves the following three stages, which are discussed in the coming sections:

1. Pre-migration
2. Migration
3. Post-migration

Pre-migration

In the pre-migration stage, you collect the databases' inventory, assess these databases for potential incompatibilities, and plan for migration. In case you are going to do a heterogeneous (such as when migrating from Oracle to Azure SQL Database) migration, then you need to convert the source database schema to match the target database. This stage has the following phases:

- **Discover**   This phase is mostly required when you are planning to migrate databases in bulk, such as migrating all databases from an on-premises environment. In this phase, you scan your network and collect information about your on-premises databases, such as server hostname, IP address, database version, and features in use. For the discovery of on-premises databases, you can use the following tools:

- Microsoft Assessment and Planning (MAP) Toolkit
- Azure Migrate

- **Assess** To successfully migrate the databases and develop a migration plan, you must thoroughly assess the source database. In this phase, you try to identify the gap or incompatibilities between the source and target databases. For assessment, you can use the Data Migration Assistant (DMA) tool. Some of the objectives of the assessment are:
  - Identify migration blockers.
  - Identify breaking changes.
  - Identify the effort required to fix issues (breaking changes, migration blocker).
  - Consider the possibility of decommissioning unused databases.
  - Consider consolidation of databases.
  - Analyze the technical and business dependency of the application/databases on other applications, databases, and services. It is helpful to group these databases into a single wave of migration.
  - Consider migration downtime.

- **Convert** When you do a heterogeneous migration, you need to convert the source schema to match the target database. For example, when migrating from Oracle to SQL server, you need to convert the Oracle database schema to the SQL server database schema. To perform this schema conversion, you can use the SQL Server Migration Assistant (SSMA) for Oracle.

- **Plan** Once the assessment is complete, the next step is to use your assessment result and plan the migration. In the planning phase, you need to accomplish two things:
  - **Choose a target database** The essential thing in the planning is to choose the target database based on the current database attributes, such as database size, ease of management, scalability, availability, features used in the database (for example, SSIS, SSRS, or SSAS), and total cost of ownership (TCO). TCO was covered in Chapter 1, "Design monitoring." The TCO calculation helps you understand the tentative Azure hosting cost and benefits for the database you plan to migrate. It also provides a comparison between on-premises datacenter cost and Azure cost. The TCO calculation also helps you choose the target database. Suppose you have budget constraints at your business unit level or organization level. In that case, you can select an appropriate target database based on application needs as well as the budget. You can also use the TCO calculator to see how much you can save after migrating to Azure, making a better business case when you present it to the stakeholders.
  - **Choose a migration method and tool** You can migrate databases online or offline. In the offline method, you take downtime in the application and then migrate source databases to the target Azure databases. You can also use an online method

with minimal downtime for the migration. Please refer to Table 5-6 to choose a migration method based on the acceptable downtime.

TABLE 5-6 Migration method versus acceptable downtime

Criticality	Acceptable Downtime	Migration Method	Migration Tool
High	Near-zero downtime	Transaction replication	SQL Server Management Studio (SSMS)
Medium	Small maintenance window	Online and offline migration	Azure Database Migration Service (DMS)
Low	Large maintenance window	BACPAC export/import	Azure portal and SQL Server Management Studio (SSMS)

Migration

Once you complete the necessary activities of the pre-migration stage, you can start the migration stage. This stage has the following phases:

1. **Migrate schema**   In the assessment phase, you identified compatibility issues and fixed them. Now your database schema is ready to migrate to the target database. First, you create an Azure target database and then migrate schema using Data Migration Assistant (DMA). For heterogeneous database migration, you can use SQL Server Migration Assistant to migrate schema.

2. **Migrate data**   After migrating schema, you can migrate data using the DMA or DMS service. For heterogeneous database migration, you can use SQL Server Migration Assistant to migrate data.

3. **Sync data**   For online migration, once you complete the full load, you need to sync incremental data. You can use the DMS service to sync your incremental data.

4. **Cutover**   For online migration, once you are done with a full load, and there are no pending changes for the incremental load, then you can complete cutover using the DMS service.

> **NEED MORE REVIEW?**   **MIGRATION SCENARIOS AND TOOLS**
>
> For migration scenarios and supported tools, see *https://docs.microsoft.com/en-us/Azure/dms/dms-tools-matrix.*

Post-migration

After completing the migration, you need to perform the following phases:

1. **Remediate application**   After completing the migration, your application needs to connect to the target database. You need to remediate the application to consume the target database. This includes changing the connection string to refer to the target database, and changing the data access layer to use a target database-specific library.

2. **Perform test** After completing application remediation, you can perform the application's functional and performance test. You need to take a copy of the source and target databases and perform a functional validation test based on the defined scope. Similarly, you can execute a performance test against the source and target databases to compare the result.

3. **Optimize** In the optimization phase, you can fix the performance issue based on the performance test result. If you migrate your database to the Azure SQL Database, this tool provides recommendations fine-tuning your database such as identifying missing indexes. This dramatically helps to improve the performance of the application.

Data migration tools

In the following sections, we look at the tools you can use in your database migration journey.

AZURE MIGRATE

We have already looked at this tool in the previous section, "Recommend a solution for migration of databases."

DATA MIGRATION ASSISTANT (DMA)

DMA is Microsoft's database assessment and migration tool, which is freely available to download, install, and execute locally. DMA supports the following sources:

- SQL Server 2005
- SQL Server 2008
- SQL Server 2008 R2
- SQL Server 2012
- SQL Server 2014
- SQL Server 2016
- SQL Server 2017 on Windows

DMA supports the following targets:

- SQL Server 2012
- SQL Server 2014
- SQL Server 2016
- SQL Server 2017 on Windows and Linux
- SQL Server 2019
- Azure SQL Database single database
- Azure SQL Managed Instance
- SQL Server running on an Azure VM

Following are the key capabilities of DMA:

- Detects compatibility issues such as breaking changes, behavior changes, deprecated features that affect database functionality in Azure, and provides guidance on how to resolve these issues.

- Allows you to migrate database schema, users, server roles, SQL Server, Windows log in, and data.

- Discover new features such as performance, security, and storage of the target database platform from which the source database can benefit after migration.

DATA MIGRATION SERVICE (DMS)

DMS is a fully managed service that helps you easily migrate schema, data, and objects from multiple on-premises sources to Microsoft's Azure platform. The key capabilities of DMS include the following:

- Migrates databases, including user objects at scale with near-zero downtime.

- Simple and easy process to understand and implement database migration.

- Standard pricing tier for small to medium business workloads (offline migration only).

- The Premium pricing tier supports offline and online migrations (also called "continuous migration") for business-critical workloads that require minimal downtime. The Premium pricing tier is generally available.

- It is resilient and self-healing.

- Automates migration using PowerShell cmdlets.

SQL SERVER MIGRATION ASSISTANT (SSMA)

SSMA is Microsoft's database migration tool for heterogeneous migration, which is freely available to download, install and execute locally. SSMA supports the following source and target databases:

- **Source**
  - Access
  - DB2
  - MySQL
  - Oracle
  - SAP ASE
- **Target**
  - SQL Server 2012
  - SQL Server 2014
  - SQL Server 2016
  - SQL Server 2017 on Windows and Linux
  - SQL Server 2019 on Windows and Linux
  - Azure SQL Database

- Azure SQL Managed Instance
- Azure Synapse Analytics

The key capability of SSMA is that it provides a simple and easy tool to automate the migration of databases to Azure from Oracle, MySQL, DB2, Microsoft Access, and SAP ASE.

Recommend a solution for migrating data

Cloud adoption is gaining traction. Over the past decade, many organizations have already moved to the cloud or are in the process of moving to the cloud. One of the critical stages in cloud migration is the migration of data. Microsoft offers a variety of services to migrate data from on-premises to Azure. Let's look at data migration solutions.

Storage Migration Service

Storage Migration Service is a graphical tool for migration of storage to Windows Server on Azure. It collects data from Windows and Linux servers and migrates it to a newer server or Azure VM. It also has an option to maintain the server's identity in the target environment so that apps and users can access it without changing their links or paths.

This data migration is a three-step process:

1. Collect inventory of servers—gather files and configuration.
2. Transfer data.
3. Cut over to the new servers.

The key features of the Storage Migration service include the following:

- It provides a user interface with a graphical workflow.
- It collects inventory of multiple servers and their data.
- It's scalable, consistent, and fast.
- It can manage multiple migrations using Windows Admin Center.

Azure Data Box

Azure Data Box is a family of products designed to transfer a massive amount of data. This family includes the following products:

- Azure Data Box
- Azure Data Box Disk
- Azure Data Box Heavy
- Data Box Edge
- Data Box Gateway.

Azure Data Box, Azure Data Box Disk, and Azure Data Box Heavy are designed to transfer data offline by shipping disks/appliances to Microsoft datacenters. These products are suitable for one-time initial bulk transfer or periodic upload. Table 5-7 quickly outlines the features of these products.

TABLE 5-7 Azure Data Box products

	Azure Data Box	Azure Data Box Disk	Azure Data Box Heavy
Total devices per order	1	Up to 5	1
Total capacity	100 TB	40 TB	1 PB
Usable capacity	80 TB	35 TB	800 TB
Supported Azure Storage services	Azure Block Blob, Page Blob, Azure Files, or Managed Disk	Azure Block Blob, Page Blob, Azure Files, or Managed Disk	Azure Block Blob, Page Blob, Azure Files, or Managed Disk
Interface	1x1/10 Gbps RJ45, 2x10 Gbps SFP+	USB/SATA II, III	4x1/10 Gbps RJ45, 4x40 Gbps QSFP+
Encryption	AES 256-bit	AES 128-bit	AES 256-bit

Azure Data Box Gateway and Azure Data Box Edge are online data transfer methods. Azure Data Box Edge is a hardware appliance provided by Microsoft to be placed at the on-premises end. It acts as a cloud storage gateway that links the on-premises world to Azure Storage. It caches data locally, and then it uploads it to Azure storage.

Azure Data Box Gateway is a virtual appliance that is deployed into an on-premises virtualized environment. You can write data locally using the NFS and SMB protocols, and then this device uploads the data to Azure Storage.

Azure File Sync-based migration to hybrid file server

A hybrid file server allows you to share your file content across multiple locations and securely store data into centralized cloud storage. You can use Azure File Sync to seamlessly synchronize your files between your local server and Azure Files. The migration process consists of the following phases:

1. Identify the required number of Azure File Shares. Provision an on-premises Windows server.
2. Provision Azure Storage Sync service.
3. Provision Azure Storage.
4. Configure Azure File sync on Windows server.
5. Copy files using RoboCopy.
6. Cut over.

IDENTIFY THE REQUIRED NUMBER OF AZURE FILE SHARES

For synchronizing your local files to Azure File Share, you need a Windows server. A single Windows server (or cluster) can sync up to 30 Azure File Shares. If you are planning 1:1 mapping between the on-premises share to the Azure File Share, you need a single Windows server. If you have more than 30 local shares, then you need more than one Windows server. If possible, you can group your local shares and store the data into one Azure File Share.

Azure File Sync supports up to 100 million items (files and folders) per Azure File Share, but the best practice is to have 20–30 million in a single share. If your local share contains more than 30 million items, we recommend that you split this data into multiple Azure File Shares.

Azure File Share is provisioned within a storage account. Hence, the storage account is a scale target for IOPS and throughput. Also, there are additional IOPS and throughput limits on Azure File Share.

> **NEED MORE REVIEW?** **AZURE FILES AND STORAGE ACCOUNT LIMITS**
>
> For Azure Files and Storage service limits (such as throughput and IOPS), see *https://docs. microsoft.com/en-us/azure/azure-resource-manager/management/azure-subscription- service-limits.*

> **NEED MORE REVIEW?** **MICROSOFT-PROVIDED MAPPING TEMPLATE**
>
> To arrive at the number of Azure File Shares mapping with your local shares, you should con- sider the above points and then perform a mapping exercise using a Microsoft template at *https://download.microsoft.com/download/1/8/D/18DC8184-E7E2-45EF-823F-F8A36B9FF240/ Azure%20File%20Sync%20-%20Namespace%20Mapping.xlsx.*

PROVISION ON-PREMISES WINDOWS SERVER

It is recommended that you provision Windows Server 2019 or Windows Server 2012 R2 on- premises based on the mapping completed in the previous step using the Microsoft-provided mapping template. You can also use a Windows server failover cluster instead of a single server.

PROVISION AZURE STORAGE SYNC SERVICE

Provision the Azure Storage Sync service in the Azure region closest to your location. Also, use the same region for Azure Storage.

PROVISION AZURE STORAGE

Provision your Azure Storage Account in the Azure region closest to your location. Also, use the same region used for the Storage Sync service. Please refer to the mapping sheet refer- enced in the previous Need More Review for the number of the required storage account to be provisioned.

INSTALL THE AZURE FILE SYNC AGENT

Install the Azure File Sync Agent by performing the following steps:

1. Disable Internet Explorer Enhanced Security Configuration.

2. Install this PowerShell module:

```
Install-Module -Name Az -AllowClobber
Install-Module -Name Az.StorageSync
```

3. Install Microsoft Sync Agent.

CONFIGURE AZURE FILE SYNC ON WINDOWS SERVER

Configure Azure File Sync on Windows server by performing the following steps:

1. In the Storage Sync service, create a new sync group for each Azure File Share.

2. Select the newly created sync group and select **Add Server Endpoint**, enter the required information such as Registered Server, Path, Cloud Tiering, Volume Free Space, Initial Download Mode, and Create Server Endpoint.

COPY FILES USING ROBOCOPY

Use RoboCopy to copy files from your local shares, NAS appliance, and Linux server to the Windows server that already was configured with Azure File Sync.

CUTOVER

Follow these steps:

1. Once the initial file copy completes, run RoboCopy one more time. This will copy the new changeset that happened after the last run.

2. Now take your source file location offline or change ACLs so that users cannot modify or add new files.

3. Finally, create a share on the Windows server folder and change DFS-N deployment to point to it.

Chapter summary

- An ARM template is Microsoft's native solution to provision resources quickly in Microsoft's Azure.

- Ansible is an open-source automation tool that is designed for provisioning, configuration management, deployment, orchestration, continuous delivery, and security automation.

- Chef is an open-source infrastructure automation tool for configuration management, deployment, and compliance.

- Puppet is an open-source automation tool for configuration management and continuous delivery.

- Terraform is an open-source automation tool by HashiCorp for provisioning and configuration management.

- An Azure VM is fully Infrastructure as a Service (IaaS), which provides a virtual processor, memory, storage, and networking resources along with the operating system of your choice.

- Azure App Service is a fully managed Platform as a Service (PaaS) to deploy an enterprise-grade web application.

- Azure Service Fabric is a Platform-as-a-Service (PaaS) facilitating the development, packaging, deployment, and management of highly scalable microservices and containers.

- Azure Function is a Function as a Service (FaaS), which abstracts underlying infrastructure and operating systems and allows you to execute smaller tasks at scheduled times or when they are triggered by external events.

- Azure Batch is a managed service designed to run large-scale parallel and high-performance computing (HPC) batch jobs in Microsoft's Azure Cloud platform.

- Containers provide immutable infrastructure for your application. They allow you to bundle your application code, libraries, dependencies, and configuration as a container image.

- Azure Automation is a cloud-based, cost-effective automation service on Microsoft's Azure Cloud platform.

- Azure Virtual Network is a foundational building block for your private network in Azure.

- A hub-and-spoke network topology isolates workload while sharing services, such as identity, connectivity, and security.

- Azure Virtual WAN is a Microsoft-managed networking solution that provides end-to-end global transit connectivity.

- Azure provides various native network security services such as Azure Firewall, Azure Web Application Firewall (WAF), and Azure Front Door.

- Third-party networking offerings play a critical role in Azure, allowing you to use brands and solutions you already know, trust, and have the skills to manage.

- Azure Application Gateway is an application-layer load balancer (OSI layer 7) that allows you to load-balance traffic to your web applications.

- Web Application Firewall (WAF) provides centralized protection of your web applications from common exploits and vulnerabilities.

- Azure Bastion is a native-platform (PaaS) service that provides secure RDP/SSH connectivity to your VMs.

- Azure provides various solutions for network connectivity, such as virtual networks, ExpressRoute, VPN Gateway, virtual WAN, virtual network NAT gateway, and Azure Bastion.

- Most enterprise customers have hybrid connectivity needs. ExpressRoute service enables the extension of on-premises networks into Azure over a private connection that is facilitated by a connectivity provider.

- Microsoft provides an optimized branch to the Azure virtual network connectivity service known as Azure Virtual WAN.

- With service endpoints, traffic from your virtual network to specific Azure PaaS services always remains on the Microsoft Azure backbone network.

- While selecting Azure compute service, consider service limits, cost, SLA, and regional availability, along with the critical capabilities of each compute service.

- Azure Container Instances allows you to spin up containers rapidly so you can deploy dev/test and small-scale containerized applications.

- Azure Kubernetes Service (AKS) is a fully managed container orchestration system that is recommended for your production workload.

- Azure provides a variety of serverless choices to design consumption- and event-based microservices to leverage the cloud platform's full potential.

- Azure App Configuration is a recommended service that centrally manages application settings for microservices-based applications.

- Azure ARM Templates, Azure Pipeline, and Azure Automation are the recommended services to automate infrastructure and the application deployment lifecycle.

- You should use Azure API Management (APIM) as a managed service to publish and manage REST APIs for cloud-based applications.

- Azure Migrate is the native tool for assessing and migrating to Azure. Azure Migrate assesses on-premises infrastructure, applications, and data for migration to Azure.

- Data Migration Service (DMS) is a fully managed service that helps you easily migrate schema, data, and objects from multiple on-premises sources to Microsoft's Azure platform.

- Storage Migration Service is a graphical tool for migration of storage from the Windows server or to Azure.

- Azure Data Box is a family of products designed to transfer a massive amount of data.

Thought experiment

Now it is time to validate your skills and knowledge of the concepts you learned in this chapter. You can find answers to this thought experiment in the next section, "Thought experiment answers."

As a Cloud Solutions Architect, you need to recommend a solution for a department in your company that wants to use a website that serves two types of content: images and dynamically rendered webpages. The website must be secure, geographically redundant, and it should serve its users from the closest and lowest latency location to them. Additionally, the default VM pool serving the dynamic content needs to talk to a back-end database hosted on a high-availability cluster.

Thought experiment answers

Following are the critical technical characteristics that must be addressed by this solution:

- **Multi-geo redundancy**   If one region goes down, Traffic Manager routes traffic seamlessly to the closest region without any intervention from the application owner.

- **Reduced latency**   Because Traffic Manager automatically directs the customer to the closest region, the customer experiences lower latency when requesting the web page contents.

- **Independent scalability**   You can separate the web application workload by type of content, which allows the application owner to scale the request workloads independently of each other. Application Gateway ensures that you route traffic to the right application pools based on the specified rules and the application's health.

- **Internal load balancing**   Because the load balancer is in front of the high-availability cluster, the application would be connecting to only the active and healthy endpoint for the database. The load balancer delivers connections to the high-availability cluster and ensures that only healthy databases receive connection requests.

- **Security**   Transport Layer Security (TLS), previously known as Secure Sockets Layer (SSL), is the standard security technology for establishing an encrypted link between a web server and a browser. This link ensures that all data passed between the web server and browsers remains private and encrypted. Application Gateway supports both TLS termination at the gateway as well as end-to-end TLS encryption.

Index

SYMBOLS

12-factor app, 193

A

AAD (Azure Active Directory)
    application integration, 65–66
    application property configuration, 67–68
    authentication support, 65
    conditional access policies, 28–30
    enterprise applications, 66–67
    identity score, 51–52
    logs, 12
    managed identities
      in Azure App Service, 65
      Azure support for, 64
      system-assigned versus user-assigned, 63
    SSO (single sign-on), 26–28
access control
    Azure AD access reviews, 40
    certificates, 61–62
    conditional access policies, 28–30
    IAM (Identity Access Management), 47
    keys, 60–61
    policy inheritance, 5
    RBAC (role-based access control), 45–47
    secrets, 59–60
access tokens, 42
accessing Azure Storage
    authorization for, 104–105
    with AzCopy.exe, 107
    programmatically, 105
    securing with firewall, 105
    through Azure portal, 107
    through Azure Storage Explorer, 107
    through Microsoft Visual Studio Cloud Explorer, 107
    from VNets, 105–106

account key rotation in Azure Storage, 108
accountability in cost management, 3
ACI (Azure Container Instances), 162
action groups in Azure Monitor, 20
activity logs, 12
AD Connect Health, 38–39
ADF (Azure Data Factory), 89, 93–95
ADLA (Azure Data Lake Analytics), 99
ADLS (Azure Data Lake Storage), 98–99
agent-based visualization, agentless versus, 199
agentless visualization, agent-based versus, 199
AHB (Azure Hybrid Benefits), 80
AKS (Azure Kubernetes Services), 162, 192
alerts in Azure Monitor, 20
Always Encrypted feature, 88
Ansible, 152
API integration, 194–196
APIM (Azure API Management), 194–196
application deployment, 193–194
Application Gateway, 180–181, 187
Application Insights, 17, 19
Application Map, 19
application migration
    with Azure Migrate tools, 201–203
    strategies for, 200–201
application monitoring, 17
application security
    Azure Key Vault
      certificates, 61–62
      commands, 62
      described, 58
      keys, 60–61
      regions, 62
      secrets, 59–60
      vaults, 58–59
    conditional access policies, 68
    custom logos, 69

D

Plug into learning at

MicrosoftPressStore.com

The Microsoft Press Store by Pearson offers:

- Free U.S. shipping

- Buy an eBook, get three formats – Includes PDF, EPUB, and MOBI to use with your computer, tablet, and mobile devices

- Print & eBook Best Value Packs

- eBook Deal of the Week – Save up to 50% on featured title

- Newsletter – Be the first to hear about new releases, announcements, special offers, and more

- Register your book – Find companion files, errata, and product updates, plus receive a special coupon* to save on your next purchase

 Pearson